MW01009168

Research Genres Across Languages

At present, Web 2.0 technologies are making traditional research genres evolve and form complex genre assemblage with other genres online. This book takes the perspective of genre analysis to provide a timely examination of professional and public communication of science. It gives an updated overview on the increasing diversification of genres for communicating scientific research today by reviewing relevant theories that contribute an understanding of genre evolution and innovation in Web 2.0. The book also offers a much-needed critical enquiry into the dynamics of languages for academic and research communication and reflects on current language-related issues such as academic Englishes, ELF lects, translanguaging, polylanguaging and the multilingualisation of science. Additionally, it complements the critical reflections with data from small-scale specialised corpora and exploratory survey research. The book also includes pedagogical orientations for teaching/training researchers in the STEMM disciplines and proposes several avenues for future enquiry into research genres across languages.

Carmen Pérez-Llantada is Professor of Applied Linguistics at the University of Zaragoza, Spain. Her research interests include genre analysis, English for Academic Purposes, academic writing, and digital genres in multilingual science communication.

THE CAMBRIDGE APPLIED LINGUISTICS SERIES

The authority on cutting-edge Applied Linguistics research

Series Editors   2007–present: Carol A. Chapelle and Susan Hunston
1988–2007: Michael H. Long and Jack C. Richards

For a complete list of titles, please visit: www.cambridge.org

Recent titles in this series:

Research Genres Across Languages
Multilingual Communication Online
Carmen Pérez-Llantada

Validity Argument in Language Testing
Case Studies of Validation Research
Edited by Carol A. Chapelle and Erik Voss

Doing English Grammar
Theory, Description and Practice
Roger Berry

Learner Corpus Research Meets Second Language Acquisition
Bert Le Bruyn and Magali Paquot

Second Language Speech Fluency
From Research to Practice
Parvaneh Tavakoli and Clare Wright

Ontologies of English
Conceptualising the Language for Learning, Teaching, and Assessment
Edited by Christopher J. Hall and Rachel Wicaksono

Task-Based Language Teaching
Theory and Practice
Rod Ellis, Peter Skehan, Shaofeng Li, Natsuko Shintani and Craig Lambert

Feedback in Second Language Writing
Contexts and Issues 2nd Edition
Edited by Ken Hyland and Fiona Hyland

Language and Television Series
A Linguistic Approach to TV Dialogue
Monika Bednarek

Intelligibility, Oral Communication, and the Teaching of Pronunciation
John M. Levis

Multilingual Education
Between Language Learning and Translanguaging
Edited by Jasone Cenoz and Durk Gorter

Learning Vocabulary in Another Language
2nd Edition
I. S. P. Nation

Narrative Research in Applied Linguistics
Edited by Gary Barkhuizen

Teacher Research in Language Teaching
A Critical Analysis
Simon Borg

Figurative Language, Genre and Register
Alice Deignan, Jeannette Littlemore and Elena Semino

Exploring ELF
Academic English Shaped by Non-native Speakers
Anna Mauranen

Genres Across the Disciplines
Student Writing in Higher Education
Hilary Nesi and Sheena Gardner

Disciplinary Identities
Individuality and Community in Academic Discourse
Ken Hyland

Replication Research in Applied Linguistics
Edited by Graeme Porte

The Language of Business Meetings
Michael Handford

Reading in a Second Language
Moving from Theory to Practice
William Grabe

Modelling and Assessing Vocabulary Knowledge
Edited by Helmut Daller, James Milton and Jeanine Treffers-Daller

Practice in a Second Language
Perspectives from Applied Linguistics and Cognitive Psychology
Edited by Robert M. DeKeyser

Task-Based Language Education
From Theory to Practice
Edited by Kris van den Branden

Second Language Needs Analysis
Edited by Michael H. Long

Research Genres Across Languages

Multilingual Communication Online

Carmen Pérez-Llantada

University of Zaragoza

CAMBRIDGE
UNIVERSITY PRESS

CAMBRIDGE
UNIVERSITY PRESS

University Printing House, Cambridge CB2 8BS, United Kingdom

One Liberty Plaza, 20th Floor, New York, NY 10006, USA

477 Williamstown Road, Port Melbourne, VIC 3207, Australia

314–321, 3rd Floor, Plot 3, Splendor Forum, Jasola District Centre, New Delhi – 110025, India

103 Penang Road, #05–06/07, Visioncrest Commercial, Singapore 238467

Cambridge University Press is part of the University of Cambridge.

It furthers the University's mission by disseminating knowledge in the pursuit of education, learning, and research at the highest international levels of excellence.

www.cambridge.org
Information on this title: www.cambridge.org/9781108834940
DOI: 10.1017/9781108870528

© Carmen Pérez-Llantada, 2021

First published 2021

A catalogue record for this publication is available from the British Library.

ISBN 978-1-108-83494-0 Hardback
ISBN 978-1-108-79259-2 Paperback

Cambridge University Press has no responsibility for the persistence or accuracy of URLs for external or third-party internet websites referred to in this publication and does not guarantee that any content on such websites is, or will remain, accurate or appropriate.

For my family

Contents

Figures

Tables

Acknowledgements

I am most indebted to Professor Emeritus John M. Swales (University of Michigan, US), whose work has been a constant source of inspiration, above all for this book project. Even if geographical distance and other circumstances have prevented us from getting together and discussing the book informally, as I would love to have done, remembrances of his continued support and advice during and after the generous time he spent with me in my numerous research stays at the English Language Institute encouraged me to start this journey. As I hope to demonstrate with this book, genre analysis is a very useful heuristic for understanding the particulars of today's research world in relation to multilingual communication practices. This book seeks to be a humble contribution to his legacy in the field of genre analysis.

I am also indebted to Professor Wendy Ayres-Bennett of the Department of Theoretical and Applied Linguistics at the University of Cambridge, UK, whom I had the pleasure to meet for the first time in January 2019. She endorsed a short research stay at Cambridge that enabled me to draft part of the book and profit from the University library facilities. She also generously shared with me her time and her views on multilingualism to empower individuals and transform societies. I would also like to thank the anonymous reviewers of the book proposal for their invigorating observations and suggestions and Julian Chancellor for taking so much time to go through the full draft carefully, identify inconsistencies and contradictions and give me detailed and valuable feedback. I especially owe much to my commissioning editor at Cambridge University Press, Rebecca (Becky) Taylor. From the start, she gave me constant encouragement to move the book project forward until completion. She has always been very supportive of my work throughout this journey. My thanks also to Isabel (Izzie) Collins, editorial assistant, for swiftly sorting out all my queries regarding the figures included in the book and the copyright permissions in the pre-production stage. Special thanks also to all the editorial team at Cambridge University Press for their rigorous work over the production process.

I also wish to thank all the researchers who very kindly replied to my online survey research. Their generosity in sharing their valuable time and their practices and views on genres is very much appreciated. Some of their responses corroborated my previous assumptions about digital genre composing. Those that did not confirm my intuitions were also useful, as they point to new directions for future research. I would have liked to set up an online course and implement the pedagogical approaches I propose in this book, but the global pandemic of Covid-19 changed our lives and our priorities so dramatically in spring 2020 that I decided to postpone it. I am confident I will find the time in the near future to offer the course to doctoral students and early-career researchers at my own institution and, with their feedback, revise and improve the course materials and make them freely available to students and researchers worldwide.

This book would not have been possible without the support of the Spanish Ministry of Economy and Competitiveness and the European Social Fund under the project 'Ecologies of genres and an ecology of languages: the dynamics of local, cross-border and international scientific communication' (project code FFI2015–68638-R MINECO FEDER, EU), and the support of the Government of Aragon to the research group 'Comunicación internacional y retos sociales' (project code H16_20R). This book is also a contribution to the Digital Science research strand of the Institute for Biocomputation and Physics of Complex Systems (BIFI, University of Zaragoza, Spain). Thanks especially to the members of the Genres and Languages team, colleagues and friends, for sharing their thoughts and work on genres and languages and making me think deeply about how best to approach genre theory in this book.

As always, my heartfelt thanks to my family, who have supported me immeasurably throughout the research and writing.

I gratefully acknowledge permission to use the WrELFA (Written English as a Lingua Franca) corpus of the University of Helsinki (Finland) and permission to reproduce materials under Creative Commons licenses. The survey research conducted in this book complied with the ruling legislation of personal data protection (REGULATION (EU) 2016/679 OF THE EUROPEAN PARLIAMENT AND OF THE COUNCIL on the protection of natural persons with regard to the processing of personal data and on the free movement of such data, and repealing Directive 95/46/EC (General Data Protection Regulation). The survey protocols were approved by the Data Protection Office at the University of Zaragoza.

Abbreviations

AEs	Academic Englishes
AmE	American English
AoF	Article of the Future
ASNSs	Academic social networking sites
CARS	Create-a-Research-Space
CEFR	Common European Framework of Reference for Languages
DA	Data article
DDL	Data-driven learning
DiB	*Data in Brief*
EAP	English for Academic Purposes
ELF	English as a Lingua Franca
ERPP	English for Research Publication Purposes
IMRaD	Introduction, Materials, Methods and Discussion
ISI	International Scientific Indexing
JoVE	*Journal of Visualised Experiments*
L1	First language
L2	Second language
LAP	Languages for Academic Purposes
LFEs	Lingua Franca Englishes
LMS	Learning management system
NES	Native English speakers
NNES	Non-native English speakers
OA	Open Access
RGaL	Research Genres across Languages
SDGs	Sustainable development goals
SLA	Second Language Acquisition
STEMM	Science, technology, engineering, mathematics and medicine
TDFram	Eaquals Framework for Language Teacher Training and Development
WE	World Englishes

1 Research Genres in Context

1.1 Opening remarks

This book is a contribution to the existing literature on genres and English for Academic and Research Purposes. It builds on seminal work in genre studies and scholarly writing and, specifically, on John M. Swales's *Genre Analysis: English in Academic and Research Settings* (1990) and *Research Genres: Explorations and Applications* (2004). Both have been enormously influential pieces of work. Their bibliometric records – over 18,000 and 3,700 citations, respectively, according to Google Scholar at the time of drafting this book – evince a deep interest in the study of genres of scientific research communication. While *Genre Analysis* sets the theoretical foundations for the analysis of genres from text-linguistic, discourse and sociolinguistic perspectives, Swales's latter volume 'situates the research world in a wider context, discusses its various constellations of genres, reviews the status of the non-native speaker of English in that world, and reflects on possible roles for the analyst' (Swales, 2004: 1). The present book expands on these four investigative goals by critically examining the new social and sociolinguistic scenarios in which research genres today support socioliterate activity. Essentially, the book explores how, within these scenarios, research genres enable the enactment of social intentions across linguistically diverse academic and research settings.

The book also seeks to contribute an empirically informed description of genre evolution and innovation in multilingual scientific knowledge production and dissemination. To this end, it will cover a broader repertoire of web-mediated genres than that described in Swales, as Web 2.0 officially began precisely in 2004. My aim is to reflect on the interdependence of traditional and emerging genres and bring into focus the polycontextuality of the digital medium and the effects of what is called 'context collapse' (Marwick and boyd, 2011) on processes of 'genre remediation' and 'knowledge recontextualisa-tion' (Engeström, Engeström and Kärkkäinen, 1995; Spinuzzi and Zachry, 2000). While Swales's *Genre Analysis* and *Research Genres* mainly focused on issues of English in academic and research settings, this book acknowledges the functional role of English as a language for scientific communication on a global scale (e.g., English for Research Publication Purposes, ERPP hereafter) and also addresses issues of multilingual genre use for local, cross-border and global research communication.

At a time of profound social and technological transformation, the dynamics of knowledge production, distribution and consumption in global academia are undergoing dramatic changes. Because these dynamics have become more diverse, complex and multifaceted than ever before, this chapter first situates the contemporary research world in the context of ongoing globalisation processes in order to explore the outcomes of increasing global interaction and networking among researchers worldwide. Here, the concept of genre becomes a central construct to understand 'social ways of knowing and acting in the world' (Bawarshi and Reiff, 2010) and to examine aspects of scientific[1] knowledge exchange and dissemination, focusing on those genre-mediated activities that draw upon the rapidly changing technological affordances, particularly those of Web 2.0. Additionally, this chapter also reviews the critical conceptualisations of genre practices proposed by North American rhetorical genre studies to examine generic evolu-tion, innovation and change in research communication from both theoretical and empirical perspectives. In this sense, the book as a whole will be summative and, above all, forward-looking and agenda-setting for future enquiry into research genres.

This book was also motivated by the paucity of in-depth theoretical enquiry into two fundamental issues that cut across research genres and socioliterate activity today. The first is the increasing reliance on digital technologies in research communication, as discussed in key rhetorical genre studies such as those of Gross and Buehl (2016) and Miller and Kelly (2017), as well as in recent ethnographic studies that

---

[1] Although this book will focus on the STEMM (science, technology, engineering, mathematics and medicine) sciences, it will include occasional comments and references to the social sciences and the humanities. These fields are also scientific fields of enquiry. Research in literature, politics, psychology and philosophy does not generally use quantifiable data, but it nonetheless relies on data sources, analytical and critical methods and interpretive frameworks. More importantly, their research activity likewise draws on repertoires of (digital) genres and produces multilingual research outlets of various kinds. Therefore, at certain points this book will briefly address analogies across the disciplines.

have enquired into the impact of web-mediated communication on scholars' literate activity (Tusting et al., 2019). In this book I will argue that new ways of accessing and disseminating science in digital media are having a dramatic impact on current scholarly socioliterate practices. I will discuss how new social exigences account for the emergence of new genres (Kelly and Maddalena, 2016; Kelly and Miller, 2016; Luzón and Pérez-Llantada, 2019), the evolution of traditional, 'stabilised-for-now' (Schryer, 1994: 108) genres and the gradual disappearance and loss of some existing genres such as the book monograph (Abt, 2007). In subsequent chapters, I will explain the way traditional genres such as the journal article and the abstract are enriched by the technological affordances of the Internet and become 'enhanced publications' that offer authors and readers greater possibilities of knowledge access, circulation and dissemination through the multimodality and hypertextuality afforded by the digital medium (Gross and Buehl, 2016). In addition to aspects of genre remediation, it is also of interest for the genre analyst to understand how Web 2.0 has prompted the emergence of new genres and media formats (e.g., graphical abstracts, webinars, open laboratory notebooks, research blogs, podcasts and visualised experiment articles, among others) and how it impacts the text-composing process itself utilising 'visual rhetoric' and 'multimedia rhetoric' (Pauwels, 2006). Understanding genre uptakes, that is, 'how genres are taken up in certain ways and not others' (Bawarshi, 2016: 190) in the new media environment, for example through the use of multimodal and hypertextual affordances, to surpass the boundaries between expert readers and lay publics also seems a necessary investigative endeavour. Examining the world of research genres in new media environments can give us new insights into the form and substance of genres and, more importantly, into the interdependence between traditional and emerging genres, creating new genre assemblages and complex generic constellations in the digital medium. Linguistic and rhetorical approaches to genres and descriptions of the form and substance of the expanding repertoire of research genres are thus necessary to inform pedagogical practice and support researchers' professional development.

The second crucial issue that this book seeks to address relates to the implications that ensue from the linguistically diverse academic and research settings within which genres support socioliterate activity. While the existing literature has mostly focused on English-medium research communication, we are starting to see an increasing number of publications supporting the view that local, cross-border and global research communication involves multilingual practices (Corcoran,

Englander and Muresan, 2019; Lillis and Curry, 2010). We are also witnessing growing scholarly interest in bringing to the fore linguistic diversity in research communication practices (Gentil and Séror, 2014; Linares, 2019; Mauranen, 2012; Mauranen et al., 2010, 2020) and in the way multilingual digital genres enable researchers to reach both expert audiences and broader publics (Luzón, 2018a; Luzón and Pérez-Llantada, forthcoming). Theoretical research on genres in relation to plurilingual practices is very limited to date, even though it can help us better understand the outcomes of global Englishes and 'transcultural flows' (Pennycook, 2007) in contemporary academic and research settings. Issues of multilingual science production and dissemination have been under-researched and, perhaps, somewhat underappreciated at a time in which international research collaboration and networked communication have privileged English over other languages of science – see, for example, Phillipson's (1992, 2003) claims on English linguistic imperialism. To fill this gap, in this book I aim to address the transversal role of languages for academic and research communication in genre-supported activity and describe some language-related phenomena that characterise contemporary science communication. The book intends to assess the scope of what Pennycook (2007) refers to as 'increased local diversity' that results from socioliterate activity involving the use of researchers' first (local/national) language(s) and the use of other languages. Such diversity can best meet the specific language education needs of graduate students, junior and senior researchers worldwide, who increasingly need to engage in new web-mediated forms of sharing and disseminating their research work drawing on plurilingual language repertoires.

Given these considerations, the overarching goal of this book is to demonstrate that genre theory has gained momentum at a time of profound social and technological transformations. The book will examine the current debates on written genres in relation to languages for communicating research with a view to assessing the value of multilingual science online using the genre analytical lens.

1.2 Situating genres and languages

Rhetorical genre studies and English for Academic Purposes (EAP hereafter) studies define genres as frames for social action that support researchers' socioliterate activity (Bawarshi and Reiff, 2010; Bazerman, 1994; Miller, 1984; Swales, 1990, 2004). An enquiry into today's research communication therefore requires a critical examination of the broad contexts of social interaction in which genres are situated in order to understand how they are influencing the distribution and diffusion of scientific research. The conditions of globalising processes have fuelled the production and dissemination of scientific knowledge across national borders and fostered competitiveness, contributing to the progress and modernity of society (Pérez-Llantada, 2012; de Swaan, 2001). These contexts are intrinsically related to the constitutive conditions of knowledge-based societies (UNESCO, 2010), enabling the free flow of knowledge that links growth and economic development to the production and consumption of knowledge (World Bank, 2016). According to the *UNESCO Science Report: Towards 2030* (UNESCO, 2015), these conditions already involved 7.8 million researchers in 2013 and an overall production of 1,270,425 scientific articles listed in the Science Citation Index of Thomson Reuters' Web of Science in 2014. Both figures are on an upward trend.

1.2.1 Language, migration and mobility

Scholars and research staff's migration and mobility, together with the technological affordances of the Internet, have stimulated international cooperation in research and development activities across knowledge-based societies. The literature points out several benefits of international mobility. For Geuna (2015), the high demand for researchers has increased skilled migration and, in turn, researchers' productivity and the overall scientific output production of several countries. This author also observes that skilled migration results in financial gains for higher education and research institutions and greater availability of shared infrastructures. Using literature review data and data from a survey administered to UK-based researchers, Guthrie et al. (2017a, 2017b) define mobile researchers in Europe as a skilled population with a high potential to establish and maintain collaboration with other researchers worldwide. As these authors argue, mobile researchers represent increased staff expertise and skills development for both source (home) countries and destination countries (Guthrie et al., 2017a, 2017b: vi). These authors further add that the main reasons for migrant researchers becoming mobile range from personal interests in developing research networks and collaboration to professional development, career advancement and a better salary (Guthrie et al., 2017a, 2017b: 18). Interestingly, Guthrie et al.'s (2017a, 2017b: 20) study reports that patterns of mobility are related to the researchers' 'familiarity with the language and the culture of the destination country', the US and the UK being the preferred destinations of mobile researchers from Europe and Asia.

In the context of skilled migration and mobility, English remains 'the' shared language of international scientific exchange, collaboration and networking, corroborating earlier concerns regarding the predominance of English as a scientific and research language and the geopolitics of English academic writing (Canagarajah, 2002a; Ferguson, 2007, 2012; Giampapa and Canagarajah, 2017; Lillis and Curry, 2010; Phillipson, 1992, 2003). By way of illustration, the report 'UK research and the European Union: The role of the EU in international research collaboration and researcher mobility' reflects the growing international collaboration between anglophone and non-anglophone countries. While in the period 2005–2014 almost 40 per cent of the research papers published by the UK involved international co-authorship with EU partners, in 2015 such collaboration increased up to 60 per cent (Royal Society, 2011: 4). The International Collaboration Index (National Science Foundation Science and Engineering Indicators, 2016) indicates a similar trend. Nearly 40 per cent of the United States' international articles involve co-authorship with researchers from 'outer' and 'expanding circle' countries in Kachruvian terms – Brazil, China, France, Germany, Italy, Japan, the Netherlands, South Korea, Spain, Sweden and Switzerland. Supranational interests in the global outreach and excellence of research also become manifest in the EU's collaboration policies with the BRIC countries (Brazil, Russia, India and China (Boekholt et al., 2009)).

To grasp the dynamics of languages in today's research communication, we should bear in mind the important paradigm shift in the field of sociolinguistics. While the World Englishes (WE hereafter) phenomenon was initially described using the traditional scales of space and time as a phenomenon entailing the development of localised varieties of English in stable spaces across the globe (Crystal, 2003), post-globalisation brings about the need for a new paradigm, the 'sociolinguistics of globalisation' (Blommaert, 2010; Blommaert and Dong, 2010; Coupland, 2010). The 'sociolinguistics of distribution', the traditional sociolinguistic paradigm applied to the study of the structure of language and language variation and change, describes the movement of language resources in relation to horizontal and stable spaces (Wardhaugh, 1998: 12). According to this paradigm, the scales of space and time are no longer valid to explain the sociolinguistic variation of the English language because 'the mobility of people involves the mobility of linguistic and sociolinguistic resources' – hence, '"sedentary" patterns of language use are complemented by "trans-local" forms of language use' (Blommaert and Dong, 2010: 367–368). In view of the increasing collaboration and mobility in today's research world, it seems apposite to adopt Blommaert and Dong's (2010) view of 'language-in-motion, with various spatiotemporal frames interacting with one another' to understand language variation and patterns of language use in research communication and to better grasp how genres support literate activity in (socio)-linguistically diverse academic and research settings. Further, as argued in Chapters 6 and 7 of this book, it seems germane for genre analysts to focus on language variation in the English-medium practices that facilitate researchers' mobility and international collaboration and, at the same time, to bring to the fore linguistic diversity in science communication in the age of digital and social media.

1.2.2 Dynamic multilingualism

'Language-in-motion' is a useful construct to understand how the spread of English in global scientific knowledge exchange permeates genred activity across multilingual communities of researchers worldwide. In many ways, it explains different phenomena of language glocalisation in research communication. For example, EAP studies have claimed that L2 English academic writing is discursively hybrid (Mauranen, 2018; Pérez-Llantada, 2012, 2013a). Discoursal hybridisation is the term used to describe how the texts written by researchers from non-anglophone linguacultural backgrounds exhibit linguistic features and aspects of rhetoric and argumentation characteristic of the writers' L1 academic writing tradition, as well as linguistic and rhetorical resources of anglophone academic writing. These glocal variants of the English language, discussed in Chapter 4 of this book, have been conceptualised using labels such as 'academic Englishes' (AEs hereafter) (Mauranen, Pérez-Llantada and Swales, 2010, 2020), 'English as a Lingua Franca' (ELF hereafter) (Mauranen, 2012, 2018) and Lingua Franca Englishes (LFEs hereafter) (Guillén and Vázquez, 2018). They apply equally to descriptions of English language variation in written and spoken genres as well as in digital genres (Luzón, 2018a). AEs, ELF and LFEs strongly suggest that English is a language-in-motion from which distinct similects have emerged that instantiate a parallel phenomenon to that of WE at the micro-level of social interaction, namely, academic and research settings (Mauranen, 2018).

Other outcomes of academics and researchers' migration and mobility that also relate to dynamic multilingualism and corroborate the view of English as a 'language-in-motion' are language phenomena such as 'languaging' (Shohamy, 2006) 'translanguaging' (Canagarajah, 2013) and 'polylanguaging in superdiversity' (Jørgensen et al., 2011) that occur in communities of plurilingual language users. EAP studies have reported the use of multilingual repertoires in communities in which researchers use their local or national language, English, and other languages to communicate research through traditional genres of research (e.g., journal articles, abstracts and theses, to name a few) (Corcoran, Englander and Muresan, 2019; Muresan and Pérez-Llantada, 2014) as well as through web-mediated genres (Luzón, 2017, 2018b regarding research group blogs and microblogging). These practices suggest that genre-mediated action involves multilingual competence, or 'the command and/or use of two or more languages by an individual speaker' (Herdina and Jessner, 2002: 52). The conditions, constraints and consequences of using plurilingual genre repertoires for communicating science are issues that need to be investigated further to gain insight into socioliterate activity within and across (socio)linguistically diverse communities of researchers worldwide. It is also worthwhile to examine single monolingual genres and, above all, to focus on the language dynamics of interdependent genres and genre assemblages in one or more languages. Genre research, particularly in these latter aspects, is limited to date.

1.3 Commodification of science

In the wider contexts of ongoing post-globalisation and increasing migration and mobility, technological developments have emerged as one of the primary drivers of the massive increase in the production and diffusion of knowledge without any time and space constraints. It is therefore important to consider how Web 2.0 supports genre-mediated action for research communication in the broad social world that sociologist Anthony Giddens (1990) conceptualises as 'late modernity', an age of heterogeneity in global mass communication. At the macro-level of genre-mediated activity, both the production and consumption of knowledge in knowledge-based societies have become commodities, since both have a use value and an exchange value. Knowledge production is measured using bibliometric indicators such as the number of articles published in high-impact-factor journals and citation counts, and innovation and transfer indicators are used to measure countries' economic growth and the quality of the research outreach of higher institutions and that of individual researchers (Glänzel, Debackere and Meyer, 2007; OECD, 2008).

International recognition in higher education is also measured in terms of use-value and exchange-value indicators. Spencer-Oatey and Dauber's (2015) benchmarks for mapping and profiling internationalisation in higher education institutions include the following structural indicators: staff members' organisation of international conferences, participation in exchange programs and international professional associations, attendance at international conferences and seminars, delivery of conference presentations abroad, participation in internationally funded projects and research networks, multilateral projects and international cooperation contracts, publication of books and articles in internationally refereed journals and number of highly cited authors (Spencer-Oatey and Dauber, 2015). Altbach (2004: 65) provides a different example, that of leading Chinese universities whose 'local' needs remain an essential and distinct counterpart of the 'global' in the process of internationalisation. These universities mainly produce research for internal use and draw on this stock of knowledge to establish links with the outside world. Underpinning these policies lie bilingual practices.

Turning to the micro-level of genre-mediated activity, we see in the literature that supranational, national and institutional research policies have had a significant impact on the types of genres researchers today engage in. Lillis and Curry (2010: 1) contend that the pressure on researchers to publish is the outcome of research policies that act as 'systems which influence academic text production in powerful ways'. When referring to the Research Excellence Framework in the UK, Tusting (2018: 483) explains the impact of 'genre regimes of research evaluation', that is, 'systems of accountability driven by institutions' need to succeed in the national competitive research evaluation system privileging particular types of output (journal articles, and, to a lesser degree, research monographs), published in particular locations.' In short, career advancement is linked to the production of journal articles in JCR high-impact-factor journals. Regrettably, predatory journals have emerged that publish authors' manuscripts for a publication fee in cases where JCR standards are unattainable.

One useful heuristic for understanding why a genre like the journal article stands as a core genre for research communication is the theory of structuration proposed by Anthony Giddens (1986) in his work *The Constitution of Society*. Giddens explains that social interaction practices lie at the intersection of structures and agents. In the case of the journal article, we could argue that this key writing activity for scientists takes place within a well-established *patterning of interaction* among different actors (authors, journal editors and reviewers). Moreover, journal article writing responds to the expectations of diverse agents – not only scientists or expert peers but also other science stakeholders such as funding organisations and governmental bodies. The intersection of structures and agents can explain why the traditional journal article as a print genre becomes in the digital medium an enhanced publication with greater visibility and impact. The Article of the Future (AoF hereafter) best illustrates this point. In the AoF the article contents are enhanced with multimodal and hypertextual elements (e.g., graphical abstracts, embedded videos, short summaries, audioslides and external hyperlinks), creating a macrogenre formed by the core genre (the article) and extensions of this genre (the add-on genres aimed at enhancing the article contents) (Casper, 2016; Cox, 2015; Pérez-Llantada, 2013b). Another example can be found in scientific video journals such as the *Journal of Visualised Experiments* (JoVE hereafter). This journal publishes articles reporting methodological protocols along with their associated video methods articles. In these videos the scientists thoroughly explain the methodological procedures and steps followed in their study so that other researchers can replicate the study (Hafner, 2018).

Digitisation of printed texts has also improved the circulation of knowledge via digital libraries, in which knowledge is stored locally and accessed remotely. Authors are able to share their research data with other scientists in a large scale, generally open-access, research-data repositories. Some journals have prompted the emergence of the so-called data articles, described as 'brief, citable articles' that offer authors the possibility to publish an abbreviated account of the significance of their data and make their data public along with the original journal article. Open access (OA hereafter) possibilities also account for the transformation of another traditional genre, the peer review, into a digital genre, the open peer review (Breeze, 2019). Likewise, Mehlenbacher (2019a) describes the genre of registered reports, a genre that has emerged as a requirement of the 'reproducibility of science', as a response to the need to make methodological procedures more transparent and science more trustable through a two-stage peer-review process. Scientists first submit a methodology report indicating the stages of the methodological protocol and, once this report is peer reviewed and accepted, the authors submit the full article for a second-round review.

1.3.1 Science in society

The inseparability of structures and agents postulated by the structurational approach can also help genre analysts to understand why some new genres on the web have emerged as a response to actors other than peer scientists, namely, publics with diverse knowledge backgrounds and interests in science. An example of transformative practice in science communication today is the case of genres related to science education and the citizen science movement. These genres have emerged in response to new social exigences, namely, the need for enhanced collaboration, reproducible research and accountable and responsible science (Fecher and Friesike, 2014; Science Europe, 2017). Citizen science is a radically new form of production and consumption of scientific knowledge that involves close collaboration between scientists-authors and interested individuals who become project volunteers to collaborate with the researchers in the data collection and interpretation stages (Reid and Anson, 2019). Other genres that have emerged in response to more open approaches to scientific results are lay summaries and research blogs, inter alia, as well as new forms of communicating science to a non-expert, diversified public, such as lay abstracts, 60-second video narratives and crowdfunding project proposals. Internet-mediated texts distributed via social media networks such as Twitter, Facebook and Reddit are also increasingly playing a key role in disseminating science to the broad public. Social interaction through academic social networking sites (ASNSs hereafter) such as ResearchGate and Academia.edu (Jordan, 2014), as well as microblogging sites such as Facebook, Twitter, Reddit and WeChat in academia in China (*Nature Methods*, 2020[2]), are new ways scientists use to inform and debate science with experts and broader audiences. Even if they do not yet hold the same status of 'valued genres' in the existing systems of research evaluation as traditional genres such as the journal article and abstract do, they do add social value to scientific knowledge production. In the following text, I briefly introduce the context of these new practices.

Disseminating research in the public sphere seems particularly germane at a time in which the United Nations' 2030 Agenda for Sustainable Development has placed the focus on education. Digital genres such as citizen science projects, for instance, make science with and for society, by this means enabling a more participatory framework between scientists and other science stakeholders. One could further argue that this scientific practice in many ways aligns with the UN's Goal 4 – Quality Education (Ensure Inclusive and Quality Education for All and Promote Lifelong Learning). The consumption of scientific knowledge by society in general (i.e., by broad audiences) stands as a feasible way to support citizens' education in science, which may in turn help to achieve other SDGs included in the 2030 Agenda. New forms of scientific practice and engagement in genres of

[2] Science on WeChat. *Nature Methods*, 17, 863 (2020), https://www.nature.com/articles/s41592-020-0954-1

science with and for society can contribute in many ways to the global citizenship's education in issues of science and in current societal concerns such as good health and well-being, affordable and clean energy, climate action, life on land or responsible consumption and production, to name a few, as I will also try to illustrate in this book.

Under existing genre regimes, these new forms of communicating science do not benefit individual scientists' work in terms of recognition or promotion of an academic career as genres such as journal article publications do. Nevertheless, to individual researchers, above all if they are supported by the policies and principles of Open Science, citizen science could make these genres a feasible means of achieving the goals of the 2030 Agenda (Science Europe, 2017). As the scholarly literature attests, researchers can act as disseminators of science and effectively make science accessible and reachable to non-specialist audiences, hence the social impact of genres for public communication of science. By way of illustration, while admitting that TED presentations do not impact the citation count of an academic, Sugimoto et al. (2013: 2) point out that according to popularity metrics, TED Talks are 'a highly successful disseminator of science-related videos, claiming over a billion online views'. In citizen science projects, volunteers collaborating in the classification of scientific data of various kinds can be thousands (Luzón and Pérez-Llantada, forthcoming). A total of 7.8 million researchers worldwide (UNESCO, 2015) is indeed an important stock of human resources who can inform and educate society in issues of science while aiming to solve social problems. It thus seems germane to address the scope of public communication of science from a genre analytical perspective. Imbalances across world regions, such as researcher density in low-income countries (121 per million inhabitants) and high-income countries (3,814 per million inhabitants [UNESCO, 2015]), should also be acknowledged when considering the potential reach of digital genre action, even if they fall outside the scope of this book.

1.4 Languages of science

One of the main language-related debates over the past two decades has been the dominant use of English for scientific communication and, more specifically, for the publication of research outcomes in the form of scientific articles, the scientific genre par excellence. In the late 1990s and the first decade of the new millennium, the widespread use of English as the language of science was regarded by some as a critical threat. Arguments on the adverse effects of the dominance of English mainly came from the perspective of 'linguistic imperialism' (Ammon,

2006; Hamel, 2006a; Phillipson, 1992). The opponents of the predominance of English as a scientific language contended that English
spreads to the detriment of other languages of science and argued that
prior to the dominance of English, other scientific languages such as
French and German were widely used languages of research. The main
reason why English has dominated over other scientific languages is
because it has 'real or potential access to modernisation, science,
technology, etc. with the capacity to unite people within a country
and across nations, or with the furthering of international understanding' (Phillipson, 1992: 272). Yet English is also viewed as a highly
functional language in the context of knowledge exchange and dissemination. As seen in survey- and interview-based studies on attitudes
towards English over the past decades, scholars from diverse linguacultural backgrounds – for example, Bosnia, China, Germany,
Iceland, Mexico, Romania, Thailand or Turkey, to name a few –
emphasise the instrumental value of English. According to the EAP
literature, English-medium communication enables scientists to reach
an international audience, maintain international cooperation with
other peer scientists overseas, advance scientific knowledge and, at
the individual level, comply with research evaluation systems and
achieve career progression (Ferguson, Pérez-Llantada and Plo, 2011;
Flowerdew, 1999; Phothongsunan, 2016). Notwithstanding the
advantages of a shared language, the dominance of English remains
an issue that needs addressing in the genre research agenda. As
I argued elsewhere, the position of English at the top of the hierarchy
of languages for research communication purposes poses threats to the
ecology of genres itself (Pérez-Llantada, 2019). It may lead to the
attrition of genres used to disseminate knowledge in local or national
languages, especially if we consider the existing 'genre regimes' and
'systems of rewards' for research assessment mentioned previously
(Lillis and Curry, 2010; Tusting, 2018). Additionally, it raises concerns regarding the ecology of languages of science if we add an
anthropological perspective (Geertz, 1983) to the genre perspective.
Tensions between competing languages and the demise of languages
(Skutnabb-Kangas, 2000; Skutnabb-Kangas and Phillipson, 2001)
may lead to loss of knowledge of local scientific facts (Haberland,
2005; Ljosland, 2007). And there is also evidence that only the use of
the language of the local setting can preserve local knowledge of
science (see, e.g., Amano, González-Varo and Sutherland, 2016, for
the case of indigenous languages).

At the onset of this introduction, I quoted Swales's goal in *Research
Genres*, namely, to review the status of the non-native speaker of
English in academic and research settings. Two important conclusions

drawn by Swales were, first, that rather than nativeness or non-nativeness, at present it is more correct to talk about 'broadly English proficient' versus 'narrowly English proficient' (Swales, 2004: 57) and, secondly, that the 'native speaker' model is no longer viable when the ratio of non-native English speakers to native English speakers is 3:1 (Lillis and Curry, 2010). EAP research also supports the view that non-English-speaking researchers are legitimate users of English, thus making 'non-nativeness concerns' questionable. Hynninen and Kuteeva (2017) and Rozycki and Johnson (2013) offer convincing evidence that 'good/acceptable English' – that is, the use of non-standard features of English in research articles written in English by non-native English-speaking researchers – no longer hampers acceptance for publication. Then, if the use of English by non-native English speakers does not mean failure in getting research work published in English-medium journals, we can deduce, as Swales (2004) suggests, that aspects such as expertise in writing and knowledge of genre conventions are the determining factors for successful publication of primary genres of research, particularly genres involved in gatekeeping practices, such as journal articles and abstracts.

Regarding Swales's second conclusion, it is actually rather difficult to ascertain the extent to which the number of native speakers has declined. In terms of raw figures, it indeed has. According to Crystal, as of 2003, non-native speakers of English (NNES hereafter) already outnumbered the native English speakers. The estimated number of researchers worldwide (7.8 million) presumably constitutes a multilingual community formed by speakers of diverse language backgrounds. A clear-cut native or non-native divide falls somewhat short if one considers the outcomes of the ongoing migration and mobility discussed previously. As regards the language, large-scale phenomena such as AEs, ELF and LFEs, mentioned previously, evince academic English language variation and are 'essentially multilingual' in nature (Jenkins, 2015: 49). On the other hand, there are reasons to believe that the NES/NNES divide remains valid in some ways. Even if perceptions and attitudes may be influenced by ideological discourses, the particular twists and turns that researchers from non-anglophone environments experience when writing articles in English medium journals or participating in international conferences, extensively documented in the literature, in a way explain why their native-English speaking counterparts are perceived as a privileged group by virtue of their native status. Here, at least one factual argument in support of this perception is a fundamental Second Language Acquisition (SLA hereafter) principle: only about 5 per cent of second language learners develop the same mental grammar as native speakers. Echoing Selinker (1972), the reported language challenges experienced by researchers from non-anglophone linguacultural backgrounds strongly suggest that many learners' interlanguage stops developing some way short. Hence, the model of dynamic multilingualism becomes key in order to assess from the genre analytical perspective the value of plurilingual competence, both individual and collective, for producing and consuming scientific knowledge. After all, a look at the scholarly literature clearly suggests that it is only the journal article, the 'privileged' genre, which prompts the NNES researchers' perceptions of unfair play in a 'publish in English or perish' research world.

In assessing the consequences of globalisation for language use, Haberland (2005: 227) objected to the classical concept of 'domain' used to identify 'different areas of language use in multilingual societies, which are relevant for language choice'. In his view, this concept was limited to identify people's actual behaviour towards language choice because globalising processes have brought about 'multilingual societies with in-group multilingualism' (Haberland, 2005: 228). Like Haberland, it is my contention in this book that the classical concept of domain is neither fully applicable to multilingual academia nor fully explanatory of its intricate processes of socioliterate activity and definitely not always the best approach for tracking the complex and changing dynamics of language choice and multi-/plurilingual practices in science communication online. Whereas the scholarly literature has been – perhaps excessively – focused on the effects of 'Englishisation' in the domain of research communication and raised concerns towards the gradual loss of domains of other academic languages (Hamel, 2006a; Uzuner, 2008), not much attention has been placed on the fact that in contemporary academic and research settings, language choice is highly context- and situationally dependent. Genre-mediated activity in these settings, for example, article writing in international journals and participation in international conferences, is generally associated with English-monolingual practices. However, a basic search for documents in Scopus reveals rich linguistic diversity, namely, the use of fourteen different genres (articles, conference papers, reviews, book chapters, editorials, notes, letters, short surveys, books, conference reviews, data papers, business articles, abstract reports and reports) and forty-four languages, both world languages such as English, French, German, Portuguese and Spanish and other official languages worldwide, like Afrikaans, Arabic, Greek, Hebrew, Indonesian, Latvian, Malay, Norwegian or Urdu, to name a few. In this book, therefore, I would argue that language choice for research communication purposes cuts across very diverse multilingual research settings and local populations of scientists with in-group multilingual practices. Then it seems judicious to align with Haberland's revisited conceptualisation of domain and acknowledge the difficulty of circumscribing the choice of a given language within a single domain of language use.

Given the rich linguistic diversity inherent in multilingual academic and research communities across the globe, it is not possible to establish clear-cut language dominance configurations. In assessing whether English is 'one, many or none', Pennycook (2010a: 682) perceptively notes that so far we have considered languages as 'separate, countable, describable entities', while in today's globalising world it makes more sense to describe them 'in terms of local activities, resources, or practices'. As Pennycook remarks, the idea of communicative repertoires is more suitable to look at 'language in concrete social activity' (p. 683). In this book I will draw on the concepts of genres and language repertoires to examine how research genres, as 'social action' (Bazerman, 1994), support the multiple goals of research knowledge production and dissemination. Using the lens of genre theory, my aim is to disassociate genre-based social action from a specific language and, in doing so, foreground how genred activity may rely on very diverse repertoires of languages. The title of the book itself signals such an endeavour.

1.5 Aims and study design

The main aim of this book is to provide an empirically informed view of the existing ecology of research genres that supports multilingual science communication online. The broad research questions of the Research Genres across Languages (RGaL hereafter) study are the following:

- What genres support the production, circulation and dissemination of knowledge across multilingual settings?
- Do the affordances of Web 2.0 account for genre innovation and change and genre interdependence?
- Does dynamic multilingualism influence genre action?
- Is the current ecology of research genres expanding with the emergence of new modes of science communication?
- Is linguistic diversity wide in scope in science communication online?

In order to answer these questions, the study conducted for this book drew on an explanatory sequential mixed-methods design (Figure 1.1). This type of design enables researchers 'to understand the data at a

Figure 1.1 Proposed explanatory sequential mixed methods (adapted from Creswell, 2013)

more detailed level by using qualitative follow-up data to help explain a quantitative database' (Creswell, 2013: 177). This methodological approach enables the analysis of aspects of genres (e.g., remediation, hybridisation, innovation, evolution and change) and language use (linguistic diversity, language variation, language hybridity, discourse and intertextuality, and register and style). It also sought to explore the interdependence of traditional and new genres in formations of macrogenres and different types of genre assemblages. This analysis was motivated by the need to understand how research genres are shaped and constrained by new social and policy demands, such as making science more trustable in society and making scientific advances accessible to non-expert, diversified audiences. It also sought to examine how genre exemplars on Web 2.0 reflect what has been conceptualised as 'polycontextuality' and 'context collapse' in digital media (boyd, 2002; Marwick and boyd, 2011; Vitak, 2012). On the web the traditional distinction between expert and non-specialist audiences is no longer valid. As this book will seek to demonstrate, communicating science on Web 2.0 entails diversified audiences, with different interests and knowledge backgrounds.

For the study I complemented the literature review with empirical evidence from several small-scale specialised corpora. This type of corpora enables a better contextualisation of discourse (Flowerdew, 2004). Table 1.1 summarises the research data sources this book is based on. The corpora were representative of traditional genre exemplars (mainly articles and abstracts) and emerging genres on the web. It enabled the comparison of sets of genres formed by new genre exemplars and their associated antecedent genres (e.g., graphical abstracts and verbal abstracts, lay summaries and abstracts, data articles and their associated research articles, and so on) and sets of interdependent genres (e.g., short texts and abstracts, video methods articles and their associated methods articles, briefings and associated news, among others) in relation to genre ecologies. The University of Helsinki Written English as a Lingua Franca Corpus science component, SciELF (WrELFA, 2015), was also used for both analytical and comparison purposes. The selected genres of this component were journal articles and blogs.

Table 1.1 An overview of the RGaL study

Empirical research questions	**About the texts** • What are defining features ('form' and 'substance') of remediated genres and emerging genres of research in media environments? What are their communicative purposes and intended audiences? • How do the linguistic, discursive and multimodal (multisemiotic) resources of these genres reflect the polycontextuality of Web 2.0? • What are the organisational and discourse structures of emerging digital genres and to what extent do these structures resemble or differ from the structures of their generic antecedents? • How do digital genres expand, complement and/or recontextualise the information conveyed in traditional genre exemplars when forming genre assemblages? • More broadly, what is the scope of genre stabilisation, innovation and change in Science 2.0 and its impact on society? **About the producers of science** • What repertoires of genres and languages do researchers rely on for professional and public communication of science? • What strategies do scientists use to transform expert knowledge and make it accessible to non-specialist audiences? What languages (and forms of languaging) do they use? • What skills and competences are necessary to communicate science to expert and diversified audiences? • What support do these researchers need to become effective communicators of science?
Methodology and corpus/statistical tools	• Linguistic analysis • Rhetorical (move) analysis • Discourse and register analysis • Multimodal analysis • Descriptive and inferential statistical analysis • *AntcConc* (Anthony, 2019). *KfNgram* (Fletcher, 2002–2007), *Log-Likelihood Calculator* (Rayson and Garside, 2000), *Wordsmith Tools 5* (Scott, 2008), *Web-Based Lexical Complexity Analyser* and *Web-Based L2 Syntactic Complexity Analyser* (Ai, 2010–2017a, 2010–2017b)

(*continued*)

Table 1.1 (cont.)

Quantitative data sources	**General data sources** • Eurostat, OECD • Metadata from journals (views, citations, mentions, downloads, shares, comments, tweets, etc.) • Websites from STEMM magazines and journals (*Cell, Nature, eLife, IEEE Spectrum, PLoS*) • Scientific research data platforms (Dimensions) and platforms from publishers of scientific contents (Cambridge, Elsevier, Springer, Taylor and Francis) • Twitter microblogs comments (#FiridaysForFuture, #schoolstrike4climate, #ClimateStrike, #plasticwaste, #ClimateEmergency, #ClimateAction, #ClimateBreakdown #ClimateEmergency #EUBiodiversity, #UniteBehindTheScience, #scicom. hub) • ResearchGate responses to posts **Small-scale specialised corpora** • *Cell* short summaries and their associated article abstracts ($n = 100$) • *Nature* short summaries and their associated article abstracts ($n = 100$) • *eLife* short summaries and their associated article abstracts ($n = 100$) • *Public Library of Science (PLoS)* abstracts and lay summaries ($n = 100$) • Data articles and their associated abstracts from *Data in Brief* ($n = 100$) • Graphical abstracts from *Journal of Environmental Management* ($n = 100$) • *Journal of Visualized Experiments* (JoVE) video methods articles and their associated written methods articles ($n = 20$) • Podcasts from *Nature* ($n = 10$) • Audioslides from computer science journals[a] ($n = 10$) • Crowdfunding projects from Precipita.com ($n = 10$) • Crowdfunding projects from Experiment.com ($n = 20$)

Qualitative data sources	• Small-scale surveys to sample populations (making a total of $n = 800$ participants)
	  o Authors of *Cell* ($n = 100$)
	  o Authors of *Nature* ($n = 100$)
	  o Authors of *eLife* ($n = 100$)
	  o Authors of *PLoS* ($n = 100$)
	  o Authors of graphical abstracts (*Journal of Environmental Management*) ($n = 100$)

(continued)

Table 1.1 (cont.)

○ Authors of *Data in Brief* articles (*n* = 100)
○ Authors of *JoVE* (*n* = 100)
○ Researchers/project launchers of Experiment.com (*n* = 100)

[a] Available at www.youtube.com/playlist?list=PLZWyFifoawUtF6vOQBtc869Ivs N5kVac0 [last accessed on 16 June 2020].

In addition, a small-scale corpus of microblog comments retrieved from Twitter accounts using hashtags on STEMM and STEMM-communication-related themes (namely, citizen science, climate change, climate emergency, health and well-being, scientific communication and Open Science) was also used for grasping the ongoing social debates about these themes and for better contextualising the rhetorical exigences posed by the polycontextuality and context collapse in digital media.

The main reason for selecting these small-scale corpora was to put together a representative sample of digital genres and enhanced publications, that is, traditional genres and their associated add-on genres (see Harmon, 2019). This was thought to be a suitable approach to track 'genre transmediality' and processes of 'transmedial gradation' (Engberg and Maier, 2015; Maier and Engberg, 2019). Also, a feasible approach to understand how expert knowledge is recontextualised, or rather 'transformed' (Gimenez et al., 2020) in media environments and, more broadly, how genres harness the affordances of Web 2.0 to reach diversified audiences. As shown in Table 1.1, all the data are gathered from several disciplinary subfields in the Science, Technology, Engineering, Mathematics and Medicine sciences (STEMM hereafter).[3] Yet it should be noted that although STEMM will be the main area for enquiry into research genres, on occasions I will refer to disciplinary cultures and disciplinary practices in fields other than STEMM. One reason to delimit the representativeness of the corpus data to the STEMM subfields was to align the study

---

[3] The specific subject areas included Biochemistry, Biophysics, Biostatistics, Biotechnology, Cancer Research/Oncology, Cell Biology, Developmental Biology, Ecology and Evolution, Genetics, Human Disease, Infectious Diseases, Immunology, Metabolism/Endocrinology, Microbiology, Molecular Biology, Neuroscience, Pharmacology/Drug Discovery, Physiology, Plant Biology, Stem Cells, Systems/Computational Biology. These areas involve the broad fields of health sciences, biomedical sciences, environmental sciences, life sciences and earth sciences.

with UNESCO's 2030 Agenda for Sustainable Development. The decision to select only some of the seventeen sustainable development goals (SDGs hereafter) of the 2030 Agenda was based on the World Federation of Science Journals interest in the theme of science communication in the following subject areas: (i) global warming and what societies can do to adapt to climate change, (ii) mental illness, science and global health, (iii) the global crisis of biodiversity and (iv) deep seabed mining.[4]

The corpora were used to carry out a broad descriptive characterisation of the existing repertoire of genres by looking at the rhetorical organisation of web-mediated genres, the strategies deployed for transforming expert knowledge across genres and languages and the linguistic and discoursal resources used to construct an identity, create proximity and engage with expert readers and broader publics. Regarding linguistic features, corpora explorations were based on aspects of vocabulary, grammar and syntax, measures of lexical and syntactic complexity and recurring phraseology. Explorations of colloquialisation and economy features aimed at identifying discourse styles and aspects of register in traditional and digital (hybrid) genres. Lastly, exploratory analyses of some sets of interrelated genres were intended to track the role of intertextuality in genre systems and by this means identify the degree of interdependence between new digital genres and their antecedent genres or associated genres forming different genre ecologies.

In order to better understand the production of genres to disseminate science to both expert and non-expert audiences, the study conducted for this book also drew on small-scale survey research on the 'producers' of those genres. The surveys were targeted at the authors of some of the genre types included in the small-scale corpora compilation (e.g., corresponding authors in high-stakes journals and in open-access journals, authors of enhanced publications and researchers involved in genres related to public understanding of science) (see Table 1.1 for further details). The purpose was to understand the researchers' professional and public science communication practices and their perceptions of Open Science, emerging digital genres and their perceived value. The emic perspective also sought to understand the scientists' text-composing strategies, the skills needed to compose multimodal texts and their views on language repertoires and bi/multiliteracy practices in disseminating knowledge to expert and non-specialist audiences – both local and more widespread.

---

[4] See www.wcsj2019.eu/five-major-themes [last accessed on 16 June 2020].

1.6 Overview of the book

This first chapter has situated research genres in today's rapidly changing technological and social contexts. The aim was to set the scene in which research genres enact social actions, particularly through new media environments, and to focus on systems of genres of research that are evolving in response to the multiple accountabilities of scientific knowledge production, dissemination and consumption today. In reviewing some of the consequences of globalisation, this introduction has briefly presented the particular conditions that post-globalisation processes – for example, skilled migration and the boost in researchers' mobility – have created in academic and research settings. The chapter has also briefly described the effects of such processes on researchers' socioliterate activity at a time of unprecedented (socio)linguistic diversity.

Chapter 2: 'Theories and Metaphors' revises some seminal definitions of 'genre' and key concepts in genre theory, such as 'genres as frames for social action', and 'intended audiences' and 'communicative purpose(s)'. The latter two are key criteria for genre identification (Swales, 1990). The intention is to introduce and reflect upon recent conceptualisations of web-mediated generified activity – for example, 'genre remediation', 'transmediality', 'polycontextuality' and 'context collapse', among others – from the perspective of structuration theory (Giddens, 1990). The chapter also expands on Swales's (2004: 68) understanding of metaphors of genre to critically address aspects of generic evolution, hybridisation and change. This chapter aligns with earlier definitions of genres as relatively stabilised entities and contends that genres tend to evolve as new social purposes surface and as the current frames of social action change. I argue that the genre analyst needs to look not only at context in terms of co-text and intertext (Stubbs, 2001) but also in terms of hypertext, because 'genre' is 'an open category at least partly bounded by constraints of time, resources, availability and access' (Swales, 2004: 72). In this chapter I coin the concepts of 'language collusion' and 'language collisions' and draw on the metaphors of genre(s) and language(s) ecologies to explain the emergence of new genres on the web, the evolution of traditional genres, the interdependence between traditional and new genres and, more importantly, the creation of complex genre assemblages that support multilingual science communication on Web 2.0. Aspects of generic innovation and some examples of how the ecology of the journal article in an online environment draws on constellations of multilingual semiotic resources illustrate the ecological approach to genres.

Chapter 3: 'Science, Genres and Social Action' frames the role of research genres within the much broader social views of Giddens' (1990; 1999) structuration theory and Russell's (1995) activity theory to show how genres act within highly articulated social systems (Berkenkotter and Huckin, 1995). The empirical orientation of this chapter seeks to validate the assumption that the processes underlying generic forms are paramount for assessing how researchers today draw on language repertoires to communicate their research work locally and globally in the physical and the virtual space. Corpus descriptions of diverse research outlets inform a critical discussion on the interrelationships between traditional genres and what Miller and Kelly (2017) define as emerging genres in new media environments. Furthering the existing literature (Büchi, 2016; Gross and Buehl, 2016), the chapter also examines how genre theory stands as a robust analytical framework to understand the multisemiotic options available for the construction of enhanced publications, above all, multimodal and hypertextual possibilities. The chapter also draws on corpus linguistics methods to describe rhetorical, grammar and discourse features of remediated genres, that is, traditional print genres that have moved to a web environment, and their associated genres in the digital medium. Analogies with concepts from the field of literary criticism serve to clarify how emerging digital genres can be conceptualised as 'generic hybrids' (Giltrow, 2017; Herring, 2013) as they draw on features of existing genres and enhance those genres using the multimodal and hypertextual possibilities of the Internet. The chapter finally addresses transformative scientific practice in science communication to illustrate emerging forms of social interaction between scientists and science stakeholders. Discussion revolves around the way the collapsing of contexts influences the form and substance of genres of public communication of science.

Chapter 4: 'Language Diversity in Genred Activity' examines the situatedness of communication practices to discuss the central role of languages in the dissemination of scientific knowledge. The concept of 'fluid societies' (Piller, 2015) and, again, Blommaert's (2010) 'sociolinguistics of mobility' paradigm serve to propose a timely definition of academic and research settings as 'fluid communities' that engage in languaging practices and multilingual genre-mediated interactions. A critical review of the status and functions of English in the language ecology of such interactions introduces some reflections on language-related aspects – translanguaging, polylanguaging, processes of language macroacquisition and coalescence of languages – that characterise generified activity. Corpus and ethnographic (survey) data are used to describe 'glocal' and 'translocal' language use and the social and technological conditions that account for the observable linguistic diversity, language variation and change in and across genres. Like others, I contend that given the diversity of linguascapes, 'English is becoming deterritorialized' and 'losing its identity as a language belonging to the inner circle [native speakers]' (Canagarajah and Said, 2011: 395; see also Canagarajah, 2007; Mauranen, 2018). In contesting the monolingual habitus and foregrounding the plurilingual realities, the chapter closes with some final thoughts on one important concern, namely, the fact that 'languages are still a major barrier to global science' (Amano, González-Varo and Sutherland, 2016).

Chapter 5: 'Genres and Multiliteracies' expands on Johns's (1997) socioliterate view of writing development to integrate this author's view within the mutually beneficial fields of genre theory/analysis and broader fields such as Second Language Acquisition, rhetoric and composition studies. Using survey research, I explore researchers' writing strategies and resources to compose traditional and emerging digital genres in one or more languages. In acknowledging the pedagogical value of individual experiences accumulated in writing practices, this chapter also attaches value to the concept of 'generic interdiscursivity' (Salö and Hanell, 2014), as prior genre knowledge can scaffold the composing process of other genres, both written, spoken and hybrid, through strategies of connectivity across discursive practice. The chapter critically supports Gentil's (2011) important claim of 'biliteracy' in genre practices, or the use of previous genre knowledge in one language to compose genres in other languages. Given the increasing popularity of multimodal digital genres for science communication, the chapter describes aspects of transmedial gradation and strategies of compression and expansion of meaning to make scientific contents accessible to lay audiences. Corpus data also illustrate aspects of multimodal rhetoric and the construction of visual scientific arguments in multisemiotic genres and in multilingual genre sets.

Chapter 6: 'Innovation and Change in Genre-Based Pedagogies' outlines some specialised language planning and course design proposals involving genre-based approaches to Languages for Academic Purposes (LAP hereafter) instruction and/or communication training. In order to be responsive to the current policy scenarios for global science – research policies, internationalisation policies and language policies – as well as receptive to the existing 'genre regimes of research evaluation' (Tusting, 2018), this chapter sketches out some aspects that instruction should take on board, placing the focus on the language and the rhetoric of traditional genres and on the use of data-driven-learning (DDL hereafter) tasks involving multilingual text-composing. I also use a fundamental heuristic for the genre analyst-practitioner, the 'rhetorical consciousness-raising cycle' (Swales and Feak, 2012), to propose some possible tasks involving the text-composing practice of remediated and web-mediated emerging genres, as well as hands-on activities for developing writing skills in ASNSs and social media networking. The chapter also provides some reflective tasks involving both familiarisation and practice with digital resources for multimodal text composing. In closing, the chapter advocates the use of assessment methods and self-assessment reflective tools that I conceptualise as 'plurilingual portfolios of genre assemblages' and 'portfolios of multiliteracies'. I believe these can foster independent, self-directed, lifelong learning and support academics and researchers' professional development throughout their lifespan.

Chapter 7: 'The Way Ahead' will wrap up the main theoretical and methodological arguments raised in the previous chapters concerning the evolutionary nature of genres in order to set an agenda for future joint research on research genres and languages of science. Some final reflections on ecological diversity, the 'multilingualisation of science' (Amano, González-Varo and Sutherland, 2016) and ways of managing language diversity in research communication will validate previous seminal conceptualisations of genre. In closing, the chapter will underline the need to deploy systematic and robust methodologies when conducting genre research, in the belief that this will give greater rigour to the outcomes of future enquiries into research genres across languages.

In reflecting on the possible futures of genres, Swales (2019: 81) contends that research on EAP genres has tended to be 'a) too textual, b) too 'thin' in Geertz's sense, c) too concerned with overall structure, d) too interested in the interpersonal and promotional aspects of research writing, and e) over-focused on our own fields of applied linguistics and ESL'. Echoing Swales's reflection, the following chapters illustrate ways in which future genre and LAP research can redress these limitations and gain further insights into the world of genres in research communication online. It is hoped that the book will be of particular interest to genre analysts, researchers in sociorhetoric, rhetoric and composition, and researchers in the field of Languages for Academic Purposes and academic writing. Because the book also raises issues of multilingualism in research communication, it may be a useful source of information to applied linguists interested in providing solutions to problems and challenges in professional communication practices and to applied sociolinguists investigating the effects of post-globalisation processes on language ecologies in academic and research settings. Language-teaching professionals and materials developers, researchers and professionals in the field of LAP pedagogy, postgraduate students and early-career researchers may also find some theoretically informed, practical approaches to learning science communication in today's rapidly changing digital world.

2 Theories and Metaphors

2.1 Beyond Swales's *Research Genres*

Over the past decade, a significant number of genre and EAP studies have focused on issues relating to research genres across linguacultural contexts and discussed genre-mediated practices in relation to language use and language variation and change. In this section, I carry out a systematic literature review of the main outcomes of these studies, as their approaches all nurture from the Swalesian tradition (Swales, 2004). To conduct this review, I followed Cheng's (2019: 37) recommendation to establish clear 'inclusion and exclusion criteria and the rationales for these criteria'. Accordingly, the review includes published articles (i) that explicitly cited Swales (2004) in carrying out analyses of traditional written genres and/or emerging genres and generic hybrids (i.e., digital multimodal genres), (ii) whose main investigative goal was the characterisation of the selected genre(s) at different textual levels, the genre exemplars (texts) being written in a single language or in two or more languages and (iii) that were published in the past decade. The first criterion aimed to ensure consistency in the use of genre theory as the main interpretative framework to describe genre features. The second criterion was intended to identify and critically assess the reception of Swales's (2004) work in terms of the range of research genres and language(s) analysed. The third criterion sought to ensure the same timeframe of the selected articles and the timeliness of their results. Applying these three criteria, a Google Scholar search yielded 173 studies. Table 2.1 groups the different genres addressed in those studies into broad genre sets for ease of the discussion that follows.

The literature review clearly shows that the research article attracts the most attention, in many ways corroborating the strong impact of the neoliberal agendas of knowledge-intensive economies and the politics of knowledge production on a global scale in academic and

Table 2.1 Overview of genres and part-genres investigated

Genre sets	Genre types	Comparative %
Traditional journal publication-related genres	Research articles, research article sections (introductions, methods, results, discussions, conclusions, acknowledgements), author bionotes, abstracts, editorials	70.7
Tenure-track genres	Book reviews, book prefaces, grant proposals, research reports, prize applications, handbooks, retention-promotion-tenure reports, call for papers in international conferences, conference abstracts, conference posters, proceedings articles	13.2
Early career-related genres	PhD dissertations, part-genres of PhD dissertations (introductions, discussion sections, acknowledgements), other PhD dissertation-related genres (doctoral prospectuses, meta-genre accounts of the dissertation)	10.9
Others (add-on genres and professional genres)	Research highlights, graphical abstracts, short texts accompanying research articles, electronic posters, popular science articles, academic and research blogs, academic home pages, crowdsourcing science projects	5.2

research settings (Canagarajah, 1996; Giampapa and Canagarajah, 2017; Pérez-Llantada, 2012). As noted in the introduction of this book, publishing in top-tier journals is one major undertaking among researchers worldwide (Lillis and Curry, 2010; Tusting, 2018). As shown in Table 2.1, 70 per cent of the studies analysed exemplars of the research article or its part-genres (i.e., introduction, discussion and conclusion sections of research articles) or its accompanying genres, both traditional genres such as abstracts and author bionotes. To these we should add a very small percentage of studies on emerging genres, addressing digitally supported part-genres such as research highlights, and other add-on genres (or extensions of genres) in enhanced publications such as short texts and graphical abstracts. Broadly speaking, all these studies have contributed to advancing the understanding of aspects of genre typification, such as rhetorical organisation, move structure, recurring lexicogrammar, citation conventions and use of interpersonal and promotional features (e.g., Cortes, 2013; Kim and Lim, 2013; Okamura, 2008, to cite a few). The studies consistently claim that the research article is an informationally dense, evaluative, argumentative and highly dialogic genre. Supporting Swales (2004), the observable prototypicality of the journal article and its accompanying genre, the article abstract, confirms that both of them are 'stabilized-for-now or stabilized-enough sites of social and ideological action' (Schryer, 1994: 200).

The literature review also reveals the centrality of disseminating research in English and the hegemonic role of English for research publication purposes. Almost 60 per cent of the studies retrieved from the Google Scholar search examine the journal article genre in relation to the use of English as an international lingua franca and the challenges English poses to non-native English-speaking (NNES) researchers. The main rationale of these studies is pedagogically driven, namely, an interest in providing research data that could inform pedagogical practice. How these researchers acquire and learn genre knowledge and, as Belcher (2009: 221) puts it, 'how research space is created in a diverse research world', to get articles accepted in English-medium journals is the main focus of interest in these studies. Gladkova, DiMarco and Harris's (2015) study on clinical research publications illustrates the pedagogy-driven interest in English as an academic and research language. In stark contrast, only seven studies (less than 5 per cent of all those included in the literature review) report on features of journal articles written in L1s other than English – Arabic, Bulgarian, Chinese, Danish, German and Spanish.

These genre-based cross-linguistic studies that compare journal articles written in English and other L1s and journal articles written in L1 and L2 English varieties (a cumulative total of circa 30 per cent of all the studies surveyed, as shown in Table 2.2) explore convergent and divergent uses of lexicogrammar, rhetoric and style across academic writing traditions, as can be seen in the studies by Demarest and Sugimoto (2014), Geng and Wharton (2016) and Shaw and Vassileva (2009). These cross-linguistic comparisons acknowledge the centrality of English in international research publication practices worldwide (e.g., Buckingham, 2014; Corcoran, Englander and Muresan, 2019; Lillis and Curry, 2010). While, as another study rightly claims, the 'centre-periphery dichotomy in terms of scientific output' seems difficult to redress because it is associated with the social and economic development of each nation state (Salager-Meyer, 2008:

Table 2.2 The journal article investigated across languages/ language varieties

Languages/language varieties	No. of studies	Comparative %
English as an International Language (EIL) (linguacultural backgrounds not specified)	85	48.9
English and other L1s (Arabic, Brazilian, Chinese, French, Italian, Iranian, Malay, Persian, Portuguese, Spanish)	25	14.4
English L1 and English L2/EIL (linguacultural backgrounds: China, Czech Republic, Iran, Spain, Thailand, Turkey)	24	13.8
English L2/EIL (linguacultural backgrounds: Cameroon, Czech Republic, Indonesia, Iran, Japan, Malaysia, Portugal, Slovakia, Turkey, Vietnam)	19	10.9
English (L1 anglophone background)	11	6.3
L1s other than English (Arabic, Bulgarian, Danish, German, Spanish)	7	4.0
English L1, English L2 and L1s other than English (Italian, Spanish)	2	1.1
Korean L1 and English L2 (Korean linguacultural background)	1	0.6

121); in these studies English is described as the preferred language of science for researchers from outside of the anglophone 'inner circle' – to use a Kachruvian term (Kachru, 1986). In a way, these studies move beyond the current debate between 'Goffman's stigma' (Flowerdew, 2008) and the 'myth of linguistic injustice' (Hyland, 2016), which remains open and not uncontroversial (Politzer-Ahles et al., 2016). Notwithstanding possible issues of linguistic disadvantages, 'scholars from "smaller" languages [opt] for English because of the greater scientific impact and prestige associated with a wide international audience' (Giannoni, 2008: 97).

Lastly, pedagogical, ESL-oriented rationales for enquiring into textual and interpersonal aspects of writing in early-career research genres are found in 10 per cent of the studies reviewed. In these studies the doctoral dissertation genre is approached from quantitative (corpus) analytical methods and/or qualitative methods such as experimental classroom-based research methods and ethnomethodology – for example, case studies, written reflections and focus group interviews. Belcher (2009) and Paltridge, Starfield and Ravelli (2012) are representative of this group of studies, offering detailed accounts of advanced literacy development processes and insightful suggestions for genre-based instructional intervention.

Cheng (2019: 38) emphasises that systematic reviews have 'the potential to guide further research actions'. Considering the aforesaid literature review, the clearest gap that future research should address lies in the small number of studies that examine genres for science dissemination in digital media and digitally supported modes. As shown in Table 2.2, less than 5 per cent of the studies included in the literature review focused on remediated genres along the lines described by Bolter and Grusin (1999) and Casper (2016). Interestingly enough, the repertoire of digital genres examined in the selected studies included both digitally mediated genres targeted at expert audiences (e.g., research highlights, graphical abstracts, and the short texts accompanying research articles in online journal platforms), as well as emerging genres that disseminate science to wider audiences and the lay public (e.g., research blogs, academic homepages and science-focused crowdfunding proposals). Swales (2019: 81) himself notes this major gap in current research. It should also be said that the digital genres shown in Table 2.2 are all analysed in relation to processes of genre remediation and transmedial gradation and interpreted in relation to the effects of the polycontextuality of the digital medium (e.g., the case of genres such as electronic posters and graphical abstracts, research group blogs and crowdfunding proposals, to name a few). The studies also contend that digital genres supporting science dissemination beyond expert audiences perform multiple communicative goals – for example, informing, persuading and educating in science – since they respond to multiple science stakeholders' agendas. Studies such as those of Luzón (2011) and Mehlenbacher (2017), on academic weblogs and crowd science-focused projects, respectively, illustrate the main claims regarding emerging digital genres. Lastly, it is also worth pointing out that in these studies, the genre analytical approach cross-fertilises with studies of rhetoric, discourse and multimodality to describe and conceptualise aspects of genre innovation and evolution in online environments (see Chapter 3 for further discussion).

In the following sections, I take the reception of the Swalesian tradition forward and introduce several theorisations to describe how systems of genres and genre repertoires in new media environments relate to multilingual science communication.

2.2 The triple helix

Borrowing the perspective of Giddens's (1990) structuration theory, which foregrounds the inseparable intersection of social structures and agents, in this section I summarise some current theorisations and debates on research genres. The aim is to sketch out the main conceptual and analytical developments.

Supporting the view of genres as relatively stabilised constructs but subject to ongoing evolution and change (Bazerman, 1994; Miller, 1984; Schryer, 1994; Swales, 1990), a look at today's existing repertoire of research genres shows that genre sets, systems, repertoires and ecologies – the four types of genre assemblages proposed by Spinuzzi (2004) to investigate professional communication – remain stabilised to some extent, yet also keep on evolving. The new dynamics in the social organisation of the scientific community – nowadays, increasingly networked and computer-mediated – and the changes in its socioliterate activity as a result of the growth of techno-dependency are the main rationales for the current conceptual and analytical developments in genre theory. As digital genres have gained momentum as a result of social exigences such as the reproducibility of scientific methods and results (Mehlenbacher, 2019a, 2019b; Schulson, 2018) and the 'democratization of science' (Science Europe, 2017; Trench, 2008), important concepts and theorisations have been proposed to explain the rhetoric of digital science communication. I briefly turn to them in what follows.

Concepts such as 'genre webification' and 'genre remediation' (Miller and Kelly, 2017) have been taken up in discussions of enhanced publications resulting from the migration of different types of research outputs – articles, abstracts and reports in print format – to digital environments, as is the case of the AoF (Aalbersberg et al., 2012; Gross, Harmon and Reidy, 2002; Pérez-Llantada, 2013b). The evolutionary changes in these genres result in greater visibility and citational impact of scientists' work in the context of expert-to-expert scientific communication. In this context, the AoF, as a remediated genre, illustrates how the specialised knowledge found in journal article contents can be enhanced in a web environment by means of multimodal elements and hyperlinking affordances (Gross and Buehl, 2016). As shown in Figure 2.1, the core genre remains central, the only difference being that it interrelates with other genres and multimodal elements. This genre forms clusters with its associated traditional and add-on genres (Casper, 2016): the abstract, multimodal genres (graphical abstract/video abstracts/author videos) and elements (e.g., dynamic images and interactive graphs). The article contents are also enhanced with text-internal and text-external hyperlinked sources (related articles) (Gross, Harmon and Reidy, 2002; Harmon, 2019; Mackenzie Owen, 2007; Pérez-Llantada, 2013b; Sancho-Guinda, 2019). Because these extensions work together with the article, we

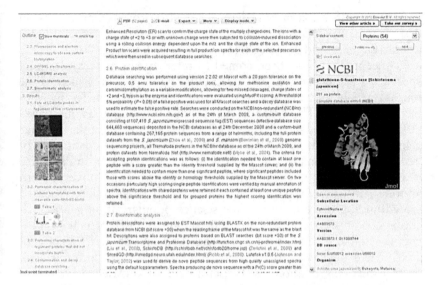

Figure 2.1 The Article of the Future, an enhanced publication (retrieved from www.elsevier.com/connect/designing-the-article-of-the-future [last accessed 7 January 2021])

could argue that the latter has become a macro-genre involving other embedded genres, as conceptualised in Systemic Functional Linguistics, and at the same time the core genre of a complex genre assemblage embedding semantic and hypertextual interconnections across interrelated add-on genres.

Another relevant conceptualisation that has been coined to describe the hybrid nature of digital genres is that of 'generic hybrids' (Giltrow, 2017; Herring, 2013). This conceptualisation applies to new genres that take the form of already existing genres — for example, traditional genres such as journal articles, laboratory notes, laboratory reports and research project proposals and grants. Processes of genre remediation have prompted scholarly interest in the rhetorical nature of generic hybrids such as electronic (digital) laboratory notebooks (Kwok, 2018), registered reports (Mehlenbacher, 2019a), video methods articles (Hafner, 2018), open-access peer reviews (Breeze, 2019) and science-focused crowdfunding projects (Mehlenbacher, 2017; Miller and Shepherd, 2004; Pérez-Llantada, 2021a), to mention a few. These genres address new rhetorical exigences in response to social and policy demands regarding the need to share data, to make scientific methodological procedures more easily reproducible and scientific results more transparent and to democratise science.

Genre webification or remediation has also provoked an interest in describing genre 'transmediality' and processes of 'transmedial gradation' (Engberg and Maier, 2015; Maier and Engberg, 2019). These are concepts that have been coined to refer to ways of transforming specialised knowledge (e.g., the contents found in genres such as the journal article and the abstract) into accessible knowledge in web-mediated genres. These conceptualisations align with Fahnestock's (1986) early theorisation on 'science accommodation' in popular genres, and Bondi, Cacchiani and Mazzi's (2015: 2) definition of 'recontextualisation', or the 'process by which some part of discourse is extracted from one communicative context and conveyed into another'. In internet genres such as research blogs, science-focused crowdfunding projects and online science popularisation genres, scientific contents are transformed and recontextualised to make meanings accessible to diversified audiences (Gimenez et al., 2020; Gotti, 2014; Mehlenbacher, 2017). Maier and Engberg's (2019) framework of 'transmedial gradation' sheds useful light on knowledge expansion and knowledge-enhancement strategies such as the use of multimodal elements and hypertextual features. As these authors explain it, multi-semiotic generic innovations form genre clusters with different levels of explanatory depth to meet the informational demands of diverse audiences and social actors. Reid (2019) also provides an insightful account of how professional writing in citizen science draws on processes of meaning compression and expansion to successfully engage citizens in scientific research.

The evolution of genres and the emergence of digital genres to communicate science has also prompted theorisation on the 'collapsing of social contexts online', to address the polycontextuality of Web 2.0 and the impact of context collapse in digital communication (Davis and Jurgenson, 2014: 478). Polycontextuality refers to the fact that Web 2.0 gives access to knowledge to audiences with diverse knowledge backgrounds, interests, expectations and epistemological worldviews. Science-related genres on the Internet adapt their substance (semantic content) and form (formal features) to new rhetorical exigences, enabling researchers, the main actors in science, to share knowledge with diverse audiences in the virtual space, with no physical constraints of space and time. Further, recent genre research shows that the polycontextuality of the medium accounts for the typified generic features of open-access peer reviews (Breeze, 2019) and the rhetoric of multimodality – as understood in Bateman's (2017) multimodal semiotic framework – that characterises genres for public understanding of science, such as research group blogs, crowdfunding projects and microblogs (Facebook, Twitter, etc.), in which the

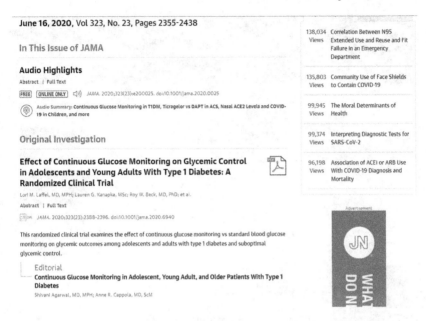

Figure 2.2 Interface of the Journal of the American Medical Association (retrieved from https://jamanetwork.com/journals/jama/issue/323/2 [last accessed on 7 July 2020])

boundaries between expert and non-specialist (lay) audiences are blurred (Mehlenbacher, 2017; Paulus and Roberts, 2018; Reid and Anson, 2019).

The ongoing evolution and increasing diversity of genres is supported by the architecture of digital platforms. Electronic platforms of STEMM journals have been improved to support this diversity of genres, the merging of semiotic modes and the semantics (or meaning-making) of multimodality. These platforms also provide possibilities of information-screening and different entry paths to access information. Figures 2.2 and 2.3 show the embeddedness of different hyperlinked genres and modes of communication – audio highlights, audio summaries, research articles, editorials, tweets, a blog with associated visuals and Facebook posts – in a single interface.

The 'collapsing of contexts', as defined by Davis and Jurgenson (2014), has important implications for multilingual science communication, particularly if we bear in mind that genre-mediated action takes place in and across very diverse linguacultural backgrounds. Given this fact, I would like to propose here the term of 'language collapse' as an analogous conceptualisation. On the one hand, it seems

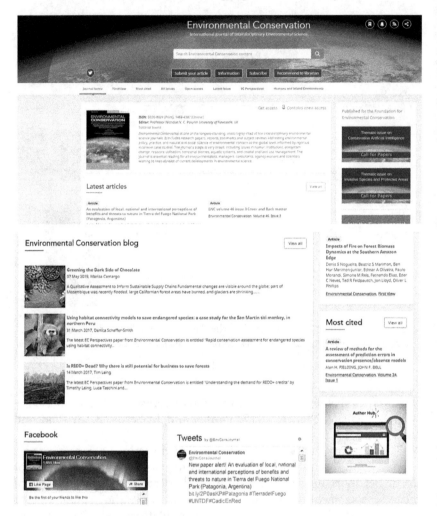

Figure 2.3 Interface of Environmental Conservation
(www.cambridge.org/core/journals/environmental-conservation [last accessed on
7 July 2020])

reasonable to support a shared lingua franca of science, and it is
likewise sensible to support multilingual science dissemination at a
time when the technological affordances of Web 2.0 increasingly
enable researchers to engage with multilingual audiences. However,
there is a possibility of language collisions or a clash of languages (i.e.,
languages colliding in the same situational context). Languages such

as Arabic, Chinese, English, French, German, Portuguese or Spanish, described by de Swaan (2001) as supercentral languages in the global language system, may intentionally or unintentionally prevail over the use of central and peripheral (local/national) languages. We could hypothesise that such language collision might cause a clash of language empires in the domain of research communication if the use of web-mediated genres is on the increase. On the other hand, it seems evident that plurilingualism has large-scale potential to address the polycontextuality of the digital medium. The digital medium might also overcome possible language collusions (e.g., the threat of English-linguistic imperialism) or conflicts of interests in language use. It may also redress language collisions if it is considered inclusive and participatory because it supports multilingual genres, an argument that I will turn to in further detail in Chapter 4. Digital genres such as blogs in research group websites exhibit translanguaging practices that enable researchers to communicate science to audiences with different lingua-cultural backgrounds (Luzón, 2018a).

I would like to make a further point here which is that genre remediation and processes of transmedial gradation are in many ways analogous to North and Piccardo's (2016: 455) concept of 'language mediation', a process of knowledge co-construction that involves 'bridging and exchange between different elements and spaces' and that focuses on 'enhancing communication and reciprocal comprehension or on bridging gaps'. As these authors explain, this concept applies not only to foreign or second language learning but also to other scientific disciplines and contexts of language use. In the Common European Framework of Reference for Languages (CEFR, Council of Europe, 2018), the skill of mediation is defined as the 'co-construction of meaning in interaction' and mediation strategies include 'linking to previous knowledge, amplifying text, streamlining text, restructuring text in the appropriate discourse culture,* breaking down complicated information,* visually representing information** and adjusting language' (North and Piccardo, 2016: 457).

Although North and Piccardo dropped some of these strategies in phase 1* or after pre-consultation** when mediation was implemented in the CEFR, all of them without exception are valid for establishing analogies with the concepts of genre transmediality and transmedial gradation. In genres such as online journal articles, graphical abstracts or crowdfunding projects, to name a few, researchers mainly transform expert knowledge into lay knowledge by summarising, reformulating and paraphrasing strategies, as we will see in Chapter 3. In other words, as part of a transmedial gradation process, researchers adjust their language, shifting from a formal academic register (and compressed discourse style) to an informal register that creates proximity with non-expert readers, which echoes to a great extent Biber and Gray's (2016) claim that formal registers in the age of mass literacy are adopting colloquial features typical of conversation, as further discussed in the following chapter. Along with the verbal message, the multimodal elements in digital genres also address the context and audience collapse of Web 2.0 through processes of 'cognitive mediation', 'facilitating access to knowledge and concepts for others' (North and Piccardo, 2016: 22). For example, the use of the spoken translation of written texts proposed in the CEFR descriptors for mediation skills resembles to a great extent the way multimodal genres and interconnected genres combine the verbal and audiovisual modes to create multi-channelled meaning-making.

In sum, the aforementioned conceptual and analytical considerations are particularly important to genre analysts to understand how the context of interaction shapes each genre in three closely intertwined axes, the 'co-text' and 'intertext' axes, as Stubbs (2001) proposes, and the 'hypertext' axis. This triple helix may yield a more holistic view of the ecology (and ecologies) of research genres that I postulate in the following section.

2.3 On metaphors of genre

Before turning to what I will conceptualise as the ecological view of genres across languages, it seems apposite to review in the following section previous metaphorical analogies that have been proposed to describe the form and substance of genres.

Previously, I referred to Giddens's (1990: 3) 'discontinuist' interpretation of modern social development and modern social institutions. The main 'discontinuities which separate modern social institutions from the traditional social orders' are the pace of change (because change is faster), the scope of change (because it is global) and the intrinsic nature of modern institutions, 'some not found in prior historical periods' (Giddens, 1990: 6). Earlier in this book I argued that scientific communication has been dramatically impacted by unprecedented and fast-paced changes in the established forms of social interconnection, hence the 'extreme dynamism of modernity' (Giddens, 1990: 16). Understanding the world of research genres from Giddens's perspective enables us to give greater attention to the contexts in which genres act as entities or mechanisms for social action that operate across linguistically and culturally diverse academic and research settings. This invites us to propose some conceptual discernments of 'genre'. In referring to the social context of genre-mediated academic and research activity, Swales (2004: 73) conceptualises such dynamism as follows:

Social purposes evolve, and they can also expand or shrink.... [T]he frames of social action can change, standards can shift, speciation can occur, nonprototypical features can occupy more central ground, institutional attitudes can become more or less friendly to outsiders, and even speech acts can give rise to different interpretations.

I tend to think that there is little one can add to Swales's definition of genres in a changing world. Given the conceptual and analytical considerations discussed in the previous section of this chapter, the extreme dynamism in online science communication remains a valid, and timely as well, approach to describe the current map of genres discussed in the extant literature. Additionally, it paves the way to portraying the current status of genres, delineating the exigences and constraints and anticipating future contingencies. Swales's (2004: 63) view of the evolutionary nature of the genre system of academic research nurtures from Fishelov's (1993) metaphor of genres as biological species (see also Swales, 2009, for further discussion). The aptness of this analogy cannot be questioned, as we see the indisputable stability of the journal article and the abstract as key genres for the production and dissemination of scientific knowledge and, in contrast, the decline of the monograph in the STEMM fields. Both are examples that result from the changing frames of social action. In internet communication, we witness striking contrasts, for example, the birth and growth of research blogs and microblogging and the decline of emerging species such as audioslide presentations, created as previews of their accompanying journal articles, but at present struggling to survive. As further discussed in subsequent chapters, we also witness an unparalleled adaptation of generic species to the digital environment and an extraordinary generic evolution, for example, in genres such as registered reports, video-methods articles and electronic laboratory notes. Laboratory life, as depicted by Latour and Woolgar (1986), revolves around similar scientific procedures, but technologies have turned the traditional paper laboratory notes into electronic laboratory notebooks that enable researchers to manage and share scientific data with other peers for reproducibility purposes. Although spoken genres fall outside the scope of this book, the aptness of the analogy of genres as biological species subject to evolution and adaptation is also evident. Conference presentations combining the verbal with multimodal material (i.e., PowerPoint presentations) were probably a source of inspiration for audioslides presentations. Lectures and seminars can now take the form of online interactive webinars. And if we look at junior researchers' practices, written PhD proposals are (sort of) compressed into spoken three-minute thesis presentations that aim to tell and sell the essence of a PhD work project. These are some instances that attest to generic speciation or diversification, an issue I will delve into in the following chapter.

In this book I would prefer to dissociate genres from the traditional views of 'context of social interaction' and, instead, associate them within a complex layering of contextual and situational frames for research genres in accord with today's shifting social and technological scenarios. This complex layering consists of overlapping and/or circumscribed 'glocal' contexts and situations that entail continuing reorganisation of social structures as a result of the agents' continuing reflexivity of the ongoing action (Giddens, 1990). These social structures and agents are those that, among other things, actually regulate the circulation of scientific knowledge. In consideration of the debates and theorisations on research genre issues put forward over past decades, and aligning with the broader interpretative frameworks discussed previously, I further expand the existing conceptualisations of 'genre' as follows:

- Genres exist in cogent form but are always moving through phases of change and development. In this sense, they are transitional but also sufficiently stabilised so that genre exemplars can be recognised and used.
- Genres retain their individual integrity and degree of stabilisation – for example, regarding generic norms and conventions and participatory mechanisms (Bhatia, 2004: 127) – even if they appropriate or borrow resources from other genres. Appropriation blurs the boundaries across genres and causes generic hybridity. Even so, their distinct generic substance and form remain stable.
- Genre is not a matter of individual action. Rather, it is socially tied to circumstances. Genres are sensitive to and shaped by contextual and social changes and, therefore, they are ultimately constrained by the different agents' expectations and exigences. For this reason, they are subject to economic, institutional, global, local and political agendas.
- The nature of genres is dynamic because it is linked to changes in social activity and instantiates, echoing Giddens, the extreme dynamism of modernity. Changes in the established orders of values attached to genres result in genre growth or genre endangerment or eventual disappearance, or otherwise in generic innovation, evolution and change.
- Although genres are basically stable, they are nonetheless somewhat spontaneous and subject to contingency. This is because they are

sensitive to situations that are inherently dynamic and fluctuating. In response to contingencies, the form and substance of genres can be altered, partly borrowed by other genres or transformed into new genres. This can be traced at both textual and rhetorical levels. Hence, contingency accounts for the emergence of new genres and the gradual disappearance and eventual loss of some genres.

- The nature of prototypical genres remains open to change because of the creation of texts with no spatial or temporal limits, more so if they draw on horizontal and vertical intertextuality, multimodality and hypertextuality. In web environments, genres are received across infinite and multiple spans of time-space; they are ingrained in the triple helix model explained previously – involving co-textual, intertextual and hypertextual intertwining axes.
- Genres are intrinsically context-based and situated. Genres cannot be interpreted as separate from their situatedness. Such separation would indicate that they have been replaced by or transformed into other genres or that they have become more complex.
- Genres entail overt and, at times, covert communicative intentions. Covert goals or 'hidden agendas' indicate that they are tied to power structures, privileged centres and agents' private interests. As Askehave and Swales (2001: 204) claim, 'communicative purpose' is an 'elusive' concept – 'complex, multiple, variable and hard to get at'.
- Genres create interdependence relationships among themselves, by this means forming complex genre assemblages (genre sets, systems, repertoires and ecologies). These assemblages instantiate the intrinsic connections between traditional and new genres, exemplifying fragmentation, echoing the condition of 'modernity' postulated by Giddens.
- Genres are flexible, adaptable to the local as well as to the global, and reflective of it at the same time. Genres also have scope for being used beyond convention (Tardy, 2016) if we look at aspects such as individual writing experiences and issues of writing and identity, thus reflecting plurality and cross-culturality.
- Genres reproduce, mirror and replicate the social appropriation of knowledge (i.e., the use and exchange value), as well as social imbalances. Not all genres are equally accessible by countries, communities or by individuals across different linguacultural backgrounds and, though beyond the scope of this book, across genders (Thelwall et al., 2019).
- Not all genres are reached universally. As Amano, González-Varo and Sutherland (2016) note, the language in which genres are enacted is one possible constraint.

- Lastly, genres are constructed upon 'narratives of science' in response to diverse contexts, and therefore they cannot be interpreted as texts in isolation. Genre exemplars are texts moving and moved by increasingly diverse contexts and agendas or, at least, are more multifaceted than they appear at first sight, as voiced by Schulson (2018) with regard to the science reproducibility crisis.

The aforementioned considerations pave the way for an ecological view of genres, one based on the conceptualisation of genres as entities that evolve because they are continually being shaped and negotiated by their users (Bazerman, 2011, 2015). In proposing this ecological view of genres, described below in this chapter, I aim to highlight generic interdependence, not simply to bring to the fore the interrelations of genres (in terms of form and semiotic meanings) in digital environments but also to underline 'the simultaneity, the inseparability of form, meaning, and action, of individual, social, and cultural context, of actual genres and genre-ness' (Devitt, 2009: 46).

There is still a long way to go to fully understand the nature of genres in the contemporary world, and the expanded theorisations outlined earlier do not underestimate, as Askehave and Swales (2001: 210) note, the fact that even sets of communicative purposes 'are not always self-evident'. For this reason, I tend to think that attributing purposes to genres necessarily requires 'text-in-context' enquiry. We need to apply the social lens to interpret genres and to ascertain their status and boundaries with other genres, because genres are not discourse categories but rather social events. The complexity of research genres implies a level of interpretational uncertainty that very much justifies the need to establish analogies and the need to see genres and contexts metaphorically. Some analogies are proposed in the following sections.

2.4 The scientific community and its ecosystem(s)

Before going deeper into the conceptualisation of 'ecologies of genres' and the study of ecological relationships among genres of research, discussed in the last section of this chapter, I would like first of all to propose a conceptualisation of the academic and research community as a whole (i.e., the world scientific community) and its diverse disciplinary communities of practice across local (physical) settings worldwide, using the metaphor of 'ecosystem' in biology and the life sciences (Major, 1969). Broadly, an ecosystem is 'a complete community of

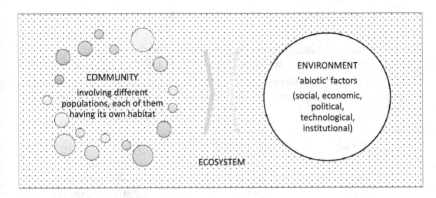

Figure 2.4 Structure of the international scientific community 'ecosystem'

living organisms and the non-living materials of their surroundings'.[1] My main reasons for establishing an analogy between the academic and research world and the 'ecosystem' metaphor are the following. Firstly, given the social and socioeconomic conditions discussed earlier in this book, the metaphorical conceptualisation seems apposite to support the view of the global scientific community as a broad ecosystem. Its 'biotic' or 'living organisms', researchers and scholars worldwide, interact with abiotic parts of the environment, that is, the established social orders and structures. Figure 2.4 illustrates both types of interaction. At the same time, members of the community interact with other biotic or living organisms within the ecosystem (namely, expert peers belonging to different populations within the community) and outside of it (science stakeholders and the public in general).

Secondly, the analogy of the global scientific community as a broad ecosystem may best capture the view of this community as a broad-based, complex integrative system. Like biological ecosystems, it has ecological stability or equilibrium. This can be seen in the dynamics of communication for knowledge exchange and dissemination. These dynamics are highly typified and routinised with respect to form and rhetorical conventions (Swales, 1990). Within the scientific community itself, populations of researchers in their specific location – their own habitat – are likewise organised at different levels. Cutting across those levels, genres support their organisational routines and

---

[1] Retrieved from Encyclopedia.com, www.encyclopedia.com/science-and-technology/ biology-and-genetics/environmental-studies/ecosystems [last accessed on 27 February 2019].

professional activity, which helps maintain a state of stability, a hierarchical social order and a disciplinary order – the latter accounting for processes of disciplinary enculturation within academic communities of practice (Berkenkotter and Huckin, 1995). Other operational levels are those that explicitly involve dialogic exchanges with other (expert) members of their disciplinary tribe, with the local population in its habitat and with and across national, cross-border and international populations.

The stability of biological ecosystems draws on their resilience or capacity to adapt themselves to new changes. If we look at the dynamics of communication, we see that the capacity to interact and maintain an ongoing flow of information has changed drastically with the growth of techno-dependency. Giltrow and Stein (2009: 3) argue that '[o]ver time, functions are realised in an increasingly stable cluster of forms. Over time language users come to recognise forms in functional contexts and are able to produce them in response to mutual expectations'. In the case of the global scientific community, the most significant changes result from the complex processes of social and technological globalisation defined in the first chapter of this book. Communicative goals are accomplished through highly conventionalised, typified genres (Swales, 1990). And while new communicative goals emerge that lead to the appearance of new genres, the latter do not completely destabilise the existing forms of communication. The case of the evolution of the scientific article in the age of digitisation has been extensively discussed. In the official blog of the Society for Scholarly Publishing, Anderson (2009) criticised the generic innovations of the Article of the Future prototypes by referring to them as merely 'lipstick on a pig'. Much more explicit is Mackenzie Owen's (2007) convincing argument of 'the illusion of a revolution'. In his view, researchers have not actually embraced new forms of interaction or more dynamic electronic peer-review procedures in electronic journals. Such resistance to change, which may be attributed to various overlapping reasons and interests – personal, institutional, even economic if we bear in mind the thrust of knowledge societies – implies generic stability and ecosystem resilience.

Perhaps the clearest analogy between 'ecosystem' and the global scientific community lies in its capacity for 'exchange'. In biological and life science ecosystems, living organisms interact with their surroundings and 'the environment affects the organism through the flow of energy' (Gates, 1968) and both environmental conditions and variables determine the survival of the organism (see also Major, 1969; Willis, 1997). By analogy, through the existing languages of the environment, scientists exchange knowledge among themselves, with their surroundings and outside of the ecosystem environment, for example, when they communicate scientific research to lay publics. Nicholas, Huntington and Watkinson (2005: online) explain this capacity for knowledge exchange using deep log analysis of researchers' scholarly journal usage (i.e., an analysis of one and a quarter million searches in a digital library). These authors conclude that '[v]iews of articles accounted for nearly one third (31 per cent) of all views' and '[a]bstracts were not only the item least requested, they were also viewed for the shortest time, about 1 second, and that kind of view time suggests a very fast scan indeed'.[2] In the introduction to this book I noted that the *UNESCO Science Report: Towards 2030* refers to 7.8 million researchers in 2013 and an increase of 23 per cent in the number of scientific articles catalogued in the Science Citation Index of Thomson Reuters' Web of Science, from 1,029,471 to 1,270,425. Hence, the fundamental rationale behind the 'ecosystem' analogy is that while in biological and physical ecosystems 'there are continuous fluxes of matter and energy in an interactive open system' (Willis, 1997: 270), in the scholarly ecosystem continuous fluxes of individuals and knowledge exchange are sustainable thanks to languages. The structures of the abiotic environment privilege some of those languages, threaten others or even endanger them.

In addition to interrelations with its abiotic environment (Figure 2.4), the community, together with the local populations and disciplinary tribes within it, also establish interrelationships within themselves as well as with other biotic populations within the ecosystem, namely, science stakeholders and the lay publics. Such interrelations entail a bidirectional exchange of information and, hence, highly dialogic social actions. While the traditional, 'sufficiently stabilised' genres of research retain their specific purposeful goals in web environments, the web also offers possibilities for generic innovation. To illustrate this point, we can go back to earlier categorisations of genres as rhetorical hybrids (Jamieson and Campbell, 1982) and to the notion of generic hybrid (Herring, 2013) discussed previously in this chapter. Web 2.0 genres for disseminating science to expert and diversified audiences do not generally rely only on verbal information. Rather, they combine visual and verbal information. By this means, they add further functionalities to their generic precedents and fulfil new communicative purposes. The graphical abstract falls under this genre typology. Its form builds upon an already existing genre with

[2] These findings are somewhat surprising, as they appear to invalidate the 'screening' function traditionally attached to abstracts (Huckin, 2001) and thus might suggest the existence of new information access practices in the age of digitisation.

clear communicative purposes and adds to it further functionality to visually convey the main findings with one single image. Figure 2.5 illustrates the conciseness of the information conveyed in graphical abstracts. Cox (2015) further adds that this genre invites authors to reflect on the novelty of their work and the most appropriate way to visualise it. More than 60 per cent of the authors of graphical abstracts surveyed for the RGaL study (a 13 per cent response rate) viewed this genre type (and other add-on genres such as author summaries and data articles) as *important/very important/extremely important* and as a way to enhance their research work. Circa 50 per cent made them available online for wider dissemination via their research group websites/blogs and academic social networking sites. These were preferred forms of dissemination compared to prepublication repositories and social media networks. Lastly, regarding text-composing, almost 85 per cent of the respondents reported they aimed at clarity and conciseness when composing them and 50 per cent at explaining the significance of the findings. Re-using a visual used in the article was not a common practice in composing this visual genre (only 7.7 per cent of the respondents did). Corpus data will be further discussed in Chapter 3.

Other examples of generic hybrids are scientific video articles such as those found in the *Journal of Visualised Experiments*. This journal publishes peer-reviewed articles that combine visual (a video) and verbal narratives with which the authors provide a detailed account of their research methodology and procedures. In this case, in addition to highlighting the value of the methodological procedures, the added functionality of the visual narrative is to provide sufficient details to reproduce the study. These video narratives will be discussed further in Chapter 3. Another example of a generic hybrid is the kind of peer-reviewed article found in journals such as *Genomics Data* and *Data in Brief*, a rhetorically hybrid genre whose aim is to describe and highlight the value of data procedures and datasets. To the best of my knowledge, data articles are a recently emerging research process-oriented genre that very much relies on genre-to-genre interdependence possibilities afforded by the digital journal platforms. As discussed later in this book, the emergence of this hybrid genre results from the growing social concern towards the transparency of methods and reproducibility of scientific results.

The variety of forms of communicating knowledge exchange in the hyperspace lends credence to the idea that researchers have, at least, two different channels for meaning-making: genres for expert-to-expert communication and genres that enable scientists to act as language mediators, transforming specialised knowledge into non-specialist contents.

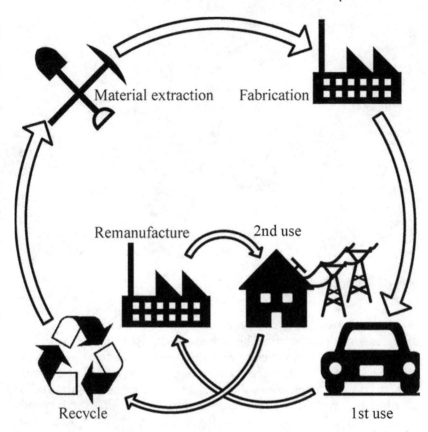

Material extraction

Fabrication

Remanufacture

2nd use

Recycle

1st use

Figure 2.5 Two examples of graphical abstracts from the Journal of Environmental Management *(under a Creative Commons license) [last accessed on 30 September 2020].*
Sources: Canals Casals, L., Amante García, B. and Canal, C. (2019). Second-life batteries lifespan: Rest of useful life and environmental analysis. *Journal of Environmental Management*, 232, 354–363, DOI: 10.1016/j. jenvman.2018.11.046. Zoboli, O., Manfred, C., Gabriel, O., Scheffknecht, C., Humer, M., Brielmann, H., Kulcsar, S., Trautvetter, H., Kittlaus, S., Amann, A., Saracevic, E., Krampe, J. and Zessner, M. (2019). Occurrence and levels of micropollutants across environmental and engineered compartments in Austria. *Journal of Environmental Management*, 232, 636–653, DOI: 10.1016/j. jenvman.2018.10.074.

We can therefore assume that, as social constructs, genres endorse two adjacent worlds, each of them having distinct sets of affordances and goals. One world revolves around hyperspecialisation of scientific and research knowledge. It involves social interactions within the

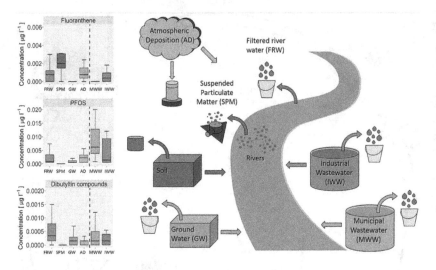

Figure 2.5 (cont.)

researchers' own habitat or with other habitats within the academic and research ecosystem. The other world is unspecialised, self-explanatory and linguistically and discoursally mediated, involving audiences outside of the scientific community ecosystem. The question is, are the social interactions in these two worlds monolingual and/or plurilingual? We could hypothesise that in each habitat the language of the physical setting is used, for example, in what Kelly and Maddalena (2016) conceptualise as 'internal' genres of science communication, such as laboratory notebooks, instructions or procedure manuals. We can conjecture that both the local language and a shared world scientific language are chosen to make the information potentially exchangeable, sharable with other scientific populations and replicable by other populations or collaborating networks. As an example, electronic laboratory notebooks may be drafted in the local language but, since concern with open data and reproducibility of research has gained momentum, they might sooner or later shift to the use of lingua franca–medium research outlets. There is still a very long way to go to fully understand plurilingual practices in digital environments.

2.5 The 'ecology' metaphor

In *Genres Across Borders*, a very inspiring online portal for genre analysts, researchers and practitioners, a 'genre ecology' is defined as 'an interacting, interdependent system or network of genres, as distinct from a series of genres with a specifically sequential series of uptakes (Erickson, 2000)' (online). Spinuzzi (2003: 21, see also 2004) uses the term 'ecology' to stress the idea of interdependences between genres. As this author explains, '[a] given genre mediates an activity, but it does not do so alone; it works in conjunction with the entire ecology of genres available'. In a similar vein, the ecological view of research genres proposed in this book supports the view of genres for mediating social action, at times working sequentially (e.g., in chains of genres) and at other times working together to fulfil a social action or to respond to new exigences. As such, ecologies of genres are dynamic, which differentiates them from other genre assemblages such as networks, systems and repertoires, as discussed a little later. Using activity theory and applying Spinuzzi's (2004) five frameworks to categorise types of genre assemblages according to the parameters of 'perspective, model of action, agency, relationship between genres and foregrounded genres', the ecologies of research genres discussed in this book can be characterised by the genre analyst as follows.

As I argued elsewhere (Pérez-Llantada, 2019), the conceptualisation of ecology (and ecologies) of genres underlines the importance of triangulating social interactions within the community and between the community and other communities and publics with the viewpoints of individuals regarding professional communication practices and genre-mediated action. Critical enquiry based on ethnographic and textographic methods would be necessary to understand the ways in which the ecology of genres of research, and/or the ecology of a particular genre (hence the use of ecologies of genres in the plural form), can model social action via expert-to-expert communication and via knowledge transformation and language mediation. In these various ecologies, the issue of agency thus becomes crucial to identify the extent to which apparently 'symmetrical agency' (Spinuzzi and Zachry, 2000) might turn out to be asymmetrical. For instance, if we take the case of peer-to-peer communication, the presumably symmetrical agency might be constrained by policymakers controlling competitive systems of rewards, or by funding agencies guiding scientific activity towards greater use of trans-scientific or parascientific genres, thus encouraging researchers to diversify their genre repertoire (Gross and Buehl, 2016; Kelly and Miller, 2016; Miller and Kelly, 2017) (see Chapter 3 for further discussion). Other asymmetries have been described in the literature, such as those between core versus peripheral countries participating in knowledge dissemination activities (see, e.g., Salager-Meyer's (2008) critical views on off-networked scholars in non-developed countries), and those related to the use of English as an additional language, as described in the literature on writing in the semi-periphery (see, e.g., Aydinli and Mathews, 2000; Bennett, 2014).

Turning to relationships between genres, the ecologies of particular genres and the genre ecology metaphor itself invite enquiry into the intertextual relations between genre chains or sequential genres 'each leading into the next' (Spinuzzi, 2004: 2). On the web, these sequences of genres are no longer standardised chains. Pretexts might be post-texts or the other way round. For example, conference presentations may be pretexts of audioslides or also sequential post-texts in a genre chain. Genre relations also reflect overlapping between genre sets, particularly among those that share some of their communicative purposes. This is the case of the abstract and the graphical abstract. Finally, examination of 'foregrounded genres', or 'official' genres (Spinuzzi, 2004) in ecologies of genres can enable the genre analyst to track the evolution and the gradual disappearance of official or major genres such as the scholarly monograph in the humanities. This used to be a key tenure-track genre, but it is no longer cited (Thomson, 2002) and whether or not it can survive is uncertain, as suggested by Knievel (2009), unless it is integrated into electronic collections or into platforms or webpages along with other genres. As Giltrow and Stein (2009: 4) note, 'from the rhetorical view of the historical contingency of genres, genres expire when the situations expire'. Other genres that are entirely unofficial to date, such as blogs or electronic lab note-books, but that have gained momentum also require further exploration from a genre perspective. The ecological view of research genres thus opens new avenues for further research that I will examine in the concluding chapter of this book.

Casper (2016) refers to the ecological basis of the online journal article genre to underline that one of the most important outcomes of digital communication technology is the interconnectedness of for-merly disparate genres within the same online environment, something that was not possible when genres were in written form. For example, if we visualise the ecology of the journal article in an online environ-ment as shown in Figure 2.6, we see that the article genre stands as the core genre, while other peripheral (add-on) genres are linked to it. Like Casper, I would argue that there is an ecological basis in this forma-tion of interconnected genres. Add-on genres (e.g., audioslides or author videos) keep emerging that complement the contents of the core genre in different ways. This formation of interrelated genres can in turn be hyperlinked to other digital genres, say, short summaries, data articles, podcasts, registered reports, open peer reviews and authors' response letters to reviewers' comments. We can speculate further on the openness of this ecology and claim that other mediatory

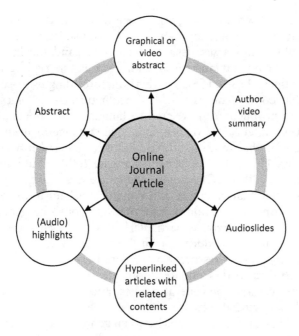

Figure 2.6 A proposed visualisation of the ecology of the journal article as an enhanced publication

relationships between the core genre and other genres or part genres are possible. For example, the journal article may relate to previous pretexts such as grant proposals, interim research project reports, data articles or registered reports that are thematically related to the journal article. We can thus presume a fair amount of intertextuality in all these instances on the assumption that such interdependence creates strong mediatory links between the genres, above all, in terms of generic substance, that is, meanings and contents. This, in fact, further supports Devitt's (2009: 44) claim of inter-genre-ality: genres 'take up forms from the genres with which they inter-act'. On a different note, the visualisation in Figure 2.6 also epitomises the impact of research policies and evaluation systems, and the existence of genre regimes, key determinants of the centrality of some types of genres over others.

A further argument for advocating the metaphor of ecology to gain a better understanding of research genres in the contemporary world is the fact that it enables us to trace the intersections of ecologies of genres with language ecologies. Like genre ecologies, ecologies of languages are subject to and constrained by social structures and agents. Because genres are 'forms of social action' (Bazerman, 1994) instantiated through language, critical enquiry is needed to identify the functionality of language repertoires in the transmission of knowledge in this ecology and assess issues of language and locality/globality, language(s) spread and language(s) endangerment in 'typified rhetorical actions' (Miller, 1984: 159). At this juncture, 'linguistic ecology', a concept that comes from the field of ecolinguistics, becomes relevant for delving into phenomena related to languages in contact, language hybridisation, linguistic diversity, language endangerment and extinction and social change (Fill and Mühlhäusler, 2001; Mufwene, 2001; Mühlhäusler, 1996, 2003; Skutnabb-Kangas, 2000). Skutnabb-Kangas and Phillipson (2001: 22) propose the concept of 'language ecology' when explaining that 'language is the major mechanism for preserving and transmitting a community's knowledge from one generation to another'. Their perspective is particularly critical towards the effects of dominant languages in education. In the present book, language ecology strictly focuses on researchers' potential use of language and language repertoires to disseminate knowledge to local audiences, both expert audiences and the general publics, and to wider social communities, including virtual communities.

Other ecological interrelations between genres and languages can be found in research genres that disseminate knowledge beyond expert audiences. The case of crowdsourcing science projects may illustrate how the ecological basis of these projects intersects with languages. The crowdfunding projects from Precipita.com[3] compiled for the RGaL project illustrate how these digital texts embrace a constellation of genres in different languages. Figure 2.7 shows the hypertextual architecture of these types of citizen science projects. As seen in this figure, the projects are formed by hyperlinked interrelated genres and draw on multisemiotic modes and hypermodal affordances. The main online proposal (highlighted in bold type) acts as the core genre. Surrounding it are an expanded project proposal, hyperlinked journal articles, researchers' bionotes, hyperlinked factsheets and professional homepages – that are either English medium or Spanish medium. Researchers draw on a predetermined genre assemblage – the one provided by the electronic platform – and diffuse knowledge using a plurilingual communicative repertoire.

We could argue that the ecology of the crowdfunding project proposal genre illustrates, borrowing Schryer's (1994) term, a 'site of competing genres'. Some are more central because of their *kairos* and

---

[3] Precipita.es is the crowdfunding platform of the Spanish Foundation for Science and Technology.

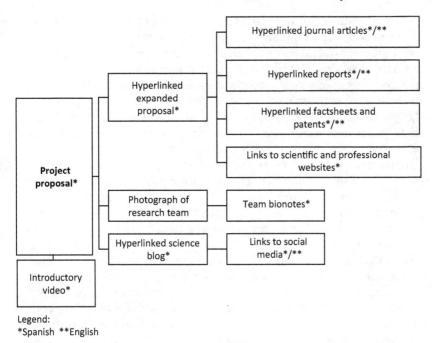

Figure 2.7 Intersections of genres and languages in an online crowdfunding project

timeliness (e.g., the online proposal and its associated introductory video). Other genres are driven by genre regimes (e.g., the first-level hyperlinked expanded proposal and the blog, and second-level hyperlinked articles (co)-authored by the project launcher and the research team), and others are more marginal (e.g., second-level hyperlinked reports, factsheets and scientific and professional websites). This genre ecology might be conceived of as a site of competing languages. Spanish is the central language, used in the main project proposal and introductory video. English is a secondary language, as the genre assemblage includes some hyperlinked English-medium genre texts. But because the coexistence of languages responds to the collapsing of contexts, this ecology instantiates neither collision nor collusion of languages. The languages have different functionalities and entail different levels of explanatory depth (Engberg and Maier, 2015). Spanish, the local or national language, is used in the crowdfunding proposal, in professional associations' websites and national-based scientific websites. The use of English and Spanish simply reflects expert-to-expert genred activity, namely, journal articles, reports and patents. If not competing, then, we could assume that both languages complement one another, instantiating polyglossia or multivoicedness in a single assemblage of genres with different communicative purposes and rhetorical intentions.

In my view, 'the complex web of relationships that exist between the environment, languages, and their speakers' (Wendel, 2005: 51) can be subsumed in the metaphors of 'ecologies of genres' and 'ecologies of languages' deployed throughout this book. I will therefore describe how generified social practices within and outside of the scientific ecosystem can in many ways redress potential threats to minority languages and local languages, for example, through the upsurge of new genres or through generic innovation and webification of traditional genres. I will argue that multilingual genre ecologies may open a window for preserving and promoting language and ethnocultural diversities in knowledge production and dissemination processes and, by this means, support Skutnabb-Kangas and Phillipson's (2001) claim that 'the contributions of local communities to global knowledge' are as legitimate and indispensable as those in the global (international) sphere. As further discussed in the subsequent chapters, stability, adaptability and diversity of genres and languages are crucial aspects when communicating science online within the academic and research ecosystem and with its abiotic environment.

2.6 Understanding genre assemblages

This section introduces some relevant interpretative theories and frameworks that will set the grounds for the analysis of some genre assemblages in Chapter 3. Many of them are borrowed from the fields of literary studies and applied in postmodern criticism. The aim is to review some early theoretical conceptualisations that align with genre theories and can be helpful for exploring aspects of genre change and evolution. These theories and frameworks can also provide complementary insights into genre hybridisation and the scope of inter-genreality, for example to identify how generic forms are shared among interconnected genres (Devitt, 2009: 44). My main line of argument in reviewing these theories is that, in conceptualising genres, we need to complement the description of different types of genres by looking at levels of meaning-making that can uncover the interrelations of genres forming online genre assemblages. Understanding such interrelations between or among genres in these assemblages could give a more accurate view of the rhetorical functionalities of each genre type.

In order to better grasp the nature of contemporary research communication, we can also draw on Giddens's (1990) concept of 'modernity's reflexivity'. As this author explains, reflexivity is one of the features that characterises the post-traditional order of things (see also Bauman, 2000), an order that has been strongly influenced by the advances of science and technology. Giddens (1990: 144) argued that modern societies are dynamic because they use information and new scientific knowledge in reflexivity processes that involve 'the dialectical interplay' of the local and the global. For Giddens (1990: 38), reflexivity processes entail continuing examination and restructurings of social practices 'in the light of incoming information about those very practices, thus constitutively altering their character'. These reflexivity processes could account for the reported generic evolution, innovation and change taking place in researchers' socioliterate activity today. It is through these processes that aspects of social action, including knowledge production, distribution and dissemination practices, are susceptible to revision by the actors – the agents – of social life. Giddens (1990: 38) further stated that '[i]n all cultures, social practices are routinely altered in the light of ongoing discoveries which feed into them'. The genre transformations described in the previous section of this chapter illustrate how, even if genres have their own generic integrity, the boundaries between them have become fuzzier in current social and technological scenarios, a point already made by Bhatia (2004) regarding professional communication.

If we move on from the contextual to the textual, Genette's (1997) concepts of 'paratexts', 'publishers' peritext' and 'thresholds of interpretation' in literary theory are also inspiring and apt in the analysis of research genres in relation to the dynamics of genre change. A paratext is the term used to refer to the conventional texts accompanying a book, for example, dedications, forewords, prefaces, notes, blurbs or illustrations that 'form part of the *complex mediation* between book, author, publisher, and reader ... part of a book's private and public history' (Genette, 1997: 169, my emphasis). This concept can be useful to understand generic representations of social actions on the web. Digital genres and visual elements such as graphical abstracts, three-dimensional images, interactive graphs and maps in online journal articles would qualify as paratexts in genre assemblages or groupings of interdependent genres (Engberg and Maier, 2015). As peripheral generic elements, they have paratextual value but, unlike printed books, these are formats supported by the affordances of digital technologies. Digital paratexts challenge and actually blur the traditional linearity of the main text and different thresholds of interpretation of such text and, ultimately, the reception of the text. In Chapter 3 these concepts will be applied to the analysis of digital genres.

Bakhtin's (1981, 1986a) theory of heteroglossia and intertextuality is another relevant framework with which to address the transformation of scientific genres and genre innovation and evolution in Web 2.0. Bakhtin's (1986a) notion of 'heteroglossia' or 'multilanguagedness' refers to the 'multiple variations of languages and *ideas/perspectives within* those languages' (my emphasis). If we navigate the digital landscape, heteroglossia is a suitable term to define the functionalities of interdependent genres forming genre assemblages, as well as a helpful heuristic to explain the effects of the polycontextuality of the medium and the possibilities for multilanguagedness in genre assemblages. In Bakhtinian theory, an utterance reflects the appropriation of others' utterances to fulfil specific communicative intentions. That is, an utterance appropriates 'qualities such as perspective, evaluation, and ideological positioning' (Bakhtin, 1981: 262–263). By analogy, in genre assemblages, emerging genres may take up the perspective, evaluation and authorial positioning of their generic antecedents. But they may also not do so if they want to construct different narratives to target different audiences. For instance, in his analysis of acknowledgements, home pages and bionotes, Hyland (2018: 2) concludes that because these genres are 'neither strictly academic not entirely personal', the way the writer's 'discoursal self' is expressed in these genres is different from that of traditional genres. Figure 2.7 illustrates different ways of expressing agency and authorial identity across the genres forming the assemblage.

Bakhtin's conceptualisation of the novel as a genre that is 'unique in that it is able to embrace, ingest, and devour other genres while still maintaining its status as a novel', hence preserving its distinct identity, can also be set in parallel with the view of major research genres as unique. For example, in enhanced publications, the online journal article maintains its generic integrity despite being interconnected with add-on digital genres constellating around it. Another possible analogy of multilanguagedness in interconnected digital genres such as crowdsourcing science projects would be the term 'multi-register-ness' to refer to the use of different registers – formal, less formal and conversational – in enhanced publications and in emerging digital genres such as citizen science projects and crowdfunding projects and their associated hyperlinked texts, for example, journal articles, reports, blogs and microblogs like Facebook, Twitter or Reddit. Multiregisterness, supported by the hyperlinking affordances of the electronic platform, is thus a rhetorical response to the polycontextuality of the medium. I would further add that hybrid genres themselves embed multiregisterness (see Chapter 3). The polyphony of registers instantiates 'science accommodation' (Fahnestock, 1986) and the transformation of expert knowledge to reach larger publics (Bondi, Cacchiani, and Mazzi, 2015; Orpin, 2019).

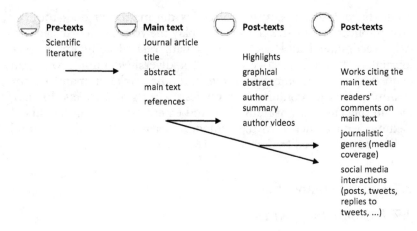

Figure 2.8 Genre uptake and horizontal intertextuality in PLoS-*enhanced publications*

Bakhtin's (1981) theory of intertextuality, which introduces concepts such as 'adaptation' and 'transposition' and refers to 'the text unbound' and 'absorption and transformation of one text into another', in point of fact applies to aspects of genre evolution and innovation. In digitally mediated research genres, analogous transformations of one text into another can be useful to understand sequential genre uptake in relation to enhanced publications. As seen in Figure 2.8, these transformations do not entail reciprocal intertextuality but rather horizontal intertextuality, reflecting connections between previous texts and a main text and between the main text, its immediate post-texts (i.e., its add-on genres) and its subsequent post-texts once the main text is published and available online.

From this figure we can presuppose that there are explicit intertextual connections between the main text and their pre-texts – what Fairclough (1992: 117) labels as 'manifest intertextuality'. The intertextual links between the main text and immediate post-texts (the add-on genres) and their post-texts would rather fall within the subcategory of 'constitutive intertextuality' or 'interdiscursivity', involving the transformation of monomodal into multimodal texts (visual and verbal) (Fairclough, 1992: 125) while retaining part of the 'substance' of their corresponding main texts and appropriating features of other discourses (Bhatia, 2004: 50). Moreover, if we relate issues of genre, intertextuality and social orders (Briggs and Bauman, 1992) with transmediality (Bateman, 2017), or the activity of transforming and repurposing the meanings in this sequential genre uptake, we unveil different rhetors and, hence, different voices. While the main text's pre-texts represent scientists' voices, as the main text does too, the post-publication post-texts bring into play the voices of journal editors (who recommend and select articles with related contents), science journalists (for media coverage) and a diversified public, who can express their own interest in the text and make it manifest, for example, through comments or replies to posts and tweets. In sum, the interdependences of traditional and emerging genres in the digital medium lend credence to the ecological basis of the online journal article, as advocated by Casper (2016).

2.7 Sites of competition

2.7.1 Competing genres

Studies on genre, rhetoric and communication acknowledge the role of activity systems in relation to textual production, textual practices in context and broader aspects of professional (disciplinary) communication (Bazerman, 2004a; Bazerman and Prior, 2004; Schryer, 2011; Yates and Orlikowski, 1992). These studies support the view of genres as 'typified communicative actions characterized by similar substance and form and taken in response to recurrent situations' (Yates and Orlikowski, 1992: 485). Schryer (1994) further argued that disciplinary environments are 'sites of competing genres' in disciplinary spaces. Bazerman and Prior (2004) and later Schryer (2011), among others, contend that texts organise activity by reproducing conventionalised speech acts and genres. The genre repertoires are nonetheless subject to change because the actors (agents) of the social context raise new rhetorical exigences that originate new practices. As Bazerman and Prior put it, 'social formations are *established, negotiated, enacted and changed* through communicative practice' (p. 3, my emphasis).

The structurational paradigm was criticised for not establishing a sufficient balance between enabling and constraining aspects, in particular, for giving more attention to the former than to the latter. Recent scholarship in genre, rhetoric and communication studies contends that this paradigm has two significant caveats. The first one relates to agency. In the context of research communication, there is evidence that scientists draw on an expanding repertoire of genres and that these genres are constituted and shaped by various social actors or agents whose decisions influence the processes of production and consumption of scientific knowledge. The remaking of existing practices is in fact manifest in the case of traditional genres that have moved to web environments. As a result of agents in the system other than scientists (e.g., decision-takers and policymakers, funding organisations and sponsors and publishers), traditional genres such as the journal article and the abstract are stable-enough forms that support scientists' communication practices that have undergone innovation and change in the transition from print to online forms.

Other factors constraining researchers' communication practices revolve around the existence of 'genre hierarchies' (Swales, 2004: 16) in 'professional practice' (Schryer, 1994: 106). As an example, both Swales and Schryer explain that Introduction – Materials – Methods – Discussion (IMRaD hereafter) texts are more valued than others (e.g., medical records) in disciplines, like medicine, that have a clear-cut division between research and practice. As another example, in the existing 'social orders' a journal article or an abstract do not need to compete with emerging digital genres, say, a graphical abstract or a research blog. At least to date, the former genres do not compete with the latter emerging digital genres, but it might be possible that Open Science and OA policies give greater value to the latter genres in the near future because of their inherent social impact and hence become competing genres. There are also constraints intrinsic to genre use, as there is a limit to variation imposed on genres so that their forms can be recognised by their users at the operational level. These constraints guarantee effective communication of scientific advancements. Open Science, which has grown in policy and practical significance, and policies giving value to open-access publications (Ball, 2016) make it easy to predict researchers' greater interest in this type of publishing option. Ninety per cent of the corresponding authors of *Cell*, *Nature*, *eLife* and *PLoS* surveyed for the RGaL project considered publishing open access *important/ very important/extremely important*.

The second caveat becomes evident if we place the focus on the affordances of Web 2.0. The Internet plays a crucial role in supporting research communication across disciplines, enabling far-reaching actions in the diffusion of knowledge to diversified audiences. But while this role should not be sidelined, at present there are social systems (e.g., supranational, national and institutional policies) across scientific and research settings that constrain or put limits on those far-reaching actions. Earlier in this volume I argued that in the context of neoliberal universities, government and institutional policymakers establish hierarchies of 'countable vs non-countable' genres, forcing researchers to produce certain particular genres instead of others for knowledge production and dissemination (Pérez-Llantada, forthcoming; Tusting, 2018; Tusting et al., 2019).

In sum, the way the structural properties of the social context impose constraints on the ecological diversity of science communication genres basically turns the academic and research ecosystem into a site of competing genres.

2.7.2 Competing languages

In the context of global multilingualism (Coupland, 2010), today's academic and research community has increasing possibilities to target diverse plurilingual and multicultural audiences. Competition among languages has mainly been addressed by critical voices that have brought to the surface the asymmetrical relations between languages as a major sociopolitical and policy dimension of research writing (Canagarajah, 2002a, 2002b; Uzuner, 2008). As stated earlier, the high Q-value attached to some central genres in researchers' activity worldwide has fuelled the increasing spread of English as an international lingua franca (Ferguson, 2007; Phillipson, 1992, 2003). From the abundant EAP/ERPP literature published in the past decade, we can deduce that there has been little competition between English 'tyrannosaurus rex' (Kuteeva and McGrath, 2014; Swales, 1997; Tardy, 2004) and other scientific and research languages. The main reason lies in the policy motivations behind research communication practices, all of them based on the assumption that English is going to be understood globally or, as claimed in some ideological discourses, that English is intrinsically valuable because it brings with it beneficial consequences to all science stakeholders, particularly to multilingual researchers (Corcoran, Englander and Muresan, 2019; Ferguson, 2012).

The Internet has been a fundamental driver in the creation of virtual sites where different languages coexist for science communication purposes. Web 2.0 thus represents a social structure that both enables and constrains not only genre-mediated activity but also language-mediated praxis. Canagarajah's (2018: 31) concept of translingual practices is pertinent here, in particular, his view of translingualism as a phenomenon that 'relates to mobile, expansive, situated, and holistic practices'. The same qualifiers apply to multilingual science communication on the Internet. Previously in this chapter I discussed how digital environments allow scientific contents to be disseminated electronically, and I outlined some of the factors that have a significant bearing on the way genres are constructed in those environments. New practices on the Internet fuelled by Open Science policies (D. Ball, 2016) and participation in ASNSs and social media networks involve the use of a shared language with the purpose of maintaining scholarly conversation and knowledge exchange. The multilingual potential of the Internet and the extent to which English competes or coexists with other scientific and research languages on the web is, to date, a relatively under-researched area. A few notable exceptions are Jeng et al. (2017), Jordan (2014), Luzón (2011) and Mauranen (2013), who have approached science blogs and ASNSs across the disciplines. However, prima facie evidence suggests that other languages coexist in virtual spaces for professional or personal networking for science purposes. For example, although English appears to be the prevailing language in Reddit r/science,[4] with 22.2 million users, along with English many other languages are used. Digital genres such as research blogs and microblogs (Twitter) are also spaces of translingual practices (Luzón, 2017; Luzón and Pérez-Llantada, forthcoming). In ResearchGate, publications are shared in several languages, revealing that many of its members, who do not have English as their native (first) language, use languages other than English to get their work published and shared widely.

Digital technologies also assist research networking and 'international knowledge mobility' (UNESCO, 2015: 14). This report underlines that 'cross-border co-authorship as indicator for international collaboration is on the rise everywhere'. Professional networking and mobility flows necessarily call for an examination of the issue of languages in competition. Both dynamics justify the utility of a lingua franca on the international stage, while in non-anglophone settings, academic and research languages other than English are circumscribed to local, national and cross-border communication. This means that science communication is not monolingual, even if the spread of English in academic and research settings has received far more scholarly attention than other languages for research communication. Scholarly interest has also been motivated by the need to find solutions to researchers' 'linguistic disadvantages' and linguistic inequality in scientific communication (Carli and Ammon, 2007) and to critically assess the consequences of such spread, for example, the increasing use of English as a threat to multilingualism (House, 2003).

A further issue that revolves around perceptions of competition of languages – or, as conceptualised previously, language collusions and collisions – lies in the existence of translingual practices and in the choice of a given language to fulfil distinct goals and target specific audiences. Hence, there is no need to strive for acknowledging one particular language over other languages. Even though the ideological discourses associated with certain languages and language policies create tensions between English and other academic languages and

---

[4] www.reddit.com/r/science/ [last accessed on 7 January 2021].

pose dilemmas regarding language choice (Plo Alastrué and Pérez-Llantada, 2015), there seems to be evidence of linguistic diversity in several science communication dynamics. To preserve such diversity, some actions can be proposed. For example, the use of alternative metrics (Harzing and van der Wal, 2009) could become a structural property of the social system, downplaying the impact of traditional metrics (i.e., citation) on researchers' careers. Alternative metrics would enhance the societal impact of online research communication and public communication of science (e.g., indicators such as reads, downloads, mentions, shares, recommendations, comments, likes and tweets). Also, because there clearly exist constraining influences from policies in place that force the production of high-stakes genres (journal articles, abstracts, conference presentations, dissertations), the promotion of emerging forms of digital communication for public understanding of science, for example prompting scientists' greater engagement in intermediary genres and trans-scientific or parascientific genres, could democratise science and make a strong point for preserving language diversity in contemporary research communication (see Chapter 3).

2.8 Chapter summary

In this chapter I have reviewed some seminal interpretative frameworks and key theoretical developments in the fields of genre analysis, socio-rhetoric and academic writing. In the light of this critical review, I have proposed a revised definition of the concept of genre to provide a rationale for viewing the scientific community as a distinct ecosystem. Using the metaphor of 'ecology'/'(ecologies)' of genre(s) and the framework of 'linguistic ecology' (Skutnabb-Kangas and Phillipson, 2001), I have also focused on issues of language ecology and linguistic diversity to foreground how genre-based socioliterate activity supports multilingual practices. The aim was to set the ground for the analysis of science communication online, the focus of attention in the following chapter.

3   Science, Genres and Social Action

3.1 Producers and consumers of science

This chapter contextualises the production and reception of genres to discuss how the social and socio-rhetorical contexts account for the way genres are characterised at linguistic and rhetorical levels. This first section will place producers and consumers of science in the broad social context. The discussion in subsequent sections will be based on the assumption that the social processes influencing generic forms can explain how producers of science draw on diverse genre repertoires to communicate their research work locally and globally, both in the physical and virtual space. Genre analysis will be applied to examine aspects of text, discourse and transmediality (Bateman, 2017; Briggs and Bauman, 1992) and to discuss the inherently dialogic nature of genres for professional (expert-to-expert) and public communication of science (expert/non-specialist). Lastly, transformative practice will be discussed to show how generified activity cuts across multilingual science communication and how genres act as frames for social action that entails languages in contact and translingualism.

Giddens's structuration theory, mentioned briefly in the previous chapter, is a useful point of departure to understand genre innovation and change in scientific communication and to better grasp how the research world is a social system with specific structural properties and structures that articulate its praxis. Giddens (1986: 169) postulated that a social system is organised hierarchically, that is, it has a social order and its established structures consist of rules and resources 'implicated in the nature of lived activities'. For Giddens, there is an 'inherent relation between structure and agency (and agency and power)' that explains that social structures do not exist separately from human agents because both enable and constrain such praxis. Evoking Giddens' theory, we could likewise claim that in today's academic and research world both the producers (i.e., the scientists) and the consumers of science (i.e., the scientists and different science stakeholders such as policymakers, funding bodies/institutions and the public as recipients of science) interact according to a social order that establishes patterns of interaction. The systematicity of these patterns explains the prototypicality of the genres.

As a social ecosystem, today's research world has structural properties (rules and resources) that are inseparable from the human agents, namely, the various science stakeholders. These agents are the ones that generate actions in the continuity of praxis, which is enacted in various discipline-specific practices (Hyland, 2012; Johns, 1997; Swales, 1990). In addition to enabling praxis, as a social system, the research world has established structures that, as Giddens (1990: 169) notes for the broader social context, 'imply rules and resources'. First, we could conceive of genre sets and genre systems as structures that support patterns of interaction so that the different science stakeholders mentioned previously can produce, disseminate and receive science. Second, because of their prototypicality, all genres impose certain limits on variation, since each genre necessarily has to adhere to its established conventions for the pursuance of its communicative purposes. Third, it is through genres that knowledge begets texts and can be received. Otherwise, action – production, dissemination and reception of knowledge – would not be recognisable by the human agents, that is, the genre users, both producers and recipients. Lastly, every genre is contingent in itself. Genre emergence, genre evolution, even genre loss account for the generation of actions in response to new exigences. In sum, the established social structures and the various agents' actions mutually influence and shape one another, in turn contributing changes in praxis.

As noted earlier, a dominant social structure, Web 2.0, also acts as a major driver of research networking, collaboration and distribution of knowledge. As human actors, researchers draw on established genres of research to exchange new knowledge digitally and advance their disciplinary fields. As a structural property of the social system, the web offers tools and resources so that actors can engage in new digital practices. As an example, there are policy priorities to incentivise Open Science and the use of social media networks to make science known and recognised by society (D. Ball, 2016; Puschmann, 2014). A drawback of this dynamic, though, may be found in the inequities between centre versus peripheral countries and in the case of off-networked scholars. For instance, Salager-Meyer (2008: 126) criticises the lack of access to the Internet that hinders the participation of researchers from developing countries in the world scientific community – hampering involvement in collaborative research, offering fewer opportunities for knowledge access and production and preventing the submission of manuscripts online.

Russell's (1995) activity theory is also a pertinent framework for understanding the current context of production and consumption of science at a time of dramatic social changes. The main rationale of Russell's activity theory is that human behaviour in social contexts consists of 'goal-directed, historically-situated, cooperative human interactions'. Activity systems are conceptualised as '(1) historically developed, (2) mediated by tools, (3) dialectically structured, (4) analysed as the relations of participants and tools and (5) changed through zones of proximal development'. Russell further explains that genres are mediational tools in activity systems. As Russell (1995: 5) observes, '[h]uman activities are complex systems in constant change, interaction, and self-reorganization as human beings collaboratively adapt to and transform their environments through their actions with tools (including writing)'. Drawing on Russell's activity theory, we could likewise argue that genred activity is historically situated and, therefore, subject to evolution and change (Prior, 1998; Swales, 2004). We see changes in the genres that come from familiar and recognisable antecedent genres (e.g., the graphical abstract and the traditional abstract) (Herring, 2013) or in features of interdiscursivity in digital science genres that merge expert discourse with other discourses, such as educational discourse and journalistic discourse (Gotti, 2014; Motta-Roth and Scherer, 2016). Doubtless, the Internet revolution accounts for the most unprecedented change in genre use (Gross and Buehl, 2016; Luzón and Pérez-Llantada, 2019; Miller and Kelly, 2017), and it is very likely that the digital publication context and Open Science will be different in the next few years.

The collaborative, goal-directed interactions that take place in current scientific knowledge dissemination and characterise human behaviour within activity systems also help us understand why genre-mediated activity between producers and recipients of science is dialectically structured. Essentially, this activity relies on grammar features that are very common in written registers 'in the age of mass literacy' (Biber and Gray, 2016), as illustrated in subsequent sections of this chapter. Scientists maintain a dialogue or juxtapose conflicting ideas with other scientists as well as with science stakeholders and society in general. This dialogue is supported by the digital media, in which networks of genres and other types of genre assemblages enable the creation of complex polyphonic (heteroglossic) narratives of science, merging the voice of the researcher, that of the community of practice and that of the individual within a single multimodal element, making manifest the relations between participants and tools.

As mediational tools, research genres are part of a complex ecosystem subject to power relations and ongoing reorganisation of social actions. Being part of the activity system, the production and reception of scientific knowledge varies across language contact situations and accounts for language variation in zones of proximal development – including virtual spaces if we understand 'zone of proximal development' from the perspective of activity theory and human-computer interaction (Zinchenko, 1996) – where two or more languages coexist. The activity system sets up translingual practices (Canagarajah, 2018: 31) across the various biotic populations that constitute the broad scientific community ecosystem. We can further claim that there exist zones of proximal development that may change the established structures of the social system. In Chapter 4, for example, we will see that physical spaces like shared infrastructures, international fora and collaborative web spaces such as repositories and ASNSs and microblogging sites enable fair participation and are open to translingualism and language contact situations.

Russell (1995: 5) observed that '[h]uman activities are complex systems in constant change, interaction, and self-reorganization as human beings collaboratively adapt to and transform their environments through their actions with tools'. Increasing generic speciation reveals such complexity.

3.2 Generic speciation

Two of the main features characterising the activity system that supports research communication in the contemporary world are its increasing speciation of genres and its 'evolutionary development' (Swales, 2004). The dramatic social and technological changes, as major driving forces, in many ways account for the fact that 'most genres are continuously evolving and so need to be periodically revisited' (Swales, 2004: 31). In particular, two interrelated facts lie behind the speciation of traditional 'stabilised-for-now' genres (Swales, 2004: 63) in the contemporary scene. One is that communicative repertoires are, by their very nature, contingent on the changes in research activity determined by political, economic, social and policy agendas and, more broadly, by post-globalisation effects, mobility and skilled migration. The second factor is that Web 2.0 has emerged as a dominant 'sphere of activity', to borrow Bakhtin's (1986b) original concept. It has dramatically impacted the way scientific knowledge circulates and is disseminated beyond traditional (printed) channels of communication, by this means extending the ecological environments of genres of research. Speciation can be traced

Table 3.1 Generic speciation in research communication forms

Traditional genres	Remediated and emerging genres
Abstract	Graphical abstract, video abstract
	Author summary, lay summary
Biostatements, curricula vitae	Academic home pages
Monograph	Electronic monograph
Doctoral dissertation	Electronic theses and dissertations (ETDs)
Laboratory notes	Electronic laboratory notes
	Video methods articles/visualised experiment papers
Field report	Brief research reports, working party reports, short reports, case reports, working group report
Report	Registered reports microblogging
Grant proposal/Proposal/Prospectus	Citizen science projects, crowdfunding project proposals
Research article/Review article	AoF and enhanced publications
	Video methods articles
	Data articles
	Featured video articles
	Audioslides
	Short texts accompanying articles
Evaluation genres (peer review reports, author response to reviewers)	Online peer reviews
	Online author response to reviewers
Forum discussion	Microblogging (Facebook, Twitter, Reddit, WeChat, etc.)
	Research group blogs
	Discussions on academic social networking sites (ResearchGate, Academia.edu, etc.)

in the ongoing changes of the existing genre systems and networks underpinning social interactions in the STEMM fields or, to be more accurate, in 'the set of genres that are *routinely enacted* by the members of a community' (Orlikowski and Yates, 1994: 542, my emphasis). For the sake of illustration and a better understanding of the subsequent empirically based discussion in the following sections, Table 3.1 showcases the possible evolutionary development of some traditional genres that have been moved to the digital environment, as well as the increasing genre diversification, 'add-on genres' (or associated extensions) and new digitally mediated written genres.

As shown in Table 3.1, major genres (research articles, abstracts, the monograph, the PhD dissertation, grant proposals and reports), minor genres (biostatements, prospectuses) and other forms of communication (discussion forums) that are 'part of the total genre network that a particular individual ... engages in, either or both receptively and productively, as part of his or her normal occupational or institutional practice' (Swales, 2004: 20) undergo processes of remediation and genre-internal diversification. For example, according to the RGaL corpus, such diversification aims to fulfil a wider range of communicative purposes in response to social concerns towards science ethics and the transparency and reproducibility of scientific methods and scientific results (Fecher and Friesike, 2014; Schulson, 2018). Additionally, web interfaces draw on hyperlinking options to virtually/physically relate these genres with other genres, by this means contributing evolutionary development in genre sets and systems. Other examples of evolutionary development can be found in lab notes and reports. Validating Herring (2013) and Miller and Kelly's (2017) conceptualisation of 'generic hybrids', the 'forms' of existing genres are borrowed by emerging genres. This is the case of the registered report, a report of a research study design that undergoes a peer review process before the study data are collected and analysed and the article submitted for publication (Mehlenbacher and Mehlenbacher, 2019). As another example, existing forms adopted by microblogging practices to reach wider audiences are defined by Büchi (2016) as 'an extension of science reporting'.

In the context of Open Science, new science-related contingencies explain the emergence of multimodal genres such as visualised experiment papers, also called video methods articles (Hafner, 2018), and 'occluded evaluative genres' (Swales, 2004: 20) that have turned into open access, such as open peer reviews. The former genres emerge as a response to the science reproducibility crisis (Schulson, 2018), while the latter give greater transparency to external processes of research assessment before the article is finally published (Breeze, 2019). These genres are already well established in the STEMM disciplines, and it seems likely that in the future we will find similar practices in other disciplinary fields.

Figure 3.1 further illustrates how the genre ecology has expanded by incorporating add-on genres, or extensions of traditional genres of scientific research. On the web, genres form more and more complex genre assemblages. Journals such as the *Journal of Environmental Management, Journal of Physical Chemistry, Solar Energy Materials, Solar Cells* and *Clinical Immunology*, to cite a few, publish articles with associated abstracts and graphical abstracts. Other journals

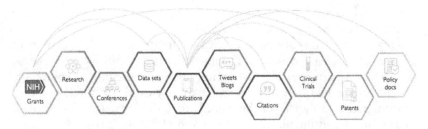

Figure 3.1 Contexts of interrelated genres
(Permission to reproduce granted under Creative Commons License. Hook, Porter and Herzog, 2018)

publish articles with associated lay summaries, author videos and audioslides, and others (e.g., *Data in Brief*) offer the possibility to publish interdependent genre texts, namely, a data article associated with a journal article, the former offering a detailed description of the data of the study and an explanation of their significance. In journals such as *Cell* and *Nature*, online articles have associated author videos and podcasts/videocasts, and Elsevier articles are complemented by video demonstrations of how to perform methodological procedures (e.g., featured videos, video articles and video case reports that describe tools and methods through visual media to enable the reproducibility of the research conducted).[1] As another example, journals such as the *Journal of Visualised Experiments* and *Fungal Genetics and Biology* publish video articles that likewise support those researchers interested in the reproducibility of their methodological procedures and research results. Generic speciation thus offers plenty of room for discussion on 'inter-genre-ality' (Devitt, 2009), as interrelated genres share some genre forms. Figure 3.1 also illustrates how other traditional genres such as lab notes and discussion forums have been taken up by new digital genres and forms of communication with audiences that have different interests and knowledge backgrounds in science. The traditional laboratory note (document) defined by Latour and Woolgar (1986: 69) has now been taken up by digital lab notebooks in response to researchers' need to deal with 'increasing volumes of data' and address 'concerns over reproducibility, as well as more stringent requirements on data management from funding agencies' (Kwok, 2018: 269). Other emerging genres such as citizen science projects and crowdfunding science-focused projects, that borrow some features from the traditional genres such as the journal

---

[1] For further information, see www.elsevier.com/authors/author-resources/research-elements [last accessed on 12 September 2020].

article and research grant proposal (Mehlenbacher, 2017), also attest to today's increasing generic speciation.

Finally, it seems apposite to draw attention to other genres in Figure 3.1, such as books and monographs and doctoral dissertations, which undergo neither innovation nor change in digital environments, except for the fact that they increasingly rely on the hypertextual and multimodal affordances of the web. Unlike the journal article (Buehl, 2016; Gross and Buehl, 2016; Gross and Harmon, 2016), they maintain their form and substance and remain to date as stand-alone genres in the online environment, with no add-on genres extending them.

3.3 Genre innovation and hybridisation

Before delving into issues of genre innovation and hybridisation, I would like to refer to two very influential social views on societal change, that of communication theorist Marshall McLuhan (1987: 62) and that of sociologist Zygmunt Bauman (2000) on 'liquid modernity' or 'late modernity'. Both views are important to understand the social and technological contexts shaping genre texts. McLuhan (1987: 56–61) views societal change as resulting from 'materials in continuous process of transformation at spatially removed sites' and contends that the digital media fragment the way we perceive and interpret information. Particularly relevant given the scope of this book is McLuhan's description of the digital medium as a 'translator', 'a way of translating one kind of knowledge into another mode'. For Bauman, the Internet has changed the patterns of human agency and structures (institutions), as well as people's interactions. In effect, highly developed global economies are characterised by fragmentation, discontinuity and permanent change brought about by the information revolution. As he puts it,

> The change in question is the new irrelevance of space .... In the software universe of light-speed travel, space may be traversed, literally, in 'no time'; the difference between 'far away' and 'down here' is cancelled. Space no more sets limits to actions and its effects, and counts little, or does not count at all. (Bauman, 2000: 117)

Analogies based on both influential perspectives are described in the following sections in relation to processes of genre remediation, innovation and change.

3.3.1 Implosive mosaics

Asserting Bauman's contention, we could argue that the technological possibilities of Web 2.0 have radically transformed genres and brought about unprecedented changes in the production and reception of science. The 'irrelevance of space' postulated in contemporary social theory (Bauman, 2000) likewise applies, by analogy, to traditional genres that have been moved to the web and to digital genres that have emerged. On the web, space is no longer a constraint on the diffusion of knowledge (Giltrow and Stein, 2009; Miller and Kelly, 2017). Here, the notion of 'implosive mosaic' that McLuhan (1987) used to describe combinations of semiotic modes (images and text) seems apt as a metaphorical representation of the way in which knowledge is accessed on online science-related platforms, journal websites and science magazine websites. By the same token, it can also metaphorically represent the way assemblages of genres are created in enhanced publications (Aalbersberg et al., 2012; Gross and Buehl, 2016; Gross, Harmon and Reidy, 2002; Harmon, 2019). The technological advances in the science-related platforms, journal websites and science magazine websites used as a general source for this book best illustrate the fragmentation of information in the virtual space. Instead of displaying a single linear text, these platforms give access to fragmented knowledge, often taking the form of distinct genres, resembling a mosaic. For example, Dimensions (https://dimensions.ai), a scientific research data platform that targets heterogeneous publics – for instance, researchers, higher education institutions, governments and publishers – lists on its screen several genre types that these publics can choose to access research: research publications, grants, tweets, blogs, clinical trials, patents and policy documents.

Evoking genre interconnections, the Dimensions platform provides access to different genre sets: research career-related genres (articles, chapters, books and grants), research-process genres (clinical trials, case studies), professional genres and genres of accountability (patents, policy documents and white papers) and social media genres (blogs and tweets). The different science stakeholders can 'identify and/or monitor research trends' (cited literally from the Dimensions platform) by choosing their preferred navigation procedure, access points and reading paths. Additionally, the platform provides linkages based on scholarly citation indexes and funding acknowledgements, which enables users to track the citation and impact of stabilised-enough genres (journal articles, books, grants), aspects that are fundamental drivers of scholarly communication. As Hook, Porter and Herzog (2018: online) remark, the information 'acquires the power of adaptability to multiple uses' and is designed 'to give the user a much greater sense of context of a piece of research'. Interestingly, the website architecture developers use an ecological metaphor to emphasise the possibilities of contextualising and interrelating different genres – '[s]cholarly citation engines have begun to play an increasingly important part of the *academic ecosystem*' (Hook, Porter and Herzog, 2018: online, my emphasis).

The interdependence of traditional genres and emerging electronic genres is also worth discussing in relation to the concept of polycontextuality and the way groupings of science-related genres are displayed on a single interface in the digital medium. Scientific magazines tend to draw on self-contained, mosaic-like platforms with hyperlinked information in diverse genre formats. A good example is the interface of *Scientific American*, an impressively far-reaching in scope, multilingual magazine that is 'published in 14 languages with 9.5 million print and tablet readers worldwide, 10+ million global online unique visitors monthly, and a social media reach of 7+ million'.[2] On this platform, the main menu allows readers to search across topics (the sciences, mind, health, technology and sustainability) and across genres, modes and media, such as video series (e.g., 60-Second Science videos or Bring Science Home videos), 60-second science podcasts, opinion articles and publications (books) from *Scientific American* collections. The coverage of topics thus satisfies audiences with diversified interests. Instantiating the effects of the collapsing of contexts in Web 2.0 (Büchi, 2016), this platform offers not only STEMM scientists but also other interested readers the possibility to filter the search results by selecting genres and modes and media with different levels of informational depth – namely, articles, videos and podcasts.

The websites analysed also exemplify how the digital space does not set any limits on knowledge access and interaction between producers and consumers of knowledge. The architecture of the *Public Library of Science (PLoS)* interface is also a useful example to illustrate the interdependence of genres in the digital medium and, from a theoretical standpoint, to support Spinuzzi's (2004: 1) claim that 'genres work together in assemblages' or 'complexes'. In *PLoS*, a data search engine offers free access to more than 200,000 peer-reviewed articles. It is through hyperlinking options that emerging and traditional genres create a complex genre system that, to borrow Bazerman's (1994) words, enacts different social intentions. Readers can access the associated article by clicking on the *PLoS* editor's summaries located below the journal article title (Figure 3.2). This genre system is related sequentially through hyperlinking, and, interestingly, it encompasses

[2] www.scientificamerican.com/page/about-scientific-american/ [last accessed on 16 December 2019].

Figure 3.2 First-level layer of information in PLoS *interface (https://journals.plos .org/plosgenetics/*
[last accessed on 22 June 2019], permission granted)

'the full set of genres that instantiate the participation of all the parties' (Spinuzzi, 2004: 3), in this case the different science stakeholders (editors and authors).

The concepts of context collapse and genre transmediality are also key to understanding the interrelatedness of genre systems in web environments. In the *PLoS* interface, the short summaries are first-level texts, hence easily identifiable at first sight, and the journal article or featured article containing specialist (expert) content constitutes a

Figure 3.3 Visual interface of the online article (https://journals.plos.org/ plosgenetics/ [last accessed 12 June 2020]).
Source: Xue, Y., Chiu, J. C. and Zhang, Y. (2019). SUR-8 interacts with PP1–87B to stabilize PERIOD and regulate circadian rhythms in Drosophila. *PLoS Genetics*, 15(11), e1008475. https://doi.org/10.1371/journal.pgen.1008475 [This is an open-access article distributed under the terms of the Creative Commons Attribution License]

second-level layer of meaning-making. From this we can deduce that the hyperlinking affordances assist what Maier and Engberg (2019: 131) define as levels of explanatory depth and processes of transmedial gradation. As these authors argue, the hypertextual affordances serve to bridge the gap between the different informational layers of online genres. Evoking the mosaic metaphor, the second-level article, containing the highest level of explanatory depth, can be accessed via fragmented texts or part-genres (Figure 3.3). Such fragmentation reveals aspects of generic stabilisation and innovation. On the one hand, the interface displays the part-genres of the journal article (abstract – introduction – results – discussion – materials and methods), pointing at stabilisation. On the other, the author summary, which 'consists of an adapted abstract for easier understanding' (Breeze, 2016: 50), adds innovation to the traditional article structure.

It is also worth looking at the horizontal tabs on the interface (signalled with a circle), which give access to the surrounding context of the article. As seen in the figure, some of the tabs give access to information on readers' interest in the article (i.e., different types of metrics such as information on views, citations and discussion threads). Other tabs invite readers' comments or welcome submissions of information on news media or blog coverage of the article, illustrating once again the interdependence relations with online genres that reach the general public. It is also worth noting that the interface integrates a link to information on the peer review process. Some articles published in *PLoS* have open-access peer review reports, a rhetorical hybrid. It is the policy of this journal 'to give transparency' to this research evaluation process through this hyperlinked extension.

Other platforms show similar structural arrangements, likewise exemplifying the effects of the collapsing of contexts in digital research communication. *eLife* sciences,[3] a platform supporting Open Science and technology innovation, also illustrates an implosive mosaic of genres. As seen in Figure 3.4, the right-hand side of the interface displays hyperlinks to feature articles and insights, or brief articles that resemble science popularisations. The left-hand side of its interface displays information on the latest research in the form of article titles and short texts (one-sentence long) that are associated with second-level hyperlinked full research articles. Although one might expect that these short texts would have a screening function for expert readers, the main function attributed to traditional IMRaD abstracts (Huckin, 2001), they rather 'advertise a paper's contribution' making it evident that they also target the lay public, hence 'indicat[ing] a kind of "democratisation" of the scientific community' (Ayers, 2008: 22).

The second-level hyperlinked articles can also be accessed as sectioned texts. Some of these tabs are conventional article sections (Introduction – Results – Discussion – Materials and Methods). Others illustrate how occluded genres such as reviewers' reports are made available online 'in the interests of transparency' (quoted literally as appearing in the *eLife* platform). Accordingly, the tabs give access to online editors' decision letters with the acceptance summary after peer review, as well as authors' detailed responses to revisions.

---

[3] https://elifesciences.org/ [last accessed on 6 January 2020].

Figure 3.4 Screenshot of eLife
(https://elifesciences.org/ [last accessed on 21 December 2019] permission to reproduce granted under the terms of the Creative Commons Attribution License)

One might further add that, in addition to giving transparency, open peer reviews and responses to reviews are useful material for genre analysts and LAP practitioners who can exploit them for pedagogical purposes (see Chapter 6). One last example of an interface integrating traditional and new genres is *IEEE Spectrum*, advertised as an engineering magazine to keep up to date with 'the latest engineering and computer science advances in context'.[4] This platform also includes tabs to a variety of genres, ranging from special reports, blogs and multimedia genres (podcasts, slideshows and videos) to technology blogs by editors and freelance contributors, and professional resources (webinars and whitepapers). Its technological affordances are similar to those discussed previously in relation to other platforms.

---

[4] https://spectrum.ieee.org/ [last accessed on 6 July 2020].

In sum, the effects of context collapse on digital media, as discussed by Marwick and boyd (2011), determine innovation and change and at the same time reveal the interdependence relations among traditional and emerging genres in the virtual space. McLuhan's vision of the digital medium is picture-perfect. In today's research world, 'the digital medium dissolves frontiers for human individuals and for traditional textual configurations for the sake of efficiency and practicality'.

3.3.2 *Constellations of semiotic resources*

There has been considerable discussion in the literature on the use of visual support in written genres. The seminal guide *Scientists Must Write* states that the function of visuals is to 'attract attention', 'stimulate and interest the reader', and 'help and inform' (Barras, 1978: 107). A further and far more recent description of visuals in the journal article genre can be found in Desnoyers (2011: 155). This author notes that the specificity of the visuals is associated with a particular article type. Accordingly, while tables with quantitative data abound in enquiry-based research articles, and review articles rarely contain qualitative tables, organigrams are widely used in theoretical papers and histograms, and photographs recur in experimental papers. In the digital age, visuals have changed dramatically, and, thus, understanding visuals-to-genre correspondence becomes a challenging endeavour for genre analysts, who now need to examine such correspondence not only within single genres but also within web-supported genre assemblages.

I argued earlier that one central issue that accounts for the remediation or web adaptation of traditional genres and for the emergence of new genres is the combination of written texts with other semiotic resources, mainly visual resources. Rhetorical and genre studies that enquire into the semiotics of genres underline that the representation of knowledge in web-environments involves multi-channelled meaning-making processes (Giltrow and Stein, 2009; Gross, 1990; Harmon, 2019; Miller and Kelly, 2017; Prior, 2009; Tannen and Trester, 2013). This can be seen in the various semiotic resources that accompany the enhanced publications and open-access articles of the RGaL corpus – from 3D images and interactive graphs to add-on genres such as audioslides, author summaries, author videos, graphical abstracts and video abstracts (Pérez-Llantada, 2013b; Plastina, 2017; Yang, 2017).

Little generic innovation is observed in the latter two genres, audioslides and video abstracts. Supporting Yang (2017: 24), audioslides are 'appendants', consisting of a five-minute visual and audio (the researcher's voice) synopsis or overview of the article contents. According to the small-scale corpora of audioslides compiled for the RGaL project, this genre reproduces in a web-cast format the macro-structural organisation of the article, either the IMRaD structure or the problem-solution pattern (Hoey, 1983). While interest in audio-slides, which emerged in 2013, appears to have declined, video abstracts 're-articulating the meaning of the article abstract' (Plastina, 2017: 57) are becoming more prominent. This means that genres can be altered and their substance transformed into other genres, but contingency can also lead to the emergence of new genres and the gradual disappearance of some others. In the case of these two genre exemplars, the multimodal affordances of Web 2.0 contribute little innovation or change. The visuals per se do not entail any persuasive goals. Hence, like Mackenzie Owen (2007), we can claim that enhanced publications are merely 'the illusion of a revolution'. The core genre, the journal article, remains in cogent form. In other words, it retains its individual integrity and stabilisation, and innov-ation simply involves enhancement through visual contents. Yet, from a cognitive standpoint, these constellations of multisemiotic resources in enhanced publications exhibit at least one further functionality. They make information easier to process because it is conveyed through two different channels or modes, the visual and the verbal (or aural in the case of the audioslides genre) (Harmon, 2019; Makenzie Owen, 2007). Evoking the Gricean maxims of clarity, brev-ity and simplicity, the 'increased level of detail and clarification' provided by a visual element facilitates cognitive processing of information and 'contributes to the effectiveness of the discourse' (Roque, 2017: 28).

   The evolution of the online journal article thus depends on the innovations introduced by interdependent genres. For example, the constellating genres in the journal article ecology adopt some of the structures and features of generic precedents, thus becoming 'generic hybrids' (Herring, 2013). Audioslides adopt the rhetorical organisa-tion features of their associated journal articles, for example the IMRaD and Problem-solution patterns. We can therefore argue that the existing genre is then 'reconfigured' (Herring, 2013) in the digital medium but its form remains familiar to the users of this genre, in this case the journal article. But despite such resemblances, it seems that if scientists do not perceive a clear functionality (and practicality) in a genre, it might disappear or be taken up by other genres with clearer communicative purposes and utility. This could explain the emergence of other generic multimodal hybrids such as graphical abstracts and video abstracts, which instantiate the ongoing evolution of the online journal article ecology.

The use of graphical abstracts has long been a common practice in disciplines such as chemistry and engineering, dating back to the 1970s in 'the then multilingual chemistry journal *Angewandte Chemie*' (Hendges and Florek, 2019: 64). In the past decade, there has been an increasing use of this genre in some disciplinary fields. For example, Yoon and Chung (2017) report a 350 per cent increase in the period 2011–2015 in the subfields of social and economic geography. In a cross-disciplinary survey on digital communication practices by Pérez-Llantada (2021b), graphical abstracts were associated with the Physical Sciences and Engineering fields but were considered as '*not important/somewhat important*' genres in comparison with articles, abstracts and research grants. Yoon and Chung (2017: 1371) claim that variation in graphical abstracts mainly relates to the different types of content visualisations. The RGaL graphical abstracts appear to confirm these authors' claims. The abstracts analysed either give a synthetic view of the study or an overview of the methodological procedures followed or a synthesis of the most significant findings or just a visualisation of the key finding. The RGaL graphical abstracts exhibit a variety of visual forms. Circa 30 per cent are flow diagrams representing relationships (e.g., sequential processes such as means-end, cause-effect or reason-result) and almost 20 per cent use a flow diagram along with (pie) charts with the key findings (see examples in Figure 2.5 in Chapter 2). A further 20 per cent provide an overview of the article, indicating study area-methodology-results or purpose-experiment-results. Of the remaining graphical abstracts, almost 25 per cent include a visual representation of the study, sometimes accompanied by text with explanations, and less than 10 per cent are pictures and photographs illustrating key aspects.

The use of multisemiotic resources in enhanced publications points to the intricacies of ascribing communicative purposes in genre categorisation. Askehave and Swales (2001: 209) already anticipated that 'technological advance affects the way in which genre-exemplars are perceived and ranked in relation to their mode of transmission' and, consequently, the concept of communicative purpose has become 'more complex, multiple, variable and generally hard to get at' (Askehave and Swales, 2001: 195). In a way, the graphical abstract shares the main communicative purposes or functional goals of the traditional abstract, that of acting as all-inclusive stand-alone mini-texts, screening devices for readers and previews of the whole article (Huckin, 2001: 93). The only difference is that the visual innovation has further functionalities. The eye-catching image of the graphical abstract speaks more readily than the verbal abstract and reinforces its semantic meanings. And not only readers but also the authors themselves profit from this. Hendges and Florek (2019: 66) argue that graphical abstracts help authors 'reflect about their work and understand its fundamental conclusion'.

Given the greater prominence of visual rhetoric in emerging add-on and hybrid genres such as those discussed in this section, future research should ascertain the multiple communicative goals multimodal genre assemblages fulfil in response to social exigences.

3.4 Peritexts, paratexts and intertexts

An enquiry into genre interdependence and genre dialogism in science communication online requires consideration of the concept of intertextuality, extensively theorised in literary criticism and social sciences research (Bakhtin, 1981, 1986b; Fairclough, 1992; Genette, 1997), for several reasons. First, very diverse genre assemblages are formed on the web that integrate multiple voices, both from scientists and from different science stakeholders. Secondly, intertextual analysis enables us to explore 'a contextualized treatment of generic form' because, as Devitt (2009: 27) notes, 'genre itself still involves language, and any complete understanding of genre will need to include the language forms that serve to achieve those purposes and effects, the forms that make generic action happen'. Those language forms are conceptualised by Miller (1984) as syntactics. Lastly, intertextual and hypertextual relationships within genre assemblages can illustrate how genres work together in order to make rhetorical substance (semantics) accessible to both expert and lay audiences (or broader publics). The intertextual analysis applies the concepts of peritexts, paratexts and intertexts from the previously mentioned seminal works, and the view of intertextuality as understood in rhetorical genre studies as 'the relation each text has to the texts surrounding it' (Bazerman, 2004a: 84, see also Briggs and Bauman, 1992; Devitt, 2004).

One interesting textual source the genre analyst can use to conduct intertextual analysis is *Nature Briefing*, an electronic newsletter that contains a summary of relevant information on current issues of scientific research. This newsletter offers a selection of short snippets (or previews) of science that can be extended by clicking on a hyperlink. The hyperlinked information takes the form of traditional and emerging forms of digital communication – from research articles and research letters to podcasts and science news and views, to mention a few. In view of this, we could establish an analogy between what Genette (1997: 17) defined as the publisher's peritext of a book, 'an aspect of the production' and 'of the materialization of a text for public use' and this electronic newsletter format. Obviously, in the digital environment, the peritexts cannot be elements included on the cover of a printed book or, in this case, an article. They take the form of *Nature* research reporting summaries, news snippets with hyperlinked information. These are all short, preview texts, one or two sentences long, that act as thresholds of interpretation, that is, points of entry at which readers can decide whether or not to access further information. One of these peritextual summaries[5] in the daily briefing looks like this:

Global warming 'unparalleled' in 2,000 years

History is littered with pockets of warmer and cooler periods, but current warming is 'not only unparalleled in terms of absolute temperatures, but also unprecedented in spatial consistency within the context of the past 2,000 years', says new research from climate-change scientist Raphael Neukom and his colleagues. Neukom tells the *Nature Podcast* how he determined that, for more than 98 per cent of the globe, the warmest period has been within the past 100 years.

Nature Podcast | 19 min listen
Reference: *Nature* paper

The sequential genre uptake goes as follows. This short summary is intertextually associated with a hyperlinked daily podcast with the latest science news and two hyperlinked *Nature* papers by the same corresponding author. Both the summary and the podcast come from rhetors other than scientists, namely, journal editors. The contents of authors' articles are also taken up in online comments to the articles. In addition to hyperlinking to the podcast, the articles are hypertextually and intertextually connected to another journalistic genre, a News and Views article. The rhetors of this latter article are journalists who have taken on material from the two journal articles. Therefore, we could argue that the summary, the podcast and the journalistic article can be considered paratexts of the online articles (see Table 3.4). Genette (1997: 4) explains that a paratext is not a parallel text, but rather a 'threshold' that offers 'the possibility of either stepping inside or turning back'. On the journal interface, the editors' short summary acts as a threshold the reader has to pass through if he/she wants to access its related texts, the podcast, the two research articles and the News and Views article. By analogy with the author's

---

[5] www.nature.com/articles/d41586-019-02320-1, Daily briefing, 26 July 2019 (available online).

name, the title, the preface, and illustrations acting as paratextual elements of a book, in the digital medium the paratextual elements are 'verbal or other productions that surround a text and extend it', 'to ensure the text's presence in the world' (Genette, 1997: 4), which are hypertextually and intertextually linked to the original sources, in this case two research articles.

This linkage of hypertexts represents an interdependent genre chain created by the sequential genre uptake by different rhetors: the authors' articles and readers' comments → the newsletter short summary → the podcast short text and the News and Views. As stated earlier, this chain embeds different voices (or polyphonic discourses). The newsletter summary and the podcast short text reflect the editors' views on the rhetorical substance of the prior texts, the scientific articles. These scientific articles provide the experts' views on the topic, while the journalistic genres offer a technical/professional opinion of the science being reported. We therefore see in this genre chain an example of 'the discursive processes of text producers and interpreters, how they draw upon the repertoires of genres and discourses available within orders of discourse' (Fairclough, 1992: 213). The hypertextual affordances on Web 2.0 enable readers to navigate through generic forms with different levels of explanatory depth and different perspectives on scientific facts that seek to satisfy the various interests of the internet audiences. If we use Maier and Engberg's (2019) concept of transmedial gradation, we could further argue that this genre chain further instantiates a case of 'inverted' transmedial gradation. As shown in Table 3.4, the editor's snippet/summary and the podcast's short introductory text build on texts that have higher levels of explanatory depth: the highly specialised texts produced by the scientists. Processes of transmedial gradation can also be seen in the journalist's uptake of the contents of the scientists' articles, which are transformed into a professional (journalistic) narrative of science, the News and Views article.

Turning specifically to the intertextual uptake of contents in this genre chain, Table 3.2 shows how the contents of the two article abstracts and those of the News and Views text have been encapsulated in the editors' one-sentence summary, which captures the main idea and offers readers a repertoire of genres to access depending on their preferred interests. The table shows the lexicogrammatical profiles of the prior texts – in the case of the abstracts, characterised by syntactically elaborate phrasal structures and, in the case of the News and Views article, characterised by an agile syntax and evaluative discourse typical of journalistic prose. Intertextual analysis also reveals strategies of knowledge transformation (mediation) across contexts, a non-explicit type of intertextuality, also called 'constitutive

Table 3.2   Intertextual uptake in an online genre assemblage

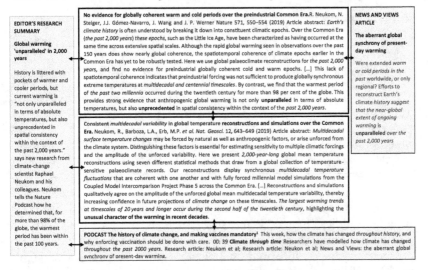

or non-manifest intertextuality'. This is one type of intertextuality in which 'the earlier words are recontextualised, and thereby given new meaning in the new context' (Bazerman, 2004b: 90). This can be seen in the extracts highlighted in bold and italics in Table 3.2. Hyperlinking has been indicated with arrows, intertextual uptake is highlighted in italics and authors' evaluation in bold type.

Interdependences between core and peripheral genres can also be found in the short summaries associated with research articles in open-access journals such as *eLife* and *PLoS*. These summaries contain intertextual material from their associated research articles and, as in *Nature*, they are merely descriptive and promotional and therefore provide no interpretation of the semantic meanings conveyed in the article. As such, they can also be considered paratexts that 'advertise a paper's contribution' to a broad public, in addition to indicating, as Ayers (2008: 22) remarks, 'a kind of "democratisation" of the scientific community'. Using Lu's (2010) web-based analyser, a comparison of the syntactic complexity indexes of both pre- and post-texts further evinces processes of knowledge transformation (Table 3.3). These indexes indicate a shift from the formal, informationally dense, discourse style of the prior texts (i.e., the article abstracts), as seen in their overall number of types (or distinct words) and type/token ratio, to the more agile, structurally elaborated and less semantically dense summaries. This shows how language assists the transformation of the

Table 3.3 Comparative statistics of short summaries and abstracts in Nature

	Short summaries	Abstracts
Tokens (running words) in text	3,849	21,966
Tokens used for word list	3,743	20,733
Types (distinct words)	1,310	3,745
Type/token ratio (TTR)	34.998665	18.062992
Average length of text (in words)	41.83695	238.76086
Sentences	98	765
Mean per sentence (in words)	38.2244873	27.10458565
Std. Dev.	10.79187202	11.16977787

generic substance (semantics) of the pre-texts into texts targeting broader publics. Syntactic measures such as the average mean (in words) per sentence further reveals 'conversations' with readers with different layers of informational depth or, to borrow Fairclough's (1992: 208) words, 'two different interpretative repertoires'. The fact that the average mean in words of sentences of the summaries is higher than that of the abstracts suggests that the former genre texts are much more explicit in meaning, differing from the 'much less explicit in meaning' – 'efficient for expert readers' – discourse style that characterises academic prose (Biber and Gray, 2010: 2).

There are other genre networks and systems that would be worth investigating in future research along the lines discussed earlier. These include abstracts and their associated video abstracts, podcasts and their associated articles, video methods articles and their associated summaries and abstracts, or lay summaries and their associated science-related videos and articles, to name a few. They reflect sequential knowledge transformation and 'a rhetor's uptake of meanings from the original text' (Smart and Falconer, 2019: 201), by this means widening the range of possible interpretations for the diversified audiences.

3.5 Narratives, stories and styles

From the increasingly wide range of research genres supported by Web 2.0 today, there are two that particularly invite reflection on various theoretical and analytical considerations. Because they are fairly recent genres, to date little research has been done on these online narratives compared to the large number of studies analysing other digital genres and media (see, e.g., Breeze, 2019; Kuteeva and Mauranen, 2018; Luzón, 2013; Mauranen, 2013; Orpin, 2019). For these reasons, and for the sake of conciseness, it is worth discussing these two genre narratives that are becoming more salient in research settings as a result of emerging social agendas: video methods articles and registered reports. Both fall under the category of hybrid genres, as described by Herring (2013) and Miller and Kelly (2017) and emerged as a result of new social exigences. The antecedent genres of these two emerging genres pose rhetorical constraints on these narratives, both in their form and substance (Jamieson, 1975; Jamieson and Campbell, 1982). Unlike traditional genres, their main focus is not on scientific findings themselves, but on the actual scientific methods, reflecting a new social exigency, namely, greater concern towards research processes and assurance of the rigour and quality of those processes. It is therefore of interest to explore aspects of text, register and style in these narratives to understand the genres' responses to such exigences and, from a different standpoint, the effects of the polycontextuality of the digital medium in the construction of both genre texts.

Visualised experiments articles, also known as protocol videos (Pasquali, 2007) or video methods articles (Hafner, 2018), have a clear generic precedent or, rather, part genre, the methods section of the experimental journal article. Drawing on data from a corpus of eleven video methods articles, Hafner (2018: 15) explains that this genre attempts to compensate for the fact that 'the addition of digital elements to research articles (e.g., embedded video) fails to add significant meaning to the genre, perhaps indicating a poor match between the affordances of digital media and the communicative purposes of the academic writers'. While his claim is true to some extent, from a genre perspective there does seem to be a certain degree of evolution and innovation in its very nature resulting from the rhetorical exigences of the genre by diverse science stakeholders' demands relating to the reliability of scientific findings and the reproducibility of science (Schulson, 2018), as noted earlier.

The different Swalesian rhetorical moves and steps of these video articles resemble the rhetorical organisation conventions of methods sections in experimental articles (Swales, 1990, 2004), hence maintaining the typified features of its generic precedent. Therefore, we could argue that the main innovation of this genre lies in its multimodal affordances and their distinct functionality. While we can affirm that the main communicative purpose of this genre is the same as that of its precedent, to report scientific protocols and methodological procedures efficiently, by relying on two modes, the visual and the verbal, this genre enhances the reliability and credibility of the reporting of such procedures. In other words, through the visual support, the verbal narrative gains in informational depth and level of detail, including information on the physical context in which the experiment was carried out. It is also worth noting that the video-based 'story' is narrated by different actors (e.g., the first author or corresponding author of the article, co-authors, a voice-over narrator or off-camera commentator). In the example given in Table 3.4, the lead author first introduces the study and provides the context, the rationale and the aim of the experiment. Afterwards, a voice-over narrator gives the instructions for carrying out the methodological protocol. In this example, this latter narrator's account is taken up by a co-author, who, instead of using the merely instructional discourse of the voice-over narrator, highlights an important aspect to bear in mind. The polyphony of voices gives dynamism to the narration, while aiming to grab the viewer's attention.

The written methods articles associated with these video methods articles – totalling 99,904 running words – include a summary, an abstract and the main text. The main text is divided into introduction, protocol, results and discussion sections, hence replicating the traditional IMRaD section (Swales, 1990). Regarding lexical complexity, the overall corpus of video transcripts scores 7,377 types and a type/token ratio (TTR) of 7.99. As for syntactic measures, the texts have an average of 19.31 words per sentence (with a standard deviation of 10.44). At a text-linguistic level, the language of these narratives appears to be more personal than the discourse style characterising academic prose (Biber et al., 1999). In this sense, it is worth noting the frequency of the first person pronoun *we* (13.71 occurrences per 10,000 words) as a marker of subjectivity. This pronoun collocates with research-processes verbs (e.g., *we have a ...*, *we describe the protocol*, *we observed...*, *we found ...*). Other recurring features in the protocol section are directives, that is, informal instructions expressed with action verbs (e.g., *start, choose, prepare ...*), the possibility modal *can* (30.08 occurrences per 10,000 words), followed some way behind by *will* (9.0), *should* (8.2) and *must* (4.5) and the discourse marker *then* (11.5) signalling stages in the protocol. Here, again, the role of intertextuality is also worth commenting on briefly, as these texts contain intertextual signposts that indicate to readers/viewers when to look at the accompanying video, as shown in the following two video extracts (signposting expressions marked in italics).

This kind of lung US sign is known as a spared area. You can find two lung points in this condition. The presence of a spared area generally suggests mild PTX (*please also see Video 6*).

In the case of tension PTX, continuous air drainage with a chest tube can be used with the infant in a supine position (Figure 4C). In moderate PTX, if thoracentesis is indicated, the site of needle insertion can be anywhere in the field where lung sliding is absent (Figure 5, *Video 3*).

Table 3.4 Rhetorical moves of a video methods article[a]

Video segment	Narrators	Purposes	Excerpts
Title	First (corresponding) author (senior researcher)	Inform and persuade the validity of the method	This method can help us answer key questions in the biochemistry field such as the proteolytic modification of proteins as well as a characterisation of inhibitors, and proteases and peptides. The main advantage of this technique is that it allows a rapid screening of the proteolytic activity of proteases on peptides....
Designing and preparing the peptides	Voice-over narrator	Inform about stages involved in the design and preparation	The first step in peptide design is to acquire the sequence of the fusion protein of interest from a public database such as NCBI or the Virus Pathogen Database. Choose the protease recognition site preceding the fusion peptide and include 2–3 amino acids upstream and downstream of this sequence....
Preparing the fluorescence plate reader	Voice-over narrator	Inform about steps to be taken in subsequent stages	Begin this procedure by turning on the plate reader and waiting until the cell test is finished. Next, open the operating software on the attached computer and make sure it is connected with the plate reader.... *(continued)*

87

Table 3.4 (*cont.*)

Video segment	Narrators	Purposes	Excerpts
Preparing the assay	Voice-over narrator [interrupted by a novice researcher]	Inform about steps to be taken Highlight essential information to be taken into account	Prepare the appropriate assay buffers for the proteases as described in the test protocol. ... [It is essential to use a black plate as the assay plate to prevent fluorescent leakage from adjacent wells ...]
Data analysis	Voice-over narrator	Inform about steps to follow when analysing the data	Prior to starting the data analysis, save the experiment file. Click on Export and export the file as a .txt. Import the .txt file into a spreadsheet ...
Results: Mutations in the cleavage site alter activity of furin and cleavage efficiency	Co-author (junior researcher)	Report on main findings	A furin cleavage assay of human MERS-CoV EMC/2012 S2' site and camel-derived double mutant strain HKU205, along with single mutant variants of EMC/2012, revealed that the EMC 2012 peptide was efficiently cleaved while almost no cleavage of the S2' peptide of the HKU205 strain occurred.
Conclusion	Co-author or first author	Provide the main conclusions	Following this procedure, western blot analysis or immunofluorescence assays using the full-length protein of interest can be performed to verify protein cleavage or in this case if cleavage results in a fluorogenic version of the viral fusion protein.

As Pasquali (2007: 713) explains, this genre helps scientists 'improve the critical analysis of scientific procedures' regarding the rigour of their methodological protocol and supports peer reviewers, who have further information to assess the scientific method and the quality of the authors' findings more accurately. Pasquali (2007: 713) further stresses the value of these multimodal narratives by arguing that 'it has always been difficult to reproduce some experiments by relying solely on the published text'. Considering the contextual constraints of this genre, it is understandable that the rhetorical and linguistic hybridisation of this multimodal narrative is a direct response to the expectations of different science stakeholders; 'the credibility of a video relies on the honesty and integrity of the author, the reliability and robustness of the method of its recording, the trustworthiness of the publishers, and the controls and standards operating in the scientific community' (Pasquali, 2007: 714).

The registered report genre also invites reflection upon the issue of giving greater transparency to the research process when reporting scientific communication today. As stated in Chapter 2, a registered report consists of a pre-publication report of the methods section and it is submitted for review before the study data are actually collected (Mehlenbacher, 2019a). Because they are also 'a direct response to the contemporary replication crisis' (Mehlenbacher and Mehlenbacher, 2019: 43), these reports strictly focus on the introduction and methods of a research study. The genre thus aims to ensure the reliability of the methodological procedures. In other words, the focus is on research methods and not research results (Mehlenbacher and Mehlenbacher, 2019). Publishers themselves emphasise that the double peer-review process increases the transparency of published research by having the scientists' 'proposed methods and analyses reviewed, prior to conducting the actual research'.[6] Mehlenbacher's (2019a: 50) case analysis of 32 stage 1 protocols and 77 stage 2 reports from the journal *Royal Society Open Science* (available at the Open Science Framework's Zotero) attests to this fact. As this author notes, '[r]egistered reports appear to follow the IMRaD logic of research articles in the sciences, first Introducing the research, then providing Methods, Results, and Discussion'. Yet the genre fulfils a different social action, namely, to give greater transparency to scientific results and 'to produce more replicable research' (Mehlenbacher and Mehlenbacher, 2019: 43). The

---

[6] https://authorservices.wiley.com/author-resources/Journal-Authors/submission-peer-review/registered-reports.html [last accessed on 25 December 2019].

editor for registered reports at *Cortex, European Journal of Neuroscience and Royal Society Open Science* accentuates the worthiness of this research process–oriented multimodal (and polyphonic) narrative by noting that '[b]ecause the study is accepted in advance, the incentives for authors change from producing the most beautiful story to the most accurate one' (quoted exactly as in the Center for Open Science platform).[7] Given the contextual exigences of the genre, we may assume that, rather than just being beautifully (and persuasively) told, the story needs to be accurately articulated.

3.6 Transformative practice

I argued earlier that the existing geopolitical and socioeconomic agendas stand at the core of scientific knowledge production, dissemination and knowledge transfer, where knowledge is 'defined not through what it is, but through what it can do' (Gilbert, 2005: 35) and where codes of practice on knowledge transfer aim at sustainability, economic recovery and social welfare (Pérez-Llantada, 2012). In Chapter 2 I mentioned that, at present, the new digital dynamics of knowledge transfer extend much more widely, moving beyond traditional science popularisation genres and by this means contributing generic speciation. We can in fact trace current attempts to compensate for the excessive focus on scholarly conversation exclusively circumscribed within the scientific community by using genres that bring together scientific research and society (see, e.g., *UK Concordat for Engaging the Public with Research*).[8] Bonney et al. (2009) use the term 'public participation in scientific research' to refer to a wider range of participatory approaches, such as citizen science, crowdsourcing and community-based research. For Eitzel et al. (2017: 1), citizen science projects involve 'the inclusion of members of the public in some aspect of scientific research', a measure for incentivising public engagement in science research and, more broadly, for the democratisation of science (Stilgoe, Lock and Wilsdon, 2014; Trench, 2008). Follett and Strezov (2015) propose a classification of these projects dividing them into three types: contributory, collaborative and co-created. Interest in promoting publicly engaged science thus accounts for the emergence of trans-scientific genres of science whose main functionalities are to inform and educate in science – what

---

[7] https://cos.io/rr/ [last accessed on 6 July 2020].
[8] www.ukri.org/files/legacy/scisoc/concordatforengagingthepublicwithresearch-pdf/ [last accessed on 2 January 2020].

has been conceptualised as scifotainment, infotainment and edutainment (Kelly and Maddalena, 2016; Mauranen, 2013; Mehlenbacher, 2017; Veltri and Atanasova, 2015) (see Chapter 2). Broadly speaking, these are all multisemiotic genres supported by Web 2.0 that no longer fall within the specialist domain but rather enable scientists to reach out to the public domain by recontextualising scientific information to satisfy the interests of a heterogeneous audience – blogs, TED-talks, crowdfunding projects or microblogging in social media networks (Büchi, 2016; Mehlenbacher, 2017; Miller and Shepherd, 2004; Orpin, 2019; Reid and Anson, 2019; Smart, 2011; Sugimoto et al., 2013). More importantly, given the scope of the present book, these genres support multilingual communication dynamics, since many scientists worldwide rely on language repertoires to diffuse science in their language contact zones. Moreover, these genres act as frames of language contact because they allow scientists the possibility to alternate between more than one language (Luzón, 2018a, 2018b).

As in other genres discussed in this chapter, the effects of polycontextuality (Spinuzzi and Zachry, 2000) can be seen in the way emerging digital genres supporting practices that empower transformation are shaped. A case in point is the science-focused crowdfunding project proposal. As the literature explains, this genre is a direct response to current agendas that support public involvement in scientific research and, more broadly, the democratisation of science. These exigences determine the specific shape of the genre. The RGaL corpus of Experiment.com proposals reveals that the form and substance of this generic hybrid relies on two existing typified texts: the grant proposal and the research article. In the platform interface, the proposals echo the rhetorical information organisation structure of the traditional journal article – the IMRaD pattern (Swales, 1990, 2004). Each section is visualised in the form of tabs: Overview – Methods – Lab Notes – Discussion. Other platforms such as Consano, Crowd.Science or GoFundMe, to mention a few, draw on other well-established conventional rhetorical organisation patterns, for example, the General-specific and the Problem-solution patterns, as also pointed out by Mehlenbacher (2017). In view of the recent literature, the recurrence of patterns strongly suggests gradual genre stabilisation (see Luzón and Pérez-Llantada's (forthcoming) analysis of citizen science and crowd science projects and Pérez-Llantada's (2021a) study of Spanish crowd science projects).

The Overview section of the Experiment.com proposals draws on the prototypical moves of the Swalesian Create-a-Research-Space (CARS hereafter) model for research article introductions (Swales,

Table 3.5 Top 25 high-frequency 3-grams in Experiment.com proposals

Rank order	*n*-Gram	*f*	Rank order	*n*-Gram	*f*
1	will be used	15	14	of this project	6
2	be used to	13	15	for this project	5
3	allow us to	9	16	of the study	5
4	project is to	9	17	one of the	5
5	the amount of	8	18	the use of	5
6	the end of	8	19	by the end	4
7	as well as	7	20	have the	4
8	in order to	7		potential	
9	this project is	7	21	in the field	4
10	we hypothesize that	7	22	it is expected	4
11	will allow us	7	23	we plan to	4
12	goal is to	6	24	we will also	4
13	goal of this	6	25	we will use	4

Notes:
Cut-off level of 5 and a minimum frequency of 10 per 1,000 words.
Bold type indicates clausal bundles.

1990): setting the research scene, identifying a research knowledge gap or problem and explaining how the researchers are going to address that gap or problem. At the lexicogrammatical level, the top twenty-five high-frequent 3-grams retrieved with Fletcher's (2002–2007) software *KfNgram* include formulaic sequences such as *will be used, we plan to, we will also* (Table 3.5), indicating that the Overview texts allow the writers to state how they plan to fill the gap or solve the problem. The fact that these texts exhibit almost similar percentages of clausal and phrasal formulaic sequences (56 per cent clausal and 44 per cent phrasal fragments) shows that they are linguistically distinct from the academic written register, characterised by a very high frequency of phrasal bundles and a structurally compressed discourse style (Biber and Gray, 2016; Hyland, 2009, 2010).

The hybrid nature of this genre becomes perhaps more salient if we further explore the differing measures of lexical and syntactic complexity across the different sections of the proposals. Using Scott's (2008) *Wordsmith Tools* lexical analysis tool, the Overview texts score a type/token ratio of 22.18, very similar to that of Lab notes (22.96) but slightly lower than those of Methods (30.74) and Discussion sections (33.13), indicating greater lexical diversity in these latter two sections. Using Lu's (2010) automatic syntactic complexity analyser, the Overview and Lab notes sections again show fairly similar scores in syntactic measures such as the mean sentence length, length of T-unit, mean length of clause, amount of coordination and subordination, degree of phrasal sophistication and overall sentence complexity (Table 3.6).

In Table 3.6, divergences are found too. The Discussion texts show the shortest average sentence length (12.1 words per sentence), whereas the average number of words per sentence of the Methods texts is 25.3. The use of verb phrases, a typical linguistic feature of a colloquial style, scores highest in Discussions (139.50) and lowest in Methods (85.01). Discussions also score highest in the average number of clauses and Methods lowest (99.55 vs 57.33). The same trend can be observed when comparing the number of T-units, highest in Discussions (a total of 117.91 T-units) and lowest in Methods (40.73), which suggests that the Methods texts are characterised by a compressed style (resembling the style of academic prose) and the Discussion texts by an elaborate discourse style, typical of the conversational register.

These project proposals further instantiate hybridisation and innovation at the level of rhetoric along the lines described by Kelly and Miller (2016) and Mehlenbacher (2019b) for parascientific genres. For example, if we look into the Methods section/tab of the proposals, we see it provides a succinct account of the research protocols, but by no means does it enable the reproducibility of the research, at least not in the same way as the methods sections of grant proposals and journal articles do. Although in the corpus analysed there seems to be some variation (not all projects have information in the Methods section/tab and there is some variability in terms of length and reporting style in those proposals that do), this section can be broadly defined as a promissory account of the methodological protocol expected to be followed. Notwithstanding the possible variations in length and reporting style, all the Methods sections include a short summary of the method and its main rationale, a statement of potential challenges and a pre-analysis plan. The recurring use of the modal *will*, expressing purpose and intentionality to carry out the proposed actions if funding is obtained, contrasts with the conventionalised use of the simple past tense for the reporting of article methods sections (Swales, 2004). The Lab notes section/tab links to second-level hyperlinked mini-texts that very much resemble blog posts (see Luzón and Pérez-Llantada, forthcoming). Despite their name, which evokes traditional laboratory notebooks, their main function is not to keep a detailed record of the different steps in lab procedures.

Table 3.6 Measures of syntactic complexity across rhetorical sections

Index	Overview	f/1,000 words	Methods	f/1,000 words	Lab notes	f/1,000 words	Discussion	f/1,000 words
Word count	11,593		5,058		13,098		3,104	
Sentences	566	48.82	201	39.74	648	49.47	271	87.31
Verb phrase	1,257	108.43	430	85.01	1,564	119.41	433	139.50
Clause	847	73.06	290	57.33	1,073	81.92	309	99.55
T-unit	598	51.58	206	40.73	702	53.60	366	117.91
Dependent clause	244	21.05	76	15.03	366	27.94	79	25.45
Coordinate phrase	370	31.92	145	28.67	360	27.49	73	23.52
Complex nominal	1,561	134.65	681	134.64	1,476	112.69	351	113.08
Mean length of sentences	20.940935		25.30903		20.3259759		12.1457706	
Mean length of T-unit	19.828085		24.38795		18.6613103		13.5231471	
Mean length of clause	13.965555		17.01244		12.2730		10.3546294	
Clause per sentence	1.523805		1.51043		1.69106035		1.16835294	
Clause per T-unit	1.43961		1.46665		1.54734138		1.30292941	
Dependent clause per clause	0.28383		0.2819		0.33056035		0.24037647	

Dependent clause per T-unit	42,564	0.43971	0.545541379	0.33095294
T-unit per sentence	1.060035	1.03508	1.09207586	0.90821765
Complex T-unit ratio	0.33334	0.34941	0.42307931	0.23937059
Coordinate phrase per T-unit	0.632015	0.65807	0.48858103	0.31048235
Coordinate phrase per clause	0.452145	0.46586	0.31585517	0.23763529
Complex nominal per T-unit	2.6665	3.28834	2.15334828	1.57261765
Complex nominal per clause	1.876085	2.32969	1.41299828	1.17671176

Resembling blogging, this section provides general information on the team's actions or achievements, or to give the project backers updates of the research in progress and/or appeal to their emotions (e.g., by thanking them for their support and interest). The discourse style of the Lab notes is characterised by the use of colloquial features very frequent in the conversational register, for example, personal pronouns (first person exclusive *we*) and oblique forms (*our, us, you*), interjections (*hi*), exclamatives (to express emotions) and coordinators (*and*) (Biber et al., 1999: 438), as shown in the following two examples.

Hi supporters. Thank you for taking this journey with us! We have refined our protocols for collecting bio specimens and are reviewing our data analysis plan so we get the most impact from your support to predict psychogenic seizures. The team is excited to get started!

Thank you to all who have donated and made our dreams a reality! We are very excited to complete the experiment and see where our valuable technology can take us. In the coming weeks once the funding goes through we will begin to set up for testing. We will be keeping everyone updated as things proceed. Thanks again!

Similar linguistic features are used in the Discussion ('Join the conversation,' as the platform reads), which very much resembles a discussion forum. Far from being a traditional discussion section of, say, an empirical journal article, this section borrows the form of science-related thematic fora in Reddit, Twitter or Facebook and science blogs, as described in Barbieri (2018), Luzón (2017) and Mauranen (2013). The main functionality of this section is to establish a channel so that the project launcher can maintain a dialogue with his/her followers. The following thread of short Twitter-like responses in a Discussion section ('Join the conversation' in the platform) illustrates this point.

(Backer 4)

Save seals it is very good...

(Researcher 2)

Yes! Very important. Thank you!

(Backer 3)

This is a really important study, and a great group doing the work! As a fellow researcher with harbor porpoises and harbor seals in the Salish Sea, I am very interested in these results, thanks for doing this important work!

(Researcher 1)

Thanks again Cindy! We will definitely keep everyone up to date on the project and share results!

(Backer 3)

Great work guys! Can't wait to see the results.

(Backer 2)

A good plan to study our impact on this shared planet.

(Backer 2)

This is a detail of our marine world that needs attention.

(Backer 1)

Good luck with this project! Looking forward to seeing your results.

(Researcher 1)

This is such an important and timely research topic, and Dr. Stephanie Norman is such a great asset to all the stranding networks in the Pacific NW Region – I hope you will join me in backing this project, even if you can only give $5 or $10, every donation matters. THANK YOU to all the great backers and supporters who have donated thus far!

The inherent dialogism of these projects becomes manifest in the way proximity with readers, as defined by Hyland (2005, 2010), is created in this section. In the previous examples, the researchers use boosters and evaluative language to achieve interpersonal goals, namely, to convey credibility and professionalism – or, as Hyland (2005: 173) puts it, constructing 'a credible representation of themselves and their work by claiming solidarity with readers', in this case, the support (and the funding) from the project backers.

Though falling outside the scope of this book, as argued elsewhere (Luzón and Pérez-Llantada, forthcoming), it is also worth noting the use of (audio)visual (multimodal) elements in the different sections, which creates a persuasive appeal (Paulus and Roberts, 2018). If we examine the rhetorical functionality of the different types of visuals (images, photographs and videos) accompanying these proposals, following Bateman (2017) we can see that argumentation is built upon two semiotic modes: the verbal and the visual. The two modes work together so that scientific advances can reach broader publics. Earlier in this book I stated that appeals for scientists' responsibility to popularise scientific research and trigger public responses to current issues of societal concern, such as climate change, environment, health and well-being (Kirilenko and Stepchenkova, 2014; Loroño-Leturiondo and Davies, 2018; Smart, 2011), has become a matter of urgent priority in national and supranational agendas (Fujun, 2013; Gunnarsson and Elam, 2012; UNESCO, 2015) – hence the need to further investigate multilingual transformative practice drawing on 'a social conception of genre' (Smart and Falconier, 2019: 201).

Being 'situated genres' (Kjellberg, 2009), crowdfunding projects, blogs and public microblogging have the capacity to inform and educate in science and establish a direct dialogue with the consumers of science from diverse language backgrounds drawing on technological affordances. Although these genres are shareable and easily diffused, their popularity remains questionable. Even if they are much easier to disseminate and may have a high social impact, as Harmon (2019) notes, '[t]he question is whether or not these merits outweigh the extra time and expense (by both authors and publishers) to implement such features'. Future changes in the value orders of the existing agendas may result in either increasing interest, and hence stabilisation, in the emerging genres discussed in this chapter or in their eventual disappearance (or genre death), as is happening in the case of the monograph in the humanities, for example (see Knievel, 2009; Pérez-Llantada, 2016). To recall Giddens once again (1986: 169), given the 'inherent relation between structure and agency (and agency and power)', only if transformative practice is routinised within the scientific community will genres of citizen science eventually stabilise and their forms become prototypical.

3.7 Chapter summary

This chapter has illustrated how the Web 2.0 represents a major driver of genre evolution, innovation and change. It has shown how genre analysts should be concerned with the form of genres (overall structure, linguistic features, register and discourse style) and with their generic substance, above all when genres involve interdependent semiotic systems of meaning-making. It has also underlined the need to be more concerned with the situatedness of generic actions, also paying attention to scientists' involvement in new forms of disseminating their work to diverse consumers of science.

4 *Language Diversity in Genred Activity*

Having considered aspects of genre evolution, innovation and change, in this chapter I delve into the role that language – and languages – play in the context of contemporary science communication. Here I would like to argue that in the same way that online communication has redefined and expanded the traditional genre repertoire, paving the way to the emergence of rhetorical hybrids or semiotic hybrids that (re)use features of already existing genres (Claridge, 2016; Jamieson and Campbell, 1982; Kelly and Miller, 2016; Miller and Kelly, 2017; Reid, 2019), social changes and the Internet have likewise prompted complex multilingual practices. New terms such as languaging, translanguaging, polylanguaging or polyglossia, to name a few (Baron, 2016; Canagarajah, 2018; Wei, 2018), have been coined to describe different aspects of multilingualism in today's research world. The reflections that follow combine a literature review and corpus research with data from digital social network analytics and bibliometrics and data from survey research. The aim is to illustrate the complex intersections involved in the deployment of genres and language repertoires.

4.1 Science and multilingualism

In previous chapters I discussed the current dynamics of knowledge exchange, circulation and dissemination across scholarly communities and sketched out some emerging modes of scholarly communication that have been spurred on by increasing researchers' mobility and collaboration and by the advances of the Internet. While the existing literature has mainly paid attention to English-medium communication dynamics (see, e.g., the ERPP literature), authors such as Canagarajah (2018) and Sivertsen (2018), among others, refer to 'balanced multilingualism' in academic and research settings. Sivertsen argues that while a lingua franca of science is supportive of research exchange in international forums, this lingua franca does not stand alone in the academic and research ecosystem. His main argument is that it is used along with other international languages of science, other research languages and the local language(s) of the physical setting. Sivertsen's explanation of the need for plurilingual practices in oral communication in international symposia is convincing enough to illustrate his point. If we turn to written communication, we can also observe in the literature that multilingual scholars' participation in high-stakes scientific journals does in fact already exist. Using Scopus as a source for scientometric analysis, O'Neil (2018: 162) reports a reduction in international publishing observed in countries of the inner circle and 'increasing national diversity despite monolingualism'. Stockemer and Wigginton's (2019) survey of 800 authors of scientific papers in *Springer Nature* journals indicates that approximately 60 per cent of the submissions come from non-anglophone scientists.

The extant literature also provides further evidence of multilingual science conversations in scientific publishing, specifically those addressing science-related topics that are of both global and local concern. Amano, González-Varo and Sutherland (2016: 2) searched for scientific documents published in 2014 with two keywords, 'biodiversity' and 'conservation', in sixteen languages on Google Scholar and retrieved a total of '75,513 manuscripts, of which English was by far the most frequently used language (48,600 scientific documents, 64.4%), followed by Spanish (9,520), Portuguese (7,800), simplified Chinese (4,540), and French (2,290)'. These authors' 'approaches both for compiling non-English scientific knowledge effectively and for enhancing the multilingualisation of new and existing knowledge available only in English for the users of such knowledge' mainly revolve around the use of translation of texts. Jørgensen et al. (2011) advocate the importance of promoting polylanguaging, or the use of language repertoires, to disseminate knowledge through multilingual genres, above all, drawing on the Internet affordances and on the increasingly diverse repertoire of digital genres. If we compare professional (expert-to-expert) and public communication of science, the latter, for example, in social media networking sites, we find a completely different picture, in fact one revealing multilingual debates on science-related topics. As shown in Table 4.1, there seems to exist a rich ecology of languages currently being used for communicating science-related topics of societal interest. This table summarises the results of a Google Scholar search of the keyword 'climate change' in twenty-seven languages and compares them with a similar search on Twitter to identify the social interest in this topic in lay conversation.

Table 4.1 '*Climate change*' *discussions in expert and non-specialist forums*

Language	Keyword	No. of scientific articles[a]	No. of tweets[b]	No. of retweets
Afrikáans	Klimaatsverandering	272	3	0
Arabic	تغير مناخي	48	74	46
Chinese	氣候變化 (traditional)	16,010	2,324	1,464
Czech	změna klimatu	13,800	70	34
Danish	Klimaændringer	172	17	5
English	climate change	19,200	2,970	1,915
Finnish	Ilmastonmuutos	2,910	2,970	1,564
French	changement climatique	24,600	3,172	2,080
German	Klimawandel	14,400	2,970	1,988
Italian	cambiamento climático	6,760	179	106
Japanese	気候変動	11,300	2,970	2,098
Lithuanian	klimato kaita	952	5	0
Malayan	perubahan iklim	34,000	2,896	2,483
Persian	تغییرات آب و هوا	16,400	19	8
Polish	zmiany klimatu	14,400	116	93
Portuguese	mudança climática	24,400	39	20
Romanian	schimbările climatice	1,190	36	11
Russian	изменение климата	37,100	540	387
Serbian	климатске промене	1,470	44	35
Somalian	isbedelka cimilada	1	–	–
Spanish	cambio climático	16,600	3,172	2,080
Swahili	mabadiliko ya hali ya hewa	99	18	6
Swedish	Klimatförändringar	3,330	411	233
Thai	การเปลี่ยนแปลงสภาพภูมิอากาศ	4,530	100	87
Turkish	iklim değişikliği	10,500	2,292	1,833
Ukranian	зміни клімату	22,400	27	9
Vietnamese	biến đổi khí hậu	4,030	14	1

[a] Retrieved from Google Scholar (selected period 2016–2020, raw numbers, excluding citations and patents).
[b] 7-day results (search run on 21 January 2020) retrieved with hashtag *#climatechange* (in different languages) using *TAGS 6.1.9* (Twitter Archive Google Sheet developed by Martin Hawksey).

The results lend credence to the existence of linguistic diversity in debating issues of science globally, both in expert-to-expert and lay discussion. This global reach attests to the value of balanced multilingualism, potentially beneficial as long as both discourses mutually inform one another – the expert discourse and the public discourse. Similar multilingual debates can also be found if we search for other science-related topics of social concern such as the environment, sustainability, climate change and biodiversity, life under the sea, energy-water-food, epidemiology and health care, to name a few.

If we place the focus on the ongoing science-related debates in lay discussion, quantified in Table 4.1, we see that while the demographics of social networks show an extensive use of English, other languages such as Chinese, French, Japanese, Malayan and Spanish are also widely used in these virtual exchanges. Evidence of multilingualism in lay science debates has also been reported earlier. For example, Kirilenko and Stepchenkova's (2014: 172) analysis of the geography of tweeting on climate change during the year 2012 reveals that whereas the majority of climate change discussion was led by the US, the UK, Australia and Canada, accounting for circa 75 per cent of the climate-change discussion, the remaining percentage corresponded to other languages (German, Portuguese, Spanish and Russian). Multilingualism in social media networks is also reported in Cody et al. (2015) and Bosch's (2012) account of blogging and tweeting climate change in South Africa.

4.1.1 Public understanding of science

In his article 'The roles of rhetoric in the public understanding of science', Gross (1994: 3–23) uses rhetorical analysis to distinguish between two models of public understanding of science: the deficit model and the contextual model. As Gross explains, in the former model the public plays a passive role, as it is a mere recipient of the scientific knowledge that the scientist communicates. In other words, it is a deficit model since scientists assume 'public ignorance' (p. 19) and accommodate scientific content to enhance the public's scientific literacy. Spoken and written parascientific genres such as TED Talks and science popularisation genres (Caliendo, 2012; Motta-Roth and Scherer, 2016) fall within this model. The public is a mere recipient of the information, which is modelled – and rhetorically shaped – at the scientists' own will. By contrast, as Gross further explains, in the contextual model science is co-constructed between the scientists and their publics and this action involves both of them. By engaging the public in scientific research, science becomes more trustable. It is to this latter model that genres for the democratisation of science belong, for example, citizen science or parascientific genres such as wikies, crowdfunding projects, blogs and microblogging (Kelly and Miller, 2016; Kuteeva, 2016; Luzón, 2013; Mehlenbacher, 2017). Considering this latter model, we can assume that multilingualism plays a crucial role in supporting genres in cultural contact zones (Miller, 2011; see also Miller, 1994, for a discussion on genres in relation to cultural-linguistic phenomena). Taking Gross's rhetorical perspective, we could presuppose that, although some parascientific genres are often circumscribed to local settings, they likewise reach a global audience because they are open digital genres. Therefore, the language(s) in each local setting become(s), along with genres, the instrument(s) or mediating tools that serve to connect science to society. For example, the discussion sections of crowdfunding projects discussed earlier, involving translanguaging or code switching, support this presupposition.

At this point it is worth assessing the extent to which multilingual genre-mediated activity could be beneficial to society. My contention is that it could. As long as the outcomes of scientific research are diffused among interested audiences and non-specialist publics, and as long as scientists' participation in the public sphere of communication becomes more prevalent than it is to date, science is beneficial for supporting and preserving societal welfare and sustainability. Transformative practice (discussed in Chapter 3) has the potential to lead to increased sensitisation and education of lay publics in issues of science that are of local and global concern. Here lies the value of parascientific genres and of genres whose goal is scifotainment and edutainment, as widely claimed in rhetorical genre studies and linguistics research (e.g., Reid and Anson, 2019; Gross and Buehl, 2016; Kuteeva and Mauranen, 2018; Luzón, 2013; Mauranen, 2013; Miller and Kelly, 2017; Miller and Shepherd, 2004).

Scientists' participation in the public sphere of communication paves the way to a better understanding of scientific facts, leading to a better grasp of the need to commit to key sustainable development goals such as good health and well-being, climate action, affordable and clean energy or sustainable cities and communities, to name a few. The various diffusion actions enacted through emerging genres respond to multiple rationales and multiple interests. At present, existing social and research policy agendas place an emphasis on the transferability of research or on social demands for greater transparency and accountability of scientific research, as noted in earlier chapters. Supranational research agendas such as that of the European Union stipulate the need 'to make science more attractive (notably to young people), increase society's appetite for innovation and promote formal and informal science education' (Horizon 2020 Programme, Science with and for society).[1] The scholarly literature also appeals to scientists' individual social responsibility (Loroño-Leturiondo and Davies, 2018; Shema, Bar-Illan and Thelwall, 2012) so that the interested publics can join scientists' conversations, become informed about issues of science and, if they are willing to, participate in scientific research. Hence, it seems judicious to foreground that multilingual science in digital media can support positive social change. The unprecedented developments of genres in media environments (Kelly and Miller, 2016; Trench, 2008) could lead to significant solutions to problems that affect individuals in and across local settings if scientists engage in multilingual communication. The interactivity of Web 2.0 and the erosion of boundaries between expert and non-specialist audiences are key determining factors in the knowledge co-construction process involved in the contextual model of public understanding of science. For Gross (1994), '[t]he goal is a better integration of the needs of science and its publics; the genre is deliberative. In this model, communication is not solely cognitive ... the model is not the state of science, but the situation of the public'. As Gross (1994: 6) further adds, it is 'a rhetoric of reconstruction, one that reconstitutes the fact and facts of science in the public interest'.

4.2 Are all languages equal?

In the strict sense of the word, the concept of language ecology is based on a biological approach to understanding the behaviour of language (Mufwene, 2001; Skutnabb-Kangas and Phillipson, 2001). In addition to the language ecology metaphor that I introduced in Chapter 2 to frame the exploration of language behaviour in the academic and research ecosystem, I would also like to refer to ecolinguistics (Kravchenko, 2016; Mühlhäusler, 2003), a field of enquiry that focuses on 'the nature and function of language as a mode of organisation of the living system (society)' to critically review the main arguments raised in the literature on the interactions between genres and languages of science. This critical view focuses on the language ecology of the academic and research ecosystem in relation to languages in motion, language spread, language contact and language mixing and language evolution and change in the contemporary research world.

---

[1] www.h2020.md/en/content/science-and-society [last accessed on 20 January 2020].

4.2.1 The geopolitics of languages

Research on the geopolitics of languages in academia has been associated with systems that rank languages one above the other and, in doing so, turn some languages into elite languages, an issue that has been described extensively in the literature in relation to research communication (see, e.g., the ERPP literature). There is in fact a well-established hierarchy of languages of research, based on their functionality. As stated in the introduction, the main reason why English stands at the top of this hierarchy and holds the status of a prestige language (de Swaan, 2001) is that it is a highly functional language acting as a shared lingua franca of science. Critical concerns regarding the negative effects of the 'global spread' of scientific English (Ferguson, 2007) over other languages of science have been theorised under the labels of English 'linguistic imperialism' (Ammon, 2001; Canagarajah, 2002a; Phillipson, 2003), the impact of the 'imperial tongue' (Altbach, 2007) and 'language empires' (Hamel, 2006a, 2007). As argued in the cited studies, existing language regulations across nation states and 'regimes of academic writing' (Hynninen, 2018) govern research publishing practices and determine language choice for research publishing purposes (Canagarajah, 1996, 2002b; Lillis and Curry, 2010; Tusting, 2018; Uzuner, 2008). In response to these critical perspectives, Ferguson (2012) proposes various measures at the level of language management and language policy and planning that could redress the effects of the widespread use of English and prevent the disappearance of other academic languages.

In addition to research policies, other factors play a role in the maintenance of this hierarchy of languages. One factor determining the particular mode of organisation of the academic and research ecosystem is the internationalisation and subsequent marketisation of research, fuelled by neoliberal discourses that consider research output as being 'symbolic capital' (Putnam, 2009). As noted in the introduction, this mode of organisation applies equally not only to the STEMM fields but also to other disciplinary fields (Salter and Martin, 2001) and has incited numerous critical concerns about the unfair participation of researchers belonging to non-core (or peripheral) academic communities (Bennett, 2014; Meriläinen et al., 2008; Salager-Meyer, 2008). Another factor is individuals' language choice. Duszak and Lewkowicz (2008: 108) note that non-anglophone researchers' use of their national language (Polish, in their study) 'limits the accessibility of the research to a much more confined readership'. As widely reported in the literature, researchers therefore opt for English to access international publishing markets, which in turn brings more personal and professional rewards (Corcoran, Englander and Muresan, 2019; Pérez-Llantada, 2012, 2018; Salö, 2015).

Bibliometric evidence further suggests that expert-to-expert scientific conversation in the global (international) sphere is mainly held in English. By way of illustration, using the RGaL corpus of articles from *PLoS*, an open-access journal, we observe that alternative metrics strongly suggest that English supports the diffusion of scientific publishing. For example, altmetrics show that these articles have all been read (100 per cent views) and that they have been mainly read online (17 per cent of them have actually been saved). Twenty-five per cent of the articles have been shared via Facebook or Twitter; only 2 per cent of the articles have readers' comments posted on them (all English medium), and only 8 per cent of the articles have been commented on in media coverage. Regarding this latter percentage, representing media coverage, English is the most common language. In 98 per cent of the cases the articles are discussed in English-medium blogs, while only 1 per cent is discussed in an English-medium scientific magazine (*National Geographic*) and 1 per cent in a Dutch-medium blog. In sum, in scientific publishing practices, alternative metrics show very little engagement in multilingual exchange and uptake of published work. For Gross (2016: 126), 'the zombie English spread across the learned world with viral suddenness' simply sought to redress what Gordin (2015) conceptualises as 'scientific Babel'. Diffusion within the peer-to-peer circle does reflect the privileged status of English. Therefore, whether open-access publishing further incentivises the greater use of English, hence reducing the Babel effect, remains to be seen in future research. I suspect that the growing presence of predatory journals, most of them English medium, that charge authors a fee for the fast publishing of articles without undergoing peer review points towards such a direction.

4.2.2 *The monolingual habitus*

If we take an epistemological perspective, it is possible to affirm that the prevailing position of English in scientific communication can be questioned or, at least, problematised to some extent. Salö (2015: 516) defines habitus as a term to capture 'the idea of people's biographically inculcated schemes of action and dispositions acquired through participation in routinized activities across the lifespan'. This author borrows Bourdieu's concept of 'linguistic *habitus*' to refer to 'dispositions pertaining especially to language, and, as such, as covering a range of acquired sensibilities concerning acceptability, appropriateness, correctness, and so forth' (p. 516). Using semi-structured interviews with Swedish researchers in the fields of computer science and physics, Salö observes that these researchers perceive Swedish as the legitimate language 'so long as it encompasses all participants' repertoires' (p. 511) because of their 'linguistic sense of placement', an 'ability to sense and anticipate the valorisation of linguistic goods in different markets, which reflexively allows agents to align their linguistic practices in relation to present and upcoming exchanges' (p. 517). Salö concludes that the linguistic habitus embedded in researchers' social practice (e.g., in scientific publishing practices) will therefore neither legitimise English nor privilege English over Swedish.

The linguistic sense of placement and the acquired sensibilities towards the established linguistic order (i.e., privileging English in scientific publishing) are not dissimilar to those found among virtual communities of researchers in ASNSs. By way of illustration, the analysis of threaded comments on the use of English for international publication practices and posted on the Q&A forum in ResearchGate (399 responses, and an overall number of 33,201 words)[2] shows that researchers from different linguacultural backgrounds also have a linguistic sense of placement and are able to reflect on their own translingual practices and on the value of English. As shown in Table 4.2, neutral perceptions towards English as a world lingua franca and as a language of science account for almost 45 per cent of the comments posted in this forum. Importantly, circa 37 per cent of the posts reflect perceptions of English as a valued language of science, whereas perceived English dominance represents 15 per cent of all posts. The participants' posts appear to indicate they have aligned their linguistic practices to English and have acquired sensibilities concerning its utility as a world language and as an additional language of science communication.

References to other languages in this thread of posts, both to past lingua francas and modern languages, such as Arabic, Chinese, Esperanto, French, German, Greek, Italian, Japanese, Latin, Mandarin, Russian, Sanskrit and Spanish, mentioned at least ten times each and valued highly, further suggest that using English as an additional language does not perpetuate English as the prevailing language for international scientific communication. Using Salö's (2015: 516) words, 'structures, norms, and external forces "out there" do not regulate the linguistic behaviour of individuals per se'.

---

[2] Data retrieved from www.researchgate.net/post/Do_you_think_that_English_is_a_good_language_for_science [last accessed on 25 January 2020].

Table 4.2 ELF users' perceptions towards English in ResearchGate forum[a]

Emerging themes	Comp. %	Examples of participants' posts
English as a world lingua franca	24.49	'English is a global language these days'. 'English is a universal language …' 'English is the modern lingua franca …'
English as the language of science	17.69	'English is the language of science'. 'Needless to say that nowadays English is the language of Science'.
English as a valued language of science	36.75	'English is best language for the scientific culture'. 'What is really precious is to dispose of ONE universal language for science'. 'English is a necessary and good language'. 'English IS an EXCELLENT LANGUAGE for science'.
English dominance	15.65	'English is too ubiquitous these days'. 'Sadly & gladly, English is the only language'. 'English is entrenched as the technical language'.
Miscellaneous (use of English related to linguistic advantage, or disadvantage, English and identity…)	5.44	'English is also hospitable to words and concepts from the whole world'. 'English is one of the worst languages for sciences because privileges "paratactic construction"'. 'I do admit that it took a while for English to be my thought language. English is not my "mother tongue"'.

[a] Retrieved by searching the commonest collocate in the corpus, *English is* (147 occurrences).

Given this evidence, one would argue that perhaps there has been an excessive focus in the literature on the dominance of English for communicating globally and the pressure to publish in English in highly competitive journals, while little attention has been paid to other research outlets. Understandably, researchers' pressure to publish in English or perish, that derives from the interests of neoliberal economies, has been reported in regions across the world – Asia, Africa, Canada, China, Europe, Latin America and the US (Cheng, 2016; Corcoran, Englander and Muresan, 2019; Gentil and Séror,

2014; Hultgren, Gregersen and Thøgersen, 2014; Lee and Lee, 2013; Linares, 2019; Plo Alastrué and Pérez-Llantada, 2015). That said, this literature does not fully acknowledge the pluricentricity of the English language worldwide, as compellingly argued in the field of sociolinguistics (Kachru, 1985, 1986; Pennycook, 2010a). Claims concerning non-anglophone researchers' 'stigma' (Flowerdew, 2008), or feeling of 'linguistic injustice' (Politzer-Ahles et al., 2016) and 'linguistic unfair play' (van Parijs, 2007) in English-medium academic publishing are not consistent with researchers' perceptions, for example, in the thread of posts given earlier (see also Ferguson, Pérez-Llantada and Plo, 2011). Borrowing Bourdieu's concept of habitus as a heuristic, we could argue that the impact on researchers' practice of the existing 'regimes of English academic writing' (Hynninen, 2018), which promote the prevalence of English in scientific publications, might not be so dramatic. The habitus heuristic brings to the fore the existence of translingual practices and the need to dissociate them from the discourses and ideologies of English. English is considered merely an instrumental vehicle for knowledge sharing and exchange, at least at the operational level. In proposing a utilitarian view of English as a global lingua franca, or as 'a neutral tool for communication' (Patrão, 2018: 30), linguistic diversity does play a part in 'the development of a global *lingua franca*; while simultaneously profiting from a *lingua franca*'s capacity to generate a shared plane where linguistic and cultural distinctiveness is not homogenized and diminished, but rather shines through, enabled and reinforced'.

To date, aspects related to communicating science in languages other than English have received very little attention. Considerable discussion is required to assess whether research languages actually compete or rather coexist for different purposes within the same ecological environment. In mapping future research directions on multilingual publishing practices, Curry and Lillis (2019: 5) suggest that '[s]tudies could investigate language choices at particular moments in scholars' work lives, how their publications in other languages are evaluated and rewarded, and the consequences of these choices for global knowledge production and circulation'.

4.3 Translingual practices

In the introduction to this book, I put forward the idea of an integral ecology of genres in the research world, one that is fast evolving as a result of the multiple factors that shape and constrain genre-mediated activity – historical, geopolitical, economic, institutional, social, political, educational and, last but not least, technological. In supporting the view of balanced multilingualism in scientific communication, I have also contended that many researchers today move back and forth between two or more language systems when communicating their research work. Two important concepts that have been coined to shed light on language phenomena in contemporary society are 'languaging' (Shohamy, 2017) and 'polylanguaging' (Jørgensen et al., 2011), among others. Both come from the perspectives of sociolinguistics and sociocultural linguistics and, in a way, both echo the Bakhtinian notions of multilanguagedness or heteroglossia (Bakhtin, 1986a) used for the analysis of speech acts.

4.3.1 Languaging

As Shohamy (2006: 20) explains, the term 'languaging' is used to embrace diversity in people's discursive practices. From a languaging perspective, language is 'an integral and natural component of inter-action, communication and construction'. As discussed later, the concept of languaging can likewise be applied to discursive practices in the research world. Genres operate across languages and it is through language(s) that genres enact social actions. Therefore, we could hypothesise that the deployment of the repertoire of research genres may embody a dynamic (balanced) multilingualism (Sivertsen, 2018), multilingual practices and other types of languaging such as code-switching or translanguaging (Canagarajah, 2007, 2018; de Fina, Ikizoglu and Wegner, 2017; Pennycook, 2018; Wei, 2018), the latter transcending the boundaries of language and incorporating multimodal interactions. In EAP and second-language writing studies, not much attention has been given to researchers' polylanguaging practices if compared to English-medium practices. Some notable exceptions can be found in ethnographic studies of academic writing contexts, the majority on STEMM disciplines and the social sciences (e.g., Gentil and Séror, 2014; Lillis and Curry, 2010; Muresan and Nicolae, 2015; Olmos-López, 2019). These, though, only focus on writing in English for scientific publishing purposes. However, as I noted in the introduction, while part of the researchers' activity draws on English-medium genres (e.g., writing articles for International Scientific Indexing [ISI hereafter] journals), there are other language(s) in use and translingual practices in professional and, above all, in public communication of science (Pérez-Llantada, 2019). In the RGaL corpus, for example, there is evidence of languaging in bidirectional exchanges between researchers and the public in genres supporting transformative practice (see Chapter 3). The discussion thread of the following example illustrates languaging in a virtual interactive exchange in Experiment.com crowdfunding platform. The use of two languages simultaneously is not unacceptable. Rather, it performs interpersonal functions, namely, expressing support and showing empathy:

Mucha suerte y éxitos Raquel! Muy interesante y ambicioso el proyecto ;)

Hola Raquel. Tu trabajo es super importante ahora que el estúpido de Trump quiere eliminar el apoyo económico al sector de la NASA que se dedica a estudiar el cambio climatico. Desde C.R te enviamos toda la buena vibra con este esfuerzo, y ojalá que la luz de la ciencia, la razón y el pensamiento lógico crítico triunfen cada día y logren erradicar para siempre la oscuridad de la ignorancia, el dogma y la mediocridad mental. Un abrazo!

Felicidades Raquel y al equipo! Éxito con todo!

Helping students with their research efforts with this form of crowd funding has many benefits, not only for the students being funded but increasing the general public participation. If you find this project interesting, please join me and participate. Any amount is helpful.

Hello guys,

I've known Raquel for a long time and I'm pretty excited about this project she is working on. I wish you the best and hope you accomplish your research goals.

   One further argument here is that languaging practices, instantiating polylanguaging (i.e., the use of several languages from the individuals' linguistic repertoires) are highly context and situationally dependent. Sivertsen (2018) argues that multilingualism allows scientists to bridge science and different social actors. Luzón (2018a, 2018b) explains the functionality of multilingual practices in research blogs in the natural sciences by arguing that translingual practices are an effect of the collapsing of contexts in the digital medium; English is used when addressing experts and Spanish when addressing the public. As another example, in a survey-based, cross-disciplinary study, Pérez-Llantada (2021b) finds strong associations of the use of language repertoires in public communication of science with the biomedical and health sciences fields. Thus, polylanguaging is strongly associated with parascientific genres targeting non-specialist, diversified audiences, both local and global.

4.3.2 Multisemiotic forms of languaging

To genre analysts, what may also be useful from Shohamy's theoretical perspective is that languaging is an inclusive construct involving not only verbal languaging but also other forms of languaging such as languaging through multi-multimodalities (p. 14) and languaging through visuals and images (p. 18), that is, languaging through non-verbal forms. Shohamy sees both as semiotic forms of languaging that are complementary to textual or verbal languaging. As this author contends, these non-verbal forms 'together provide a more complete picture that facilitates endless forms of existence, creation and expansion, messages and mediations in private and public space' (p. 16). To explore researchers' languaging when engaging in digital multimodal genres, in what follows, I report on data from the exploratory survey[3] of scientists involved in crowd science, namely, Experiment.com project launchers.

According to the researchers' responses, their main motivations to communicate science online through multimodal genres and media networks were personal, social and promotional: to get others excited about science (92 per cent of all responses), to build public trust in scientific research and to increase the visibility of their research (circa 80 per cent of all responses in both cases). Almost 40 per cent of the respondents to the survey had native languages other than English. They all reported multilingual practices for public communication of science, using either English (even if their first language is not English) (7 per cent) or two or more languages (31 per cent), which suggests that English may be associated not only with the domain of scientific publishing but also with that of public communication, hence supporting Haberland's (2005: 228) claim that it is difficult to establish clear-cut domains of language use. As for multimodal composing strategies in online genres, almost all (both English natives and non-English natives) avoid specialist jargon (92 per cent) and adapt expert knowledge to target diversified audiences. One respondent further noted a change of register ('I prefer to be less professional and more conversational'). Over 60 per cent of the respondents also aim to create empathy with their intended audiences. Lastly, languaging through non-verbal forms (i.e., visuals such as images, photos, videos, animations, etc.) was widely used to illustrate or clarify the information (100 per cent) and to attract the interest of the global community (almost 77 per cent of all responses). Reaching a global audience may explain why English as a lingua franca is included in the language repertoires of all researchers surveyed whose first language is not English. The last question of the survey, aiming at collecting further comments, revealed the researchers' sense of social commitment and perceptions of public

---

[3] Given that it was an external survey, a response rate of circa 16 per cent can be considered representative.

communication of science to be valuable. As one of the respondents stated, 'societal aspects and engaging a broad audience are just as important if not arguably more important than the actual science'.

Although further research is very much needed, there seems to be some evidence of languaging practices and use of language repertoires in public communication of science, instantiating (poly)languaging phenomena in online multimodal genres that support 'hybrids, fusions, multi-codes and *multi-modalities, beyond fixed and marked languages*' (Shohamy, 2006: 21, my emphasis). For Canagarajah, languaging across physical spaces means that language in a given setting or physical space cannot be considered a closed structure. In the digital medium, genre-mediated practices such as those involving public understanding and public engagement with science indeed exemplify a 'more expansive, situated, and holistic' (Canagarajah, 2018: 31) approach to science communication, one that relies on multisemiotic resources for meaning-making. Advocating balanced multilingualism can pave the way for a more holistic understanding of multilingual writing across digital genres and forms.

4.4 Language(s) coalescence

In light of the aforementioned considerations, I would argue that the scope and value of balanced multilingualism and polylanguaging in academic and research settings needs to be voiced and theorised in a more explicit and in-depth manner in future research. In what follows, I address some of the de facto effects of languages in contact within the international scientific community ecosystem. By moving from the level of the individual, explored in the previous section, to the level of society as a whole, I aim to create synergies between genre theory and the field of sociolinguistics to discuss issues of convergence (i.e., linguistic universals) and divergence (i.e., linguistic relativism) in the context of writing for research publication purposes.

4.4.1 Academic Englishes

Mauranen (2018: 106) offers a particularly rich theorisation of the phenomenon of English as a lingua franca, her main argument being that 'World Englishes and ELF are not competing realities but complementary paradigms with certain foundations in common'. Essentially, ELF is conceptualised as integrating three perspectives that 'mutually influence each other' – the cognitive, the micro-social or interactional and the macro-social perspective. These are, in fact, though with slightly different names, the same approaches that I have taken in my reflections of language diversity in genred activity: (i) language and the individual (i.e., language and individual writing processes and experiences), (ii) language at the micro level of social interaction (i.e., languages and communication within local communities) and (iii) language at the macro level of social interaction (i.e., languages for communication in and across the broad scientific community ecosystem). In what follows, I share my own views about some points of convergence and the complementarity of the WE and the ELF paradigms in relation to genres. My aim is to provide further theorisation of the possible intersections between genres and languages for research communication. For the sake of consistency, I will use the term Academic Englishes (AEs), instead of ELF, as I have used it elsewhere (Mauranen, Pérez-Llantada and Swales, 2020; Pérez-Llantada, 2015, 2019) to critically discuss written genres, both print and digital – the latter including mixed modes, that is, written/visual/aural. Figure 4.1

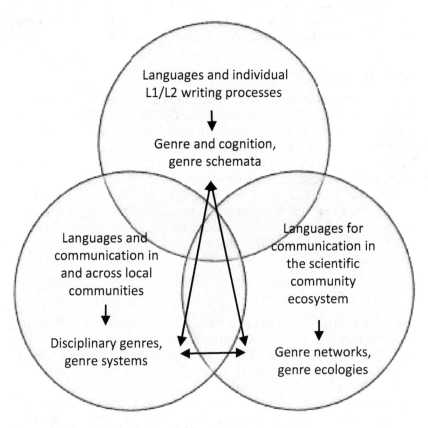

Figure 4.1 Aspects of AEs in genred activity

summarises the main interrelated approaches to AEs and research-related genred activity that I propose.

Turning first to language use at the micro level of social interaction, we can hypothesise that different languages may be in contact within localised academic and research communities within the broad scientific community ecosystem. For example, as seen in the exploratory survey research discussed earlier in this chapter, literate activity mainly revolves around prototypical disciplinary genres (Bazerman and Prior, 2004; Berkenkotter and Huckin, 1995). Considering the vast ERPP literature on non-anglophone writers, we can further hypothesise that the use of discipline-specific genre repertoires involves bi/multilingual literate practices. The main reason given by researchers from non-anglophone backgrounds to justify why they adopt English for international scientific collaboration and publishing purposes is the need for a shared language of science (Bocanegra-Valle, 2015; Ferguson, Pérez-Llantada and Plo, 2011; Gordin, 2015). English today coexists with the local language(s) used in and across each local academic setting (Canagarajah, 2007; Sivertsen, 2018). If, like Mauranen (2018: 106), we view ELF as a contact language used in the researchers' everyday professional activity, we can affirm that AEs embody second language use in contexts in which, in addition to the language(s) of the physical setting, English is one of the mediating tools for in-group communication. Such a use of English at the micro level is thus a parallel phenomenon to the large-scale sociolinguistic phenomenon of WE.

Because languages in contact situations exert a continuous influence on each other, it is possible to contend that the languages deployed in a given physical setting coalesce, eventually creating a similect, or a kind of dialectal variety. As Mauranen (2018: 109) defines them, 'similects are in essence parallel lects, that is, outcomes of each person learning a language individually, without using it as an internal means of communication in their group or language community'. What, then, are the implications for the existing language ecology in the research world? Skutnabb-Kangas and Phillipson (2001: 191) affirm the following:

[d]ominant languages are legitimated through processes of hegemonic saturation in public discourse, the media and public education to the point where their learning, involving subtractive language shift (i.e., adopting the dominant language involves loss of the first language), is accepted as natural, normal and incontestable.

Because the use of AE is widespread across local and national settings (physical spaces) worldwide, we can presuppose that the resulting parallel lects – academic English*es* – differ among themselves in very much the same way as varieties of WE do. These varieties substantiate Mauranen's (2018: 107) claim that 'notions of monolingual speakers in monolingual nation states have become plainly obsolete'. The concept of AEs or AE lects also contests scholarly debates centred on non-anglophone scholars' 'stigma' (Flowerdew, 2008; Politzer-Ahles et al., 2016) and 'stigmatising effects' versus 'the myth of linguistic injustice' (Casanave, 2008; Hyland, 2016). At present, it seems to be more pertinent and, above all, more timely, to de-centre English-only communication practices and place greater attention on multilingual communication and translanguaging and polylanguaging phenomena.

In an attempt to create synergies between the ecological paradigm and the ELF and WE paradigms, I would argue that 'Englishisation' (Phillipson and Skutnabb-Kangas, 1993) is only circumscribed to part of researchers' genre-mediated activity, namely, genres with an international outlook such as journal articles, abstracts or highly competitive grant proposals. AEs do not entail a subtractive language shift, as these varieties neither displace nor replace the original language. Rather, language contact and eventual language coalescence bring to the surface a rich and complex plurality of similects. These similects represent an additive spread of languages rather than a subtractive spread. The languages used in the physical setting permeate those similects that contain hybrid linguistic and discourse features, as we will see in the following subsection. English is used only for some purposes, and in becoming hybrid by coalescing with other languages, it neither completely replaces nor displaces them.

4.4.2 The SLA perspective

In this section I examine the use of academic English*es* from the perspective of SLA in the belief that this perspective can help us better understand the acquisition of genre skills, which 'depends on previous knowledge of the world, giving rise to *content schemata*, knowledge of prior texts, giving rise to *formal schemata*, and experience with appropriate tasks' (Swales, 1990: 9–10). As I argued elsewhere (Pérez-Llantada, 2014), we could hypothesise that researchers from non-Anglophone linguacultural backgrounds subconsciously acquire and learn lexicogrammatical formulas through incidental exposure to relevant language input. In order to trace how individuals' incidental learning processes and their previous writing experience in their L1s account for variation in L2 English writing, I used the SciELF corpus from the University of Helsinki, which comprises articles in the sciences 'that have not undergone professional proofreading services or checking by a native speaker of English'.[4] In looking at the highly frequent phraseological sequences (Table 4.3), we observe that the most recurring formulaic expressions coincide with high-frequency formulas found in Hyland's (2008) corpus and in other studies of L1 and L2 academic written English (Cortes, 2013; O'Donnell, Römer and Ellis, 2013; Simpson-Vlach and Ellis, 2010), which confirms that these writers have acquired the formal schemata of this genre. We could then assume that they might have picked them up from their reading and extensive writing practice of these genre texts.

Wu, Mauranen and Lei (2020: 10) report that the ELF articles show greater reliance on nominal phrases compared to AmE articles, a difference that these authors attribute to genre conventions, namely, the 'genre-based demands for explicitness'. These authors further contend that '[o]n average, the writers of these articles use longer sentences and clauses, more coordination (especially coordinate nouns and coordinate adjectives) but less subordination, and more complex nominal phrases but fewer verbal phrases than their AmE counterparts'. Out of these forty-six high-frequency 4-grams, almost half are nominal and complex nominal phrases, while more than half (54 per cent) are clausal sequences, suggesting that the ELF variety is different from the standard AmE variety. Furthermore, from the data in Table 4.3, it can also be observed that there is an absence of pragmatic markers in the recurring phraseology of the SciELF articles, for example, markers of modality and probability such as *may*, *might*, or *likely*, whereas these are recurring formulas in L1 English (Hyland, 2008). This might again point to glocal non-standard AE varieties resulting from languages in contact – the researchers' L1 and English as an L2. This hypothesis could be supported by contrastive rhetoric research that claims that there exist different academic Englishes (Mauranen, Pérez-Llantada and Swales, 2010), for example, AE by scholars with the following L1s: Chinese, Czech, English, Finnish, French, Italian, Spanish, Swedish and Russian. Variation at the level of the pragmatics of the language might hence pertain to the existence of cultural particulars. Lastly, language hybridisation is also manifest in various indexes of lexical and syntactic complexity. According to *Wordsmith Tools* statistics, the SciELF articles exhibit an average mean of 22.0 words per sentences. Wu, Mauranen and Lei (2020: 3) report that 'ELF authors use longer sentences, often through noun

---

[4] This is a subcorpus of the University of Helsinki's WrELFA corpus, whose texts are representative of the natural sciences, medicine, agriculture and forestry. www.helsinki.fi/en/researchgroups/english-as-a-lingua-franca-in-academic-settings/research/wrelfa-corpus [last accessed on 29 January 2020].

Table 4.3 Occurrences of most frequent 4-grams in SciELF articles

n-Gram	f	n-Gram (cont.)	f	n-Gram (cont.)	f
on the other hand	61	it is possible to	15	be explained by the	11
in the case of	52	reported in table #	15	by means of a	11
the end of the	33	shown in fig #	15	can be seen from	11
in the present study	32	the fact that the	15	in order to assess	11
as well as the	26	a wide range of	14	presented in figure #	11
one of the most	26	can be explained by	14	shown in figure #	11
at the end of	25	in figure # the	14	the analysis of the	11
shown in table #	25	presented in table #	14	the evolution of the	11
in table # the	22	the difference between the	14	to the formation of	11
is based on the	21	as a function of	13	and the number of	10
less than or equal to	21	as can be seen	13	as well as in	10
the results of the	20	can be used to	13	at the time of	10
in favour of the	19	in addition to the	13	end of the study	10
the beginning of the	19	in this study the	13	it can be seen	10
can be found in	18	an important role in	12	it should be noted	10
is one of the	17	are reported in table	12	the aim of the	10
as a result of	16	can be seen in	12	the case of the	10
at the same time	16	in the context of	12	the effect of the	10
in order to obtain	16	is the number of	12	to be able to	10
of the present study	16	it is important to	12	to the presence of	10
a large number of	15	are shown in fig	11		
are shown in figure	15	as one of the at the	11		
in this paper we	15	beginning of	11		

Notes:
At a cut-off level of at least ten times and used in at least 10 per cent of the texts.
Clausal fragments highlighted in bold.

phrase complexity, that is the use of nominals with postmodifying prepositional phrases to improve communication efficiency'. Mauranen's (2018) own conceptualisation of ELF lects as parallel variants is in many ways similar to the 'pluralistic view of englishes' underpinning other conceptualisations such as Lingua Franca Englishes that have also been proposed (Canagarajah, 2018; Guillén-Galve and Vázquez, 2018).

4.5 Macroacquisition of academic English

The ecological perspective of language evolution and change is also a useful perspective for reminding us that '[l]anguages do not in fact "spread" without agents' (Skutnabb-Kangas and Phillipson, 2011: 190). If we consider the agents, that is, the AE users, we can envisage a parallel phenomenon to the one Brutt-Griffler (2002) conceptualises as 'macroacquisition of World English'. Essentially, this author contends that societal acquisition of English and English language change are related to the worldwide spread of English and that such spread is the result of migration flows, advocating that a 'collective acquisition of English' and the acquisition of a 'collective identity' through individuals' take place through social interactions. As I argued elsewhere (Pérez-Llantada, 2019), a similar language phenomenon has taken place in the scientific community's ecosystem, leading us to presuppose that a macroacquisition process or a collective acquisition of academic English has taken place and continues to take place in today's research world.

There are several possible reasons that may account for the worldwide spread of academic English for international scientific communication. The first, already mentioned in the introduction of this book, has to do with the agents, namely, individuals' international collaboration in research as well as mobility and skilled migration. The second, as Hamel (2006b: 95) notes, is that '[t]he academic field is a sociological and sociolinguistic field of production and circulation of science. This field contains monolingual and bi- or multilingual activities and subfields', the prevailing ones being those conducted in English. Cutting across these two reasons, a third reason can be given. All individual researchers come into contact with English, specifically, with the massive production, circulation and reception of new scientific knowledge through the medium of English, fuelled by new technological advancements such as digital journal libraries that enable fast access to information and circulation of such knowledge (Nicholas, Huntington and Watkinson, 2005). One can deduce that such massive exposure to English academic texts offers rich input of

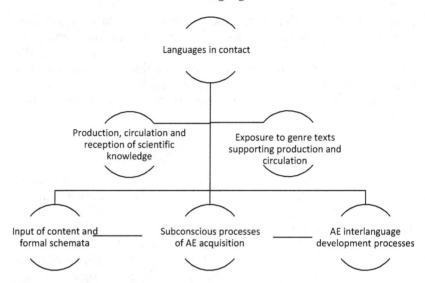

Figure 4.2 Contextual factors accounting for the macroacquisition of AE

genre text types in L2 academic English that support such production and circulation of knowledge, which might trigger interlanguage development processes in academic English. These processes, common across academic and research settings, strongly suggest a possible macroacquisition process of formal academic English (i.e., the written register), as summarised in Figure 4.2.

If, for example, we go back to the analysis of formulaic sequences reported in the previous section of this chapter, we could argue that the use of highly frequent formulas such as *on the other hand, in the case of, the end of the, in the present study, as well as the* or *one of the most*, among others, indicates that researchers may have picked up these formulas from previous exposure to them. Extensive reading and writing of research articles provides input of language forms that may be acquired subconsciously. When such input is noticed (Schmidt, 1993), it becomes 'intake', or knowledge acquired and stored in the short-term memory first and in the long-term memory afterwards. Without denying the existence of linguistic universals, I would argue that these complex psycholinguistic and cognitive processes can explain the systematic use of those academic formulas in articles written in English by researchers whose L1 is not English. In other words, the systematic use of these formulas may be the result of incidental learning and/or conscious attention to the formal schemata or patternings of this prototypical genre. Thus, we could claim that language use, no matter the ELF lect, converges towards a single macroglocal variant.

In the context of dynamic multilingualism, it is difficult to ascertain the exact degree of variation in the linguistic textualisation of the journal article genre, as we can assume that there is ongoing change. Diachronic studies such as those of Biber and Gray (2016) and Hyland and Jiang (2019) offer empirical evidence of such language change, specifically, the gradual colloquialisation of formal registers such as academic prose. Nonetheless, we can link the stability of form in this genre at both lexicogrammatical and syntactic levels across AE variants to two genre concepts: that of 'background knowledge' (Giltrow, 1994), a crucial aspect in processes of social interaction, and that of 'shared background knowledge' (Johns, 1997), used to explain cognitive processes associated with acquiring knowledge of genres by participating in a community of practice. Both concepts are in turn related to other key genre concepts, namely, 'rhetorical community' (Miller, 1984) and 'discourse community' (Swales, 1990). Because background knowledge is 'a resource shared by the producers and receivers of utterances' and relates to 'propositions unstated by a text but necessary for its interpretation' (Giltrow, 1994: 130), in selecting a given genre, the producer of this genre text assumes that the readers are going to rely on background knowledge and the specific genre schemata for interpreting the meaning of the text. Thus, a possible explanation for the systematic use of high frequency formulaic expressions is the mediating role that 'noticing', that is, awareness, intentionality and attention (Schmidt, 1993), plays between input and memory systems. As Schmidt explains, frequency is one of the factors that influence noticing of input and only what is noticed in input 'becomes intake for learning' (Schmidt, 1993: 20). The lexicogrammar formulas are recurring language input, and hence, when noticed and therefore integrated into the learner's interlanguage system, they are learned. Such cognitive processes, grounded upon extensions of SLA theories of processability, input processing and predicted linguistic outcomes (Pienemann, 2005; Pienemann et al., 2005), may account for the systematicity of language use that we find across AE variants.

This form of shared knowledge could explain the detectable regularities observed in the formulaicity of SciELF texts, as well as in their variability. On the one hand, the highly frequent use of formulaic sequences such as those listed above serve to scaffold complex nominal constructions with postmodifying prepositional phrases, to signpost readers (*in the present study, of the present study, in this paper we*) and signal visual data (*reported in table #, shown in fig #*). On the other hand, variability in language use can be found, for instance, in the expression of possibility (*it is possible to, can be explained by, can be seen in*) considering that probability and not possibility meanings are more frequent in texts written by Anglophone writers, as argued in studies on L1 and L2 academic writing (e.g., Ädel, 2006; Pérez-Llantada, 2014). Therefore, we observe two distinct dynamics here. First, background knowledge operates at the level of referential meanings and discourse organisation. Both aspects of language are crucial for interpreting the conceptual load of a given text. In effect, discourse production and reception are ensured through intercomprehensiveness, that is, a wide in scope and meaningful level of understanding of the written information in an L2 that can be comprehended by speakers from different L1s. In the case of the academic written register, the highly recurring formulaic language acts as a kind of cognitive scaffolding that facilitates the cognitive processing of the meanings conveyed in a text. Through regularities in form and substance, propositional contents are constructed first and then conceptually comprehended by the consumers of science. Further enquiry into convergent use of recurring lexicogrammar and syntactic forms in research article writing is needed to set linguistic phenomena taking place in today's scientific community in parallel with complex, and broader, sociolinguistic phenomena (Kachru, 1985, 1986). Successful attempts to codify shared features of ELF, such as Jenkins's (2000) Lingua Franca Core at the level of phonology, invite the undertaking of a similar endeavour as regards the written mode. The results of such codification could certainly have valuable pedagogical applications.

Secondly, another form of shared knowledge that intersects with the process of macroacquisition of academic English is associated with culturally bound traits, assumptions and interpretations of the group of receivers targeted by a given text. This was observed, as explained previously, in variability regarding the pragmatics of the language (i.e., the expression of possibility meanings instead of probability meanings). This second form of shared knowledge could explain what the literature on L2 learner language, perhaps not fully perceptive of this second form of background knowledge, refers to as learners' problems related to 'lack of register awareness, phraseological infelicities, semantic misuse' (Gilquin, Granger and Paquot, 2007: 319). Rather than problems, in the academic ecosystem we should regard these as instances of variation in the discoursal functionality of recurring lexicogrammar, revealing cross-linguistic influences between language systems that differ at the level of discourse pragmatics. In drawing on this background knowledge, the producers of the texts can be perceptive of possible misunderstandings that might lead to interactional gaps. To put it differently, while genre conventions lead to regularities in the way propositional meanings are conveyed and interpreted, different views of the world might lead to differing presuppositions or implicit assumptions, differing interpretations and, perhaps, even different ways of understanding the communicative goals of the genre and the social intentions that the genre enacts (see, e.g., Tardy, 2016).

The assumption that 'language users employ whatever linguistic features are at their disposal to achieve their communicative aims as best they can, regardless of how well they know the involved languages' (Jørgensen, 2010: 145) is central to our understanding of languaging phenomena in the field of sociolinguistics. Drawing on this assumption, what has been previously described in terms of '*mismatches* between what is appropriate in the author's writing culture and in scientific English' (Burrough-Boenisch, 2002: 229) or journal reviewers' *concerns* for 'lack of clarity or need for weakening claims in scientific articles written by non-Anglophones' (Gosden, 2001: 9) (my emphasis) should be considered as a manifestation of polylanguaging in the academic and research ecosystem (see also Gosden, 2003). Mauranen (2012: 29) contends that the different ELF L2 lects 'arise in parallel, not in mutual interaction'. Each L2 lect represents a distinct academic English (ELF) variety used by a group of speakers with the same L1 and, hence, exhibits similar L1 transfer features. Accordingly, AEs variants, with divergent uses of the language at the level of lexicogrammar, syntax and pragmatics, take us back to Kaplan's (1966) claim that L1 cultural thought patterns influence second language writing. Cook (2013) and Cook and Singleton (2014) also make a very clear statement about L2 users having different ways of thinking and different cognitive strategies when communicating in the L2.

As we argued elsewhere (Mauranen, Pérez-Llantada and Swales, 2020; Pérez-Llantada, 2019), academic Englishes need to be dissociated from their primary (anglophone) linguacultural roots. They should no longer be considered 'defective forms of English' (Greenbaum, 1996: 17) because their users fulfil their intended communicative goals. They illustrate a micro-level phenomenon parallel to the 'entirely natural development in the glocalisation of English' (Breiteneder, 2009: 266). Thus, in addition to codifying the single macroglocal variant to empirically assess what we mean by the use of 'good English', to date defined as acceptable and then publishable even if it contains non-canonical grammar usage (Rozycki and Johnson, 2013), the systematic codification of the distinct (pragmatic) features characterising each glocal variant could provide insights which would be useful for identifying culturally bound aspects of writing for research publication purposes. In sum, the research article genre does nothing but reflect different social and cultural worlds. Inquiring into linguistic innovations in each variant or lect, already identified in the spoken register (Cogo and Dewey, 2006), also seems desirable in future research.

Like Giltrow (1994: 148), I would underline 'the utility of genre study in cultural inquiry' for capturing the plurality of global and local discourses beyond native norms and ascertaining the extent to which research genres are different in different cultural contexts. As Canagarajah (2007: 91) asserts, 'LFE does not exist as a system out there, [but] is constantly brought into being in each context of communication'.

4.6 Language de-standardisation?

So far in this chapter I have looked at language dynamics, language diversity and language hybridity and change in research-article writing. Therefore, in order to complement the discussion, in this section I will address some language-related dynamics in processes of genre transmediality and language use in the digital medium. I will specifically comment on language as a resource supporting scientific communication in genre sets and systems on the web and assess the role language plays in digital genres regarding the polycontextuality of the digital medium.

Observing language use in the digital environment through the analysis of linguistic features in interrelated genres can shed light on the diversity of discourse styles that characterises online genre assemblages. If we use genre and discourse analysis to identify language features associated with register, we can easily spot register shift in sets of hyperlinked digital genres. A comparison of short summaries from *Nature* (3,849 words) and their corresponding abstracts (21,966 words), one of the small-scale sub-corpora of the RGaL corpus, confirms that the former genre type does not substantially differ from the latter, with regard to lexical complexity. However, if we look at the use of language as a resource to communicate scientific contents, we find certain divergences. Rakedzon et al.'s (2017: 2–8) *De-jargonizer*, a jargon-identifier tool developed to measure professional jargon and assist scientists when communicating with non-experts, shows that the vocabulary used in abstracts and lay summaries in *PLoS Computational Biology* and *PLoS Genetics* (n = 5,000) scores an average of 10 per cent and 17 per cent jargon in abstracts sand 8 per cent and 12 per cent jargon in lay summaries, indicating a lesser use of jargon in the summaries but not, as expected, 'layperson terms and a

Table 4.4 Vocabulary types in short summaries and abstracts from
Nature

	Common (high frequency) (in %)	Mid-frequency (in %)	Rare (jargon) (in %)
Short summaries	69	20	11
Abstracts	71	17	11

narrative, journalistic style' (see also Breeze, 2016). If we apply this tool to a different set of interrelated genres, the RGaL corpus of short summaries and abstracts, we observe there is actually not much difference in the percentages of jargon use in the two genre exemplars (Table 4.4). Thus far, therefore, we can deduce that the short texts effectively encapsulate the essence of the research in the same way as abstracts do and both display a similar level of explanatory depth. Then, the only difference between the two genres in relation to lexical complexity appears to lie in the time it takes a reader to grasp the essential information, much more quickly in the short texts (that score an overall average length of 41 words) than in the abstracts (238 words).

As shown in Table 4.5, from a discourse analysis perspective, neither of the two genres exhibits features associated with present-day conversation, such as contractions, progressive aspect, central modals and semi-modals, *get* passives or *help* + bare infinitive patterns (see Biber and Gray, 2016: 317). Both rely heavily on the use of economy (phrasal grammatical) features associated with informational writing, above all, complex nominal phrases, as inferred from the recurrence of *of*-phrases and prepositional phrases acting as nominal postmodifiers. Other less frequent grammar features are *-ing* clauses and *that*-complement clauses, the commonest collocates being *thereby* + *-ing*, *by* + *-ing* and *show that, demonstrate that, found that, suggesting that, report that, hypothesise that, reveal that, propose that* and *found that*. This shows that the two genres are both characterised by a phrasal discourse style, with high informational density and a high level of explicitness, which indicates that the abstracts and their peritexts (i.e., their short texts) both target an expert and not a lay audience.

The discourse style of the short summaries, acting as abstracts peritexts, can be described as an expository writing type, efficient to inform about research outcomes in a very concise way. It is nonetheless interesting to note that these texts combine lexical sophistication and phrase-level grammatical complexity with features of spoken

Table 4.5 *Distribution of linguistic features in short texts and abstracts from* Nature

		Short summaries	f/1,000 words	Abstracts	f/1,000 words	Log likelihood
Colloquial features (associated with conversation)	contractions	0	0	0	0	N/A
	progressive aspect	1	0.26	12	0.55	0.64
	central modals	25	6.50	132	6.01	0.12
	semi-modals	0	0.00	1	0.05	0.32
	get passives	0	0.00	0	0.00	N/A
	help + bare infinitive	1	0.26	0	0.09	3.81
Nominal/phrasal features (associated with informational writing)	relative clauses with *which*	8	2.08	71	3.23	1.6
	to-infinitive clauses	24	6.24	161	7.33	0.59
	-ing clause	44	11.43	258	11.75	0.03
	that noun complement clauses	31	8.05	176	8.01	0.0
	of-phrases	181	47.03	972	44.25	0.51
	prepositional phrases as nominal postmodifiers	180	46.77	962	43.79	0.59

language, such as subject ellipsis and coordination, or the process of connecting two clauses. Coordination divides the long sentences that characterise these short summaries, in a way evoking the add-on strategy typical in conversational register, or 'the process of construct-ing conversational turns from a linear sequence of short-finite clause-like segments' (Biber et al., 1999: 1068). As illustrated in the following three examples of short summaries, coordination splits the informa-tion contained in a complex syntactic structure into two main clauses. As a result, the processing effort required when reading these summar-ies is much simpler than that required for reading the sentences of the associated abstracts that typically contain subordination and comple-mentation embeddings.

The diversity in the hydraulic traits of trees mediates ecosystem resilience to drought and will probably have an important role in future ecosystem–atmosphere feedback effects.

Contrary to the hopes of policymakers, fossil fuel subsidy removal would have only a small impact on global energy demand and carbon dioxide emissions and would not increase renewable energy use by 2030.

Depletion of the DNA helicase WRN induced double-stranded DNA breaks, and promoted apoptosis and cell cycle arrest selectively in cancers with microsatellite instability, indicating that WRN is a promising drug target for the treatment of these cancers.

From this exploratory analysis of grammar and discourse style, one can conclude that the formal register employed in these two interde-pendent genres in different ways serves to strategically inform readers of the novelty of the research and grab their attention. By providing a quick summary of the main findings and conclusions, the short texts (acting as peritexts) become an effective screening device that allows the interested reader to decide whether to access the abstract and associated article for further details. More broadly, from the linguistic data given previously, it can also be concluded that the choice of standard grammar features in these two genre exemplars does not clearly align with Baron's (2016: 331) claim that '[l]anguage de-standardization has many sources, social and technological'. Digital genres related to transformative practice such as citizen science pro-jects and crowdsourcing science projects (see last section of Chapter 3) exemplify the way researchers today opt for the use of colloquial, non-formal language to engage non-specialist publics in and with science. Through a discourse style resembling the conversational register (as described in Biber et al., 1999), the writers of these genres conveyed proximity with their audiences and appealed to their audiences to prompt collaboration and funding support. In stark contrast, the rhetorical exigences in the set of genres from *Nature* explored in this chapter section are different. The recurring linguistic features do not actually compensate for lack of knowledge, and the absence of discourse strategies such as clarifications and paraphrases displays a heteroglossically disengaged mode of expression and the construal of the readership as one sharing similar views, beliefs and attitudes (White, 2003: 258–259). This is a style that is not dissimilar to that reported for journal articles, a style that indicates that the writers are 'more committed towards contents and much more collegial towards their audiences'; in short, a style that allows writers 'to open up some space for dialogism' (Pérez-Llantada, 2011: 31–32). Both the short summary and its associated abstract thus instantiate the deficit model in science communication proposed by Gross (1994). The short text establishes a threshold of interpretation that might be difficult to surpass for a non-specialist reader.

In discussing language evolution from an ecological perspective, Mufwene (2013: 66) emphasises the importance of paying attention to polyglossia so as to preserve the coexistence of several languages and fair sociolinguist equilibrium. The various language phenomena and practices discussed in this chapter in relation to the academic and research ecosystem in many ways reflect broader sociolinguistic phenomena. Paying attention to dynamic multilingualism and to polylanguaging in the research world would make linguistic diversity an effective way of resisting and redressing monoglossic (English-only) language ideologies.

4.7 Chapter summary

The reflections and explorations of this chapter have sought to show several facets of language use and language variation in genred activity. I have explored how genres intersect with languages and how genres may draw on different languaging forms at the level of the individual. I have also claimed that enquiry into language diversity can best capture multilingual science communication today. Adopting the stance of the language ecology framework, it seems reasonable to conclude that languaging advocacy for the recognition of translingual practices and, more broadly, of polylanguaging in the research world has important implications for the evolution of multilingual genre ecologies. In view of this, what needs to be looked at in depth is the skills both novice and expert researchers need to acquire in order to compose the various genres shaping the different social interaction scenarios illustrated in this chapter.

5 *Genres and Multiliteracies*

Literacy is broadly defined as the 'ability to read and write' and as 'knowledge of a particular subject, or a particular type of knowledge'.[1] In the LAP scholarly literature, the term 'literacy' has been used to refer to the competence (i.e., knowledge and skills in putting knowledge into practice) required in the activity of creating academic texts effectively. In this chapter, the term 'literacy' is preferred to the term 'competence' insofar as the former encompasses the different dimensions of writing – sociohistorical, sociocultural, linguistic, cognitive and developmental (Barton, Hamilton and Ivanič, 2000; Prior, 1998; Tusting et al., 2019). Ethnographic methods have been used to examine literacy as social practice (Barton and Hamilton, 2012; Gee, 1996) and to investigate an individual's processes of becoming literate in an academic language by acquiring writing conventions and developing expertise in composing academic texts effectively (Bazerman and Prior, 2004; Johns, 1997; Street, 1984). Ethnographies of writing contexts are also used in rhetorical genre studies to enquire into academic writing in relation to literate activity, that is, developing knowledge and skills for 'making ourselves understood and interactionally effective at a distance' (Bazerman, 2015: 89). In all these studies, writing is viewed as a process involving strategic choices. This view of writing is adopted in this chapter on the assumption that it more accurately reflects the complexity involved in writing in and about science. Both views of writing involve knowledge of genres along with rhetorical competence, digital (computer) skills, skills in composing multimodal texts and linguistic and intercultural competence. From the discussion of some existing genres in previous chapters, one can deduce that writing activity in today's research

---

[1] Cambridge Dictionary, https://dictionary.cambridge.org/es/diccionario/ingles-espanol/literacy [last accessed on 9 February 2020].

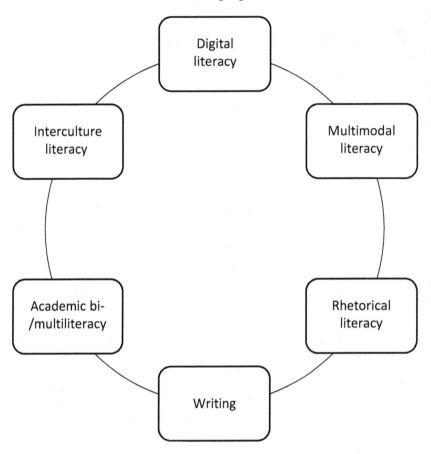

Figure 5.1 Literacies associated with writing

world is an activity that requires diverse literacies. Social action, enacted through genres, involves communicating scientific knowledge to different audiences, across languages and cultures, in different modes – visual, aural and verbal – and in different forms and media – print and online. The concept of multiliteracies encompasses the set of different skills that may be needed to communicate through different forms. In what follows, I will therefore relate writing activity to these various literacies and contend that effectively engaging in professional and public communication of science today requires a set of intersecting types of literacy (Figure 5.1).

Authors such as Johns (1997) and Bazerman and Prior (2004), among others, note that both social and contextual aspects constrain textual practices and hence influence text production. Johns's (1997) model is also insightful in that it foregrounds the key role of the community in developing literacy and the novice-senior encculturation processes that account for the implicit learning of writing conventions through observation of the seniors' writing practices. Acknowledging 'the social patterning of literacy practices' (Barton, 2001: 92; Gee, 1996; Johns, 1997), I would argue that it is not possible to dissociate writing from other forms of literacy in science communication today, because all the above literacies are ways of addressing the extant social exigences imposed on genres. Barton (2001) himself actually distinguishes between 'literacy as communication' and literacy in relation to 'values and awareness' and 'broader social relations'. As discussed in the following section, the plurality of intertwining literacies – genre, rhetorical, multimodal, digital, bi/multilingual and intercultural – underpins the view of genres articulating social actions and being shaped by social agents and structures, a claim made earlier in this book. Data from the RGaL corpus and exploratory ethnomethodology will be used to discuss what repertoires of genres and languages researchers draw upon in their everyday activities and what skills novice researchers need to acquire to communicate effectively in their everyday activities.

5.1 Revisiting territories of knowledge

In the previous chapter I discussed several languaging practices and explored the way multilingual researchers utilise language as a tool by drawing on language repertoires for professional and public communication of science. The focus was placed on ways of composing interrelated texts forming genre assemblages as well as on diverse communication practices. The exploration ranged from practices in composing traditional genres such as research articles, abstracts and peer-review reports to genres that involve multimodal composing, that is, genres that comprise different interrelated semiotic resources – verbal, audiovisual, images (e.g., blogs, homepages and tweets). Before delving into the main skills needed for straddling professional and public communication of science, I briefly sketch out the contexts that may motivate specific language and communication needs.

Changes resulting from researchers' increasing collaboration and, concurrently, greater reliance on technological developments account for parallel changes in the social context in which professional (expert-to-expert) writing practices take place. One of those changes is the merging of disciplinary knowledge in emerging interdisciplinary fields such as 'biostatistics, medical nanotechnology, and museum studies' (Swales, 2019: 81). Despite this upsurge, a search for interdisciplinary journals (the word 'interdisciplinary' being explicitly stated in their titles) in the ISI databases retrieves only 19 out of a total of 14,000 journals. Of those, some are interdisciplinary studies within a single field (e.g., different branches of chemistry or, as another example, business focused on risk and society) and some are multidisciplinary, not interdisciplinary, studies involving more than one field (e.g., social sciences and education or humanities and cultural studies) or even ranging across several disciplines (STEMM, humanities, education and social sciences). Although they are all refereed scholarly journals, some fall under the category of paywall journals, since they require a minimal processing charge for publication costs. Another changing practice in today's research world, most evident at a time when researchers are seeking to cope with the devastating impact caused by a global pandemic, can be found in multidisciplinary research. This stock of research entails joint conversations across knowledge fields so as to yield a more comprehensive understanding of the issues under enquiry. For example, research published by *eLife* covers mutually informing specialisations ranging from genetics and genomics, environmental biology, neuroscience and human biology and medicine to immunology and infectious diseases or biochemistry and chemical biology. As another example, one of the collections of *Nature* articles compiled for the RGaL corpus comprises related articles, letters, news and views, comments and outlooks on climate change and target 1.5°. These collections offer associated contents on these topics that are discussed from multifarious perspectives, from economics and nature energy to communications and geoscience. Therefore, there seems to be evidence that scientists across the STEMM disciplines are engaging in collaborative work to address complex global challenges related to health and well-being, climate change and environmental risks.

Arguably, the convergence and complementary nature of specialised knowledge fields might mean that the traditional 'territories of disciplinary knowledge', as labelled by Becher and Trowler (2001: 23), are becoming more porous and mutually penetrative, blurring the boundaries between them. This in turn suggests that the different disciplinary groupings or 'academic cultures', characterised by 'sets of taken-for-granted values, attitudes and ways of behaving, which are articulated through and reinforced by recurrent practices among a group of people in a given context' (Becher and Trowler, 2001: 23), are engaging in interdisciplinary research. I suspect that another major triggering factor for less rigid (or more porous) groupings is the benefit that the agents get out of it. Pluchino et al.'s (2019) study of interdisciplinary research in physics over a period of thirty years underscores that 'the publication-reputation-citation dynamics of the community of authors...provides more rewards to the scientists, since their productivity and their scientific impact increase with their level of interdisciplinarity'. A further point to illustrate this trend is made by Samraj and Swales (2000: 54), who use case study research on genre uptake to discuss ways to attain skills in interdisciplinary rhetoric in emerging fields such as conservation biology, a 'conceptual integration of knowledge' that writers need to achieve when composing texts. These socioliterate changes problematise well-established conceptualisations such as that of 'disciplinary identities' (Hyland, 2012; Johns, 1997), defined as the textual realisations of authorial identity that go along with the established disciplinary conventions and that stem from processes of 'disciplinary enculturation' within a given community of practice. Nowadays we are starting to witness in the research world a situation analogous to that of the contemporary social world. Local spaces where 'super-diverse' speech communities conflate (Blommaert, 2010; de Fina, Ikizoglu and Wegner, 2017), cultural contact zones exist (Miller, 2011) and situations where interactions take place become more complex as a result of 'plurilingual social formations' (Silverstein, 2015: 7).

To better situate transformative practice, a facet of research communication introduced in Chapter 3 in relation to public communication of science, we need to mention other parallel contexts and agendas, those that entail collaborative research and, like science for the public, social dialogue. Nowadays, there seems to be an outbreak of transdisciplinary research, mainly sustained upon collaboration between researchers and industry. This type of research is based on social dialogue in conjunction with the various interdisciplinary possibilities referred to earlier. The value of this research lies in crossing expert and professional boundaries, and cooperation here becomes beneficial for addressing issues of global and local social concern. What is described as 'open interdisciplinarity', that is to say, joint research cooperation between researchers and organisations, businesses and companies (see Trachtenberg et al., 2016), illustrates this practice. Using ten case studies of research collaborations on sustainability and environmental land use that draw on blogging to diffuse joint research outcomes, Trachtenberg et al. (2016) explain that the value of alliances to research complex topics calls for an integration of the fields of environmental science and policy. As these authors argue, scientific research, visible in journal publications, provides the strongest evidence and approaches to solving global challenges that current societies can rely on. Kirilenko and Stepchenkova (2014) also contend that it is through digital media genres such as blogs that science stakeholders other than scientists could get to know and benefit from the reach and impact of science communication. These arguments are germane to the pursuance of the SDGs set out in the UNESCO 2030 Agenda. A good example is the FAO's Agricultural Information Management Standards Portal (AIMS)[2] blog that openly remarks the importance of 'mak[ing] knowledge, information and research data on agriculture and related sciences available, accessible and usable' (quoted exactly as stated in the website) by enhancing digital access to knowledge through online platforms and educational programmes. The growing interdisciplinary dialogue along with the transformative potential for engaging the general public in science and scientific research, for example through citizen science projects, invite us to explore the actual communication needs perceived by researchers themselves when engaging in these practices. In the following subsection, I turn to some possible ways in which non-formal learning of the skills needed to compose genres for professional and public communication can take place.

5.2 Situated genre learning

Situated genre learning – that is, gaining genre knowledge in situational contexts – has been approached from sociocognitive and sociocultural perspectives. While the former perspective claims that generic forms of writing within a given disciplinary culture can be learned through social interaction with a situational setting (Berkenkotter and Huckin, 1995), the latter perspective postulates that social enculturation leads to learning of the values and norms inherent to specialised written communication (Bazerman and Prior, 2004). Other perspectives have contended that mastery of generic forms results from cognitive processes of perception, retention, memorisation and production (Prior and Bilbro, 2012; see also Berkenkotter and Huckin, 1995). Like Johns (2002) and Swales (1990, 2004), I tend to think that both perspectives are related closely. Both social (contextual) and cognitive factors simultaneously influence the processes of assimilation of the world view, values and conventions through awareness of the established written communication practices among peers within a researcher's community. These processes may be conscious and take place through active participation and interaction with other members of the community and, in many ways, are grounded upon the principles of learning in a community of

---

[2] See http://aims.fao.org/activity/blog/focusing-effective-science-communication-achieve-sustainable-development-goals-africa [last accessed on 1 July 2020].

practice described by Lave and Wenger (1991). Some of these principles are ongoing engagement in the activity of the community and lifelong learning (Bak and Mehmedbegovic, 2017). Both are often unrecognised in researchers' training but they nonetheless play a key role in supporting literacy development, as further discussed in Chapter 6 in relation to self-directed learning.

To learn the conventions of writing practices, a novice researcher should bear in mind that genres are 'activity types' (Swales, 1990: 42) and, therefore, contextual factors such as the sociocultural views and perceptions of the established social orders, for example the existence of hierarchies of genres, determine genre-based activity. Moreover, other community-level factors such as the existence of established conventions and standards for communicating with audiences outside the specialist community and the research world are also key aspects in novice researchers' enculturation processes. Swales (2004) explains that enculturation mainly takes place through exposure to the 'rhetorically-accessible' genres of the community. In being exposed to them, the novice researcher becomes aware of the salient textual features of those genres and perceptive of their communicative goals and intended audiences. Such genre knowledge will pave the way for later composing such texts. Berkenkotter and Huckin (1995) and Johns (1997, 2002) also explain that within this circle the junior researchers can gain knowledge of the genre schemata (both content and formal schemata) and learn to play out as full members of their disciplinary community. The only difference between sociocultural and sociocognitive factors influencing processes of disciplinary enculturation thus resides in the fact that the former pertain to the research world and the world outside it, while the latter operate at the level of the individual. Figure 5.2 summarises these intersecting factors, all of them framed within situated genre-learning processes.

Another important aspect regarding the acquisition of genre knowledge through informal and non-formal situated learning experiences concerns the cultures of the disciplines (Becher, 1981), as these cultures account for genre situatedness and genre dynamism. Each disciplinary culture has a distinct genre repertoire that its members use to engage in social interaction. Examples of such discipline-circumscribed distinctness are online genres such as graphical abstracts, mainly associated with chemistry and engineering (Hendges and Florek, 2019), and registered reports, especially common nowadays in the life and psychological sciences (Mehlenbacher, 2019a). These considerations should be taken as a rough, very simplified account, for ease of understanding, of situated genre learning. If, as Swales (2004) remarks, we view 'disciplines as bodies of conventions', it is likely that

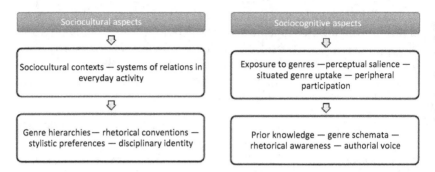

Figure 5.2 Sociocultural and sociocognitive aspects in disciplinary enculturation

researchers engaged in interdisciplinary fields profit most in situated genre learning processes, as they can gain insights into the particular ethos and recurring patterns of social interaction of the discipline(s) in which they become involved.

5.2.1 Sites of engagement

In order to learn how to write effectively, researchers need to grasp what it is they are expected to write and why the text – or genre exemplar – should be written in a particular way, in other words, what form and substance the final textual product should take (Bazerman, 2015; Bazerman and Prior, 2004). Researchers should also be acquainted with the specific contextual factors that determine the use of certain linguistic resources and with the rhetorical intentions that underlie a particular text. EAP research to date lends ample credence to the fact that for various reasons the ubiquitous research article and abstract genres take up much of researchers' time and effort in their everyday professional activity. In Chapter 2 I have pointed out that the majority of the LAP studies published in the past decade have mainly focused on journal publication-related genres, both research articles and abstracts and related genres or part genres (e.g., research article sections: introductions, methods, results, discussions, conclusions, acknowledgements), bionotes and editorials. Chapters 3 and 4 also discussed the central role of genres for journal publication purposes in genre-mediated activity, as a result of the existing systems of rewards and regulations at the national and supranational level (Tusting, 2018; Tusting et al., 2019), and the role of genres in relation to language choice decisions and language policy and planning in academic and research settings (Lillis and Curry, 2010).

Becoming acquainted with the contextual constraints impinging on researchers' genre-mediated activity and, especially, learning to write in both major and minor research genres brings to the surface the concept of 'sites of engagement', initially defined by Scollon (1998) and later taken up by Bhatia (2004, 2017). This concept, closely related to the concept of 'critical moments of interaction' (Bhatia, 2017: 117), has been applied to address the contextual constraints of discursive activity – practices and procedures – in professional communities. Bhatia (2004: 125) lists the following contextual constraints:

[T]he speaker/writer of the text and the audience, their relationship, attitude, social distance or proximity and their goals; the network of surrounding texts and linguistic traditions that form the background to this particular genre-text; the complexities of the medium in use.

The notions of critical moments of interaction and critical sites of engagement are also useful heuristics to understand how novice researchers learn what I conceptualise as 'collaborative and individual disciplinary community routines' (Pérez-Llantada, 2012: 200). For instance, we can hypothesise that novice researchers, as newcomers entering the professional academic or research community of practice, find opportunities to engage actively in different communicative events and by this means become exposed to and familiarised with the repertoire of genres that the community members use at work. They may also be able to perceive the hierarchical order of genres and the research policy regulations that shape such genre hierarchy. Additionally, they may become acquainted with issues of language choice in relation to the use of genres. In participating in professional practices, it also seems feasible that the newcomers develop literacy in written and spoken genres, at least in those genres that are more frequently employed. Perceptual salience again plays a key role here. It is likely that co-authorship, a well-established writing for publication practice in the STEMM sciences, becomes crucial in offering the newcomers opportunities to be exposed to written genres such as research articles, journal abstracts and conference abstracts. While these opportunities are commendable for fostering genre knowledge and literacy development, access and exposure to occluded genres, that is, 'those "out of sight" to outsiders and apprentices' (Swales, 2004: 19) – for example personal statements, promotion letters, grant proposals and editorial-response correspondence – are also important. It may be more challenging to acquire knowledge of those genres that are not at the top of the hierarchy of genres. The fact that they are not salient genres may make it difficult for novice researchers to grasp their communicative purposes, their intended audiences and contextual constraints and acquire their content and formal schemata.

Finally, situated learning of genres and disciplinary conventions also brings to the surface processes through which the newcomer in the discipline can become familiarised with and understand the production and interpretation of genre texts in one or more languages, as well as the specific values and ideologies attached to each language. Bazerman (2011: 226) contends that 'individuals construct meanings and consequentiality from their *perception of particular novel situations and their participant action in those situations*' (my emphasis). Perceptions of languages and awareness of ways in which languages intersect with genred activity are also part of the novices' enculturation processes.

5.2.2 Virtual community(-ies)

At this juncture, the role of the Internet and the new technological affordances should be mentioned and even acknowledged as a key determinant of literacy development processes. Open Science and open-access policies (D. Ball, 2016) offer the opportunity to have access to some of the genres hitherto defined as occluded. This would be the case of genres for expert-to-expert communication (e.g., short summaries, graphical abstracts, research reports, registered reports on research methodology or data articles, to name a few). Genres for public communication of science – for example, academic home pages, research blogs, microblogging, crowdfunding projects, inter alia – also fall within this genre category. Because this genre repertoire can be accessed online, it stands as a suitable source of input for becoming familiarised with the norms and conventions of disciplinary writing practices. This could enhance the disciplinary enculturation of newcomers and knowledge about 'how specific textual practices contribute both to the process of inquiry and the reporting of scientific research' (Wickman and Fitzgerald, 2019: 16). Hence, in the context of technological advances in digital communication, it is worth discussing the advantages of participating in virtual communities as a way of supporting novice researchers' academic enculturation beyond the local, physical disciplinary community (or in-group) a researcher belongs to. For example, in navigating open-access journals such as those of *eLife* and *PLoS*, novice researchers can get access to occluded genres such as online peer reviews, which include the reviewers' reports and the authors' responses to the reviewers' comments. Breeze (2019) reports a notable change in open-access peer-review practices, in the sense that peer reviewers' comments might be challenged – even questioned and criticised – in a transparent, open peer-review system. This is also the case of the registered report genre, already discussed (Mehlenbacher, 2019a) in relation to science transparency and reproducibility (see Chapter 2). As a form of situated cognition, familiarisation with these online genres, which were not available when journals were only in print form, can initiate apprentices into patterns of online socialisation with multilingual researchers.

The Internet can also prompt learning about publication standards and the multiple communicative purposes of emerging genres. For example, familiarisation with chains of genres (original version of the article → peer-review report → response to reviewers → final version of the article) may help early-career researchers understand the stages of the publication process, notice the differences in the use of the language in these genres and raise their perceptiveness of the value of using a shared language for international communication. In a similar fashion, they can make use of academic social networking sites (Goodwin, Jeng and He, 2014; Luzón and Pérez-Llantada, forthcoming) such as ResearchGate and Academia.edu, defined as virtual spaces that support scholarly exchange of academic achievements and informal multidisciplinary discussion. Additionally, these sites can raise novices' awareness of different types of research output both in the pre- and post-publication process – preprints of conference papers, presentations, posters, research proposals and patents. In the Physical Sciences and Engineering, arXiv.org is a popular site for preprints and can provide a way of learning the difference between a preprint and a published journal article and understanding the contextual factors shaping both genre types, namely, limitations to accessing the text due to copyright. Becoming acquainted with these repertoires of genres, which may be produced in different languages (and language varieties), can result from online engagement with virtual communities in and across disciplines.

By participating in social networking sites and social media platforms such as Facebook, Reddit and Twitter, novice researchers can also become familiarised with aspects of professional practice (Becher and Trowler, 2001: 210) such as individual scholarship vs teamwork, publishing patterns, purpose of citations, availability of outside funds, or characteristics of competition, among others. These patterns of online interaction are not stand-alone acts. 'Reads' lead to other researchers' reading interests and, as another example, 'recommendations' of research work are the result of individuals' evaluative or critical view of a particular publication triggered by a platform request for assessing others' work. In ASNSs and social media platforms, users' requests for published work prompt threads of responses. Researchers' tweets and blog posts stimulate participation in inter-action threads, 'likes' and responses to blogs. Pathos is particularly salient in the latter form of communication (Marwick and boyd, 2011). The ways in which genres are learned by participating in physical and virtual communities of practice lend further credence to the claim that the boundaries between both community types are porous and permeable.

In the subsequent sections I specifically review the range of competences and skills that are involved in the diverse genred-activity described earlier.

5.3 Genre and rhetorical awareness

Carolyn Miller (1984: 151) claims that genre knowledge is acquired by perceptions of rhetorical responses to recurring situational demands. Rhetorical skills are without doubt a crucial dimension in using research genres in today's research world, both for professional and public communication of science. Aspects of genre and rhetoric in traditional genres such as abstracts and journal articles have been extensively discussed from both theoretical and pedagogical perspectives (Feak and Swales, 2009, 2011; Hyland, 2005, 2009; Paltridge, Starfield and Ravelli, 2012; Swales and Feak, 2009a, 2009b, 2012) and also widely investigated from a contrastive rhetoric standpoint (Atkinson, 2004; Mauranen, 1993; Pérez-Llantada, 2013a; Yakhontova, 2006). This makes rhetorical literacy development a crucial aspect to assist research-ers in effective engagement in writing activity, including text-composing processes of traditional genres and emerging digital genres – both add-on genres in enhanced publications and hybrid genres. Public communi-cation of science, on the other hand, likewise draws on rhetoric and persuasion to a great extent. Gross (1994) explicitly states that one of the roles for rhetoric in writing activity oriented towards public under-standing of science is to serve as a tool for effective text composing. As this author further notes, rhetoric allows researchers to adapt the reporting of scientific research in such a way that scientific facts are comprehensible to the general public. At the same time, it allows the researcher to negotiate scientific claims taking on board (anticipating) the public's needs and interests in such scientific facts, by this means engaging the public in the co-construction of meanings. In this section I discuss several facets of research genres that can scaffold the processes of developing rhetorical literacy – that is, knowledge, skills and values and ways of interacting with one's surrounding – to engage effectively in written communication.

5.3.1 Inter-genre-ality

Swales (1990: 86) notes that 'both content and formal schemata can contribute to a recognition of genres and so *guide the production of exemplars*' (my emphasis). Here, it is worth going back to the concept 'inter-genre-ality' (Devitt, 2004: 44), mentioned in Chapter 2, to refer to the way 'genres take up forms from the genres with which they inter-act', to illustrate how recognition of traditional genres can guide the production of emerging digital genres. One emerging genre, the data article, is a good example for exploring how rhetoric is deployed in an online genre that takes up forms from a previously existing genre and how this is reflected at a textual level. Broadly, data articles can be considered an evolutionary development of traditional genres such as the research article and the abstract. The main generic innovation introduced by this genre is that it serves to report on the methodology of the research study and not on the research outcomes, as journal articles do. According to the *Data in Brief* (DiB hereafter) journal guidelines, authors are expected to explain the value of their data to the scientific community by answering the following questions: 'Why are these data useful? Who can benefit from these data? How can these data be used for further insights and development of experiments? What is the additional value of these data?'[3] Additionally, authors are also expected to comply with detailed guidelines for writing the abstract, which should describe 'the data collection process, the analysis performed, the data, and their reuse potential'. These are open-access online genres that offer researchers the possibility 'to convert supplementary data (or a part of it) into an additional journal publication' (Elsevier's *Data in Brief* journal website). According to the RGaL corpus of *DiB* articles, the rhetorical information organisation of this type of articles is as follows: title → abstract → data description → value of the data (displayed in bulleted form) → Experimental design, materials, and methods. These rhetorical categories are accompanied by detailed tables with the full data recorded for the study. Using this set of *DiB* articles (amounting to an overall total of 142,874 words), a word list generated with *Wordsmith* concordance program shows that the top lexical words are the verb *be* – *were* (1,567 occurrences), *was* (1,435), *is* (1,191) and *are* (729) – the most frequent collocates being *were/was* + action verbs related to laboratory protocols (e.g., *were/was extracted/calculate/quantified/measured*) and the

---

[3] Retrieved from www.journals.elsevier.com/data-in-brief

possibility modal *can* (459 occurrences) (e.g., *can be used, can be found*), followed by other modals but with much lower frequencies of use – *will* (98), *may* (85) and *could* (79). The former set of collocates appear to be concentrated in the Experimental design sections, where the authors provide a detailed account of the stages of the research process. Collocates with *can* tend to occur in the Value of the data section. The following is an example of a Value of data section, in which the authors foreground the validity and applicability of the researchers' study. Evaluative language such as the use of adjectives (*useful, beneficial*) and the ordinal *the first* serve to indicate the potential use or reuse of the data and to state its novelty:

- This data provides the first transcriptome of Citrus aurantifolia that merges the information from CLas-infected and non-infected leaves tissue.
- The de novo assembled transcriptome is useful as a reference transcriptome to other scientists working in the prediction and functional annotation of differentially expressed genes in Mexican lime and other acid limes.
- The RNA-seq dataset is available as raw sequence reads that can be further processed and analysed by scientists.
- This data could be useful for citrus breeding programs and the designing of novel diagnostic tools.

The analysis of the RGaL *DiB* articles illustrates how, as a generic hybrid, this online genre adopts features pertaining to existing genres, supporting Claridge's (2016: 305) contention that 'emerging genres (re)use features of established genres' (see also Herring, 2013; Miller and Kelly, 2017). We can infer from the corpus data that the rhetoric of persuasion of this online genre and the skills needed to compose these texts are not different from those involved in writing the research highlights that generally accompany online journal articles today, in terms of both layout (both are bulleted texts) and communicative purpose (highlighting value). The only difference is that, in the case of this digital genre, it is not the value of the research outcomes that counts, but that of the research processes and data collection and analysis. *DiB* article writing skills are not dissimilar either to the rhetorical skills needed to convey the novelty or 'newsworthiness' of the research in traditional article abstracts (Berkenkotter and Huckin, 1995). Swales and Feak (2009a: 21) explain that the concluding section of an abstract, as a kind of self-promotion rhetorical move, generally stresses 'the utility or applicability of the reported results'. 'Old' (i.e., previously known) rhetoric, therefore, can inspire researchers in developing skills to address the new rhetorical exigences posed by emerging digital genres, an aspect that should be borne in mind in terms of pedagogical intervention.

5.3.2 *Genre knowledge transfer*

The previous exploratory analysis of data articles showed that the genre exemplars are expected to have a sufficient degree of informativeness to ensure reproducibility and to clearly show the newsworthiness and applicability of the research. Convincing readers of the value of the data so that these data can be used and reused in subsequent research studies was also an additional functionality. Because it is always useful to the genre analyst to complement corpus data with the insiders' actual practices and perceptions towards emerging genres, it is worth summarising briefly the responses to the survey of corresponding authors of *DiB* articles (a response rate of circa 20 per cent) to have a better idea of their perceptions and possible motivations towards this new genre and their strategies in composing these genre texts.

Almost 60 per cent of the respondents reported they wrote the journal article before writing its associated data article and an additional 30 per cent co-submitted both text types, which confirms that the data article genre is an extension of the traditional genre, that is, an add-on genre that enables authors to describe research data in more detail and target research reproducibility. As almost unanimously perceived by the authors, *the important/most important* communicative purposes of the genre were, first and foremost, highlighting the value of research data and analysis, enabling others to reuse and reproduce research and making it readable because it is open access (16 responses, 94.11 per cent). The data article may also serve to increase the traffic of the associated article. Almost 90 per cent of the respondents considered this functionality *important/very important*. Another functionality was that of describing research data in more detail (82.35 per cent responded this function was *important/very important*). The respondents also perceived that this was not a genre for gaining recognition (even if the *DiB* journal is indexed in Web of Science and Scopus) and not a genre that can be used to get more citations (even if it is open access) or to make the associated article more citable. Furthermore, the respondents did not view data articles as a genre for getting more citations or publishing negative datasets and intermediate results, even if the journal encourages this latter option.

As for the skills required to compose this text, 70 per cent of the respondents referred to skills needed for explaining the significance of the data and almost 65 per cent aiming at clarity and conciseness. Almost half of the respondents stated they relied on their previous experience in writing for publication (e.g., use of formal language) to compose this genre. Given this response, we can assume that the recurring phraseology might be transferable from one genre to another. This response further suggests that researchers may be aware that prior knowledge of some genre schemata and rhetorical skills are transposable resources, in the sense that these schemata can scaffold the composing process of the data article texts. In this case, knowledge and skills of the journal article and the abstract would be transferred to data article composing. This is in fact what Salö and Hanell (2014) conceptualise as 'strategies of interdiscursivity', strategies that have also been reported in professional discourses but conceptualised as 'interdiscursive performance' (Bhatia, 2017). On pedagogical grounds, Feak and Swales (2011) also propose developing rhetorical skills for writing introductions across genres, implicitly acknowledging genre knowledge transfer and, specifically, the role of interdiscursivity in composing genres.

I can think of at least two reasons why the emergence and evolution of the data article genre deserves close attention in relation to genre literacy in future research. The first reason is theoretical. At present, the genre may in fact not yet have stabilised. Here, Miller's (1984: 152) semiotic framework, developed to characterise 'the principles used to classify discourse, according to whether the defining principle is based on "rhetorical substance (semantics), form (syntactics), or the rhetorical action the discourse performs (pragmatics)"', can be a valid framework for identification of this genre. The second reason is pedagogical and relates to how generic form shapes textual substance to fulfil the expected goals. Given its distinct textual rhetoric, along with the fact that this genre is shareable (open access) and shorter in length than other research outlets, the data article is a suitable genre exemplar for training researchers in new forms of research communication.

5.4 Academic literacy

Enquiry into academic literacy deems it necessary to focus on the interplay of language and cognition. Barton (2007: 72) explains that literacy is embedded in language and views literacy as part of general language acquisition. In the LAP literature, academic literacy is also associated with developing sociocognitive strategies and achieving skills to write disciplinary texts (e.g., Bazerman and Prior, 2004; Prior, 1998). In this literature, several aspects of academic literacy acquisition and literacy development stages have been examined to date. These are (i) academic lexis (Hancioğlu, Neufeld and Eldridge, 2008) and recurring lexicogrammar patterns, also called academic formulas (O'Donnell, Römer and Ellis, 2013; Römer, 2011;

Simpson-Vlach and Ellis, 2010), (ii) citational patterns (Hewings, Lillis and Vladimiroua, 2010; Hyland, 1999; Okamura, 2008) and (iii) metadiscourse resources and the expression of voice and author's identity (Ädel, 2006; Hyland, 2008; Ivanič, 1998). According to this literature, these aspects of literacy have been reported to be particularly challenging for novice researchers entering academia, both in their L1 and in an additional language (L2). Writers are expected to become familiarised with and understand the aforementioned aspects, as they are part of the conventions of standardised discourse in expert-to-expert communication, as well as being able to interpret their rhetorical effects (Hyland, 2009; Johns and Swales, 2002). As Bawarshi (2001: 71) contends, researchers 'actively enact and, consequently, reenact social practices, relations, and identities'. This is in fact part of their enculturation process and the way of participating effectively in the social world. Below I outline the knowledge and skills that scientists need in this context.

Studies on novice and advanced expert writing have described the cognitive processes underpinning literacy acquisition, for example, the acquisition of lexicogrammar features and the subsequent production of these features in written production (Ädel, 2006; O'Donnell, Römer and Ellis, 2013; Pérez-Llantada, 2014). Effective use of these academic formulas at a discourse level involves awareness of the pragmatic functionality of these features and their effective use of those features according to genre conventions, including discourse style and register constraints. The literature further explains that metacognitive awareness – that is, being aware of the strategies that can trigger the acquisition and learning of recurring formulaic sequences, for example through extensive reading of texts containing those formulas and/or through formal instruction, accounts for subsequent production of those features in genre texts (Negretti, 2012; Negretti and McGrath, 2018). Rounsaville, Goldberg and Bawarshi (2008: 97) also make the compelling argument that metacognition enhances literacy development by triggering an automatic transfer of general writing skills – knowledge, strategies and resources – to specific writing skills in the disciplines.

The literature also contends that metacognitive awareness helps develop and extend knowledge of citation conventions (Swales and Feak, 2009b). Citations are strategic resources that enable writers to situate a study taking the prior literature as a starting point (Swales and Feak, 2009b), create a research space following the CARS rhetorical model (Feak and Swales, 2011; Swales, 1990; Swales and Feak, 2012) and back up the author's claims and arguments (Hyland, 1999). Mastering citation practices is described as particularly challenging among early-career researchers (Hirvela and Belcher, 2001; Prior and Bilbro, 2012) and for second-language writers (Hewings, Lillis and Vladimirou, 2010). Learning citation conventions is the outcome of unintentional and/or intentional noticing and awareness of citation forms and functions. Goodrum et al. (2001) report that novice writers in the computer science field were able to recognise and identify those source document types in articles that were highly cited. Ringdal, Lossius and Søreide (2009) recommend researchers in the field of medicine to pay careful attention to compliance with publication standards in citational patterns. In addition to non-formal and/or formal learning, early-career researchers can also become acquainted with citation conventions through peripheral participation. For example, they can learn to identify the dynamics of their own publication circles (i.e., the members of their own community of practice) and others' publications via data-sharing affordances. They can also become aware of other citation dynamics such as citation circle practices and differences in citation practices in English-medium national versus international journals, as reported by Lillis et al. (2010). Unless development of these skills is supported by senior mentorship, at least prima facie it is unlikely that learning the standard citation conventions derives from mere participation in virtual communities.

There are two reasons why I specifically mention citations instead of other standard conventions such as macro-rhetorical organisation, rhetorical moves or language and stylistic choices. The first reason is the important rhetorical effects of 'academic attribution' in building convincing arguments (Hyland, 1999). The second reason is that use of citations unveils different academic writing cultures. In this respect, scholarly research reveals that processes of acquisition through conscious awareness of citation forms may lead to different pragmatics in the use of citations by writers across different linguacultural backgrounds, which renders distinct ways of modelling persuasion. For example, Okamura (2008) reports a prevailing use of integral citations in subject position in biology, chemistry and physics articles written in English by researchers from linguacultural backgrounds other than English, which differs considerably from the stylistic variation in the use of integral and non-integral citations in texts written by L1 English researchers. Developing awareness of different pragmatic nuances in the use of citations for persuading audiences can be done through formal instruction that provides rich input of cultural particulars in writing across languages.

Developing competence in projecting an authorial persona, or voice, has also been described as a crucial skill for composing academic texts (Ivanič, 1998; Matsuda and Tardy, 2007). Written language and literacy are fundamental in communicating science effectively across genres. Writers need to construct an identity at a discourse level as members of the scientific community to convey professionalism, seek acceptance and achieve recognition from their expert peers. Writing journal articles, abstracts and reviewer reports, to name a few examples of genre texts, entails the use of resources to effectively construct a disciplinary identity – 'membership', in Ivanič's words (1998) – and by this means to persuade readers and gain their acceptance of the claims made in the text (Hirvela and Belcher, 2001; Hyland, 1998; Hyland and Tse, 2005; Stotesbury, 2003). This explains why an important strand of the scholarly literature has enquired into different facets of authorial identity and the expression of voice conveyed through interpersonal – also called interactional – metadiscourse resources (Hyland, 1998) or through the language of intersubjective stance, that is to say, the deployment of either 'heteroglossic engagement' or 'disengagement' modes of expression to construct different dialogic spaces in the text (White, 2003). White (2003: 259–263) conceptualises these modes of expression as 'monoglossic' or 'hegeroglossic (dis)engagement' modes by noting that while at times writers convey overt commitment towards contents expressed in the text through bare assertions (e.g., anticipatory *it* patterns) and dialogically contractive resources (e.g., *we*-pronoun subjects), at other times they draw on dialogically expansive resources to detach themselves from propositional contents, a mode of expression that is signalled by the lack of explicit agent markers in the discourse – for example, passive constructions and inanimate subjects.

The shift from print to online writing also brings to the surface the usefulness of developing strategies to extend prior knowledge of traditional genres and to transfer such knowledge to digital genres. As argued earlier, prior knowledge of linguistic resources to convey an authorial voice and citation conventions in traditional genres can be transferred to digital text composing, for example, to add-on genres in enhanced publications. If we move beyond scientific communication circumscribed to genres such as research articles, grants and PhD dissertations, the expression of authorial stance also emerges as a crucial skill that writers need to develop to address the rhetorical exigences posed by open-access genres and hybrid genres (Gross and Buehl, 2016; Kelly and Miller, 2016; Kuteeva and Mauranen, 2018; Miller and Shepherd, 2004). Skills in constructing an authorial identity are in fact very much needed to compose science popularisation genres and hybrid genres such as research blogs, microblogs and citizen science and crowdfunding science projects, where writers project onto their texts not only a professional persona but also their own identity as individual researchers. For example, the genre literature reports that the expression of authorial voice in science popularisation genres is combined with voices of third parties in the social sectors to appeal to the audience (Motta-Roth, 2009; Motta-Roth and Scherer, 2016). Also, as already noted earlier in this book, rhetorical genre studies on crowd-funding projects from Kickstarter and GoFundMe (Mehlenbacher, 2017; Paulus and Roberts, 2018) underline how the formal language of scientific writing is transformed into a highly persuasive narrative voice that makes the 'story' sufficiently appealing to prompt funding on the part of the audience. It is also argued that in other digital genres such as research blogs, self-expression and subjectivity are mainly built upon expressions of stance, which makes the register of this genre distinct from other registers, in particular the formal register that characterises academic prose (Barbieri, 2018: 251). Aligning with Ivanič's (1998: 59) view of literacy as 'embedded in social context', we can conclude that mastering language to express voice across the repertoire of research-related genres becomes an important pedagogical target.

Before closing this section, it is also worth briefly recalling two interrelated processes underpinning writing activity, namely, bi/multi-literacy and interdiscursivity, as both have been addressed from the perspective of language, transfer and metacognition. Gentil (2011: 10; see also 2017) strongly supports the view of biliteracy as the subject's 'ability to transfer, adapt, and innovate with genres cross-linguistically'. The concept of biliteracy can be set in parallel with Cook's (2013) critical views on ELF as either central or atypical second-language acquisition. For Cook, bilingualism and multicompetence involve knowledge of two language systems either in the same mind or in the same community. Olmos-López (2019) also stresses the value of developing cognitive and metacognitive strategies when bilingual writers shift back and forth from one language to another. On the other hand, the concept of interdiscursivity previously mentioned (Bhatia, 2004) brings to the surface the view that writers can rely on the discourse strategies they use in a given genre to compose other genres. Succinctly put, literacy acquired in a given genre and/or in a given language can serve as a scaffold to compose other genres and in other languages. This is possible insofar as writers 'draw on other linguistic experiences by patching together generics from similar texts in other languages' (Salö and Hanell, 2014: 13).

5.5 Digital literacy

Supporting genre-mediated activity, digital literacy intersects with several other necessary literacies in contemporary research writing practices. Today, communicating researchers' scientific work involves engaging with different genres, modes (visual and verbal), media and languages using the affordances of the Internet. Research dissemination on the Internet requires skills to engage effectively in semiotic remediation, above all, skills in multimodal composing. And obviously, in order to construct and diffuse science online to both expert and non-expert publics, strategies for addressing the 'collapsing of social contexts online' (Davis and Jurgenson, 2014: 478) and the polycontextuality of Web 2.0, aspects already defined in Chapter 2, are also required.

5.5.1 *Semiotic remediation*

The LAP literature has been perceptive about the growing importance of digital literacy in today's research communication. Edminster and Moxley (2002) recommend that PhD students get support to engage in electronic writing of remediated genres such as print dissertations so that they can effectively present their research using the interactivity and other technological affordances of Web 2.0. Paltridge (2020) also advocates the provision of formal instruction to PhD scholars on aspects involved in writing processes, such as managing digital citations, addressing ethical issues (e.g., plagiarism and predatory publishers), knowing tools for composing multimodal genres and the possibilities offered by open-access and social media for diffusing journal publications. One interesting further argument that Buck (2012: 10) provides while investigating communication in social networks is that 'digital literacy practices must be seen within larger systems of literate activity and larger literacy ecologies'. This author observes that given the diverse audiences of these networks, writers need to successfully manage issues of identity, self and representation and rhetorical choices.

Survey-based evidence from a population of 4,000 researchers worldwide shows that online research dissemination across disciplines is increasing but that researchers do not produce online genres such as audioslides, webinars, explainer videos, author videos and so on as much as they produce journal articles because of the pressure to publish expert scholarly work (Pérez-Llantada, 2021b).[4] Yet, while this survey shows that there is, by comparison, less engagement in

---

[4] See Pérez-Llantada's (2021b) Mendeley data for descriptive statistics results from a comparison across the disciplinary spectrum – physical sciences and engineering, social sciences and education, humanities and biological and health sciences.

parascientific genres (e.g., using research blogs and microblogs, crowdfunding initiatives, TED-talks and so on) to reach non-expert audiences, the respondents unanimously affirmed that disseminating science to the lay public was crucial for responsible research and for building public trust in science (Loroño-Leturiondo and Davies, 2018; Owen, Macnaghten, and Stilgoe, 2012; Wynne, 2006). On a different note, Mogull and Stanfield (2015: 2) refer to 'the re-birth of graphical communication' that has become manifest in the emergence of multi-semiotic hybrid genres. In these genres, the craft to be learned is the effective use of the visual mode in professional communication of science, for example, in the use of visuals synthesising at a glance the main findings of a study in graphical abstracts and video abstracts (Hendges and Florek, 2019; Spicer, 2014).

For the present book, a small-scale exploratory survey on online science communication was administered to 400 corresponding authors of articles published in high-stakes journals – *Cell, Nature, eLife* and *PLoS*. The survey responses (an acceptable 15 per cent response rate, with a 95 per cent confidence level and 9.5 per cent margin of error) reveal that while digital communication skills have clearly permeated both traditional and emerging research communication, the important genres to communicate research are journal articles and abstracts. All the respondents valued these genres very highly, as seen in the cumulative total of 100 per cent of *important/very important/extremely important* responses. In stark contrast, add-on genres and emerging online genres were not perceived as important to communicate their research work: audioslides scored a cumulative total of 83.64 per cent *not important/somewhat important* responses, followed by video methods articles (with a cumulative total of 82.73 per cent responses) and electronic laboratory notebooks (76.37 per cent). According to the respondents, dissemination of research within the expert scientific community did not involve digital skills. The majority of the respondents (90 per cent) stated publishing articles in open access was *important/ very important/extremely important* for disseminating their research work, and 70 per cent valued the use of institutional repositories and personal websites with the same degree of importance. Despite their innovative (multimodal) features, almost half of the respondents attached little value to article-enhancement features and add-on genres. As also shown in Table 5.1, more than 75 per cent of the respondents considered the use of academic social media valuable to disseminate research, for example, via prepublication repositories like arXiv.org, ASNSs and social networks. Interestingly, for 75% the respondents press releases, newspapers and other mass media were also *important/ very important/extremely important* to disseminate their research.

Table 5.1 *Importance given to ways of disseminating research work (in %)*

	Not Important	Somewhat important	Important	Very Important	Extremely important
Publishing open access	0.00	10.91	30.91	27.27	29.09
Using article enhancement features (e.g., audioslides, author videos, graphical abstracts, etc.)	25.45	30.91	29.09	9.09	5.45
Depositing your publications on personal or institutional websites (to build up professional reputation)	7.27	21.82	34.55	14.55	21.82
Using prepublication repositories and social networking sites (arXiv.org, PMC, RePEc, ResearchGate, Academia.edu, etc.)	12.73	16.36	34.55	18.18	18.18
Using social media networks (Facebook, LinkedIn, Twitter, Reddit, etc.)	12.73	21.82	29.09	14.55	20.00
Using press releases, newspapers and other mass media	5.45	18.18	29.09	23.64	23.64

One important pedagogical implication that derives from these results is, first of all, the need to develop awareness of the affordances of the Internet for disseminating research and, secondly, to become perceptive of the repertoire of genres, modes and media to achieve this goal. In addition, it is worth noting that the majority of the survey respondents (90 per cent) considered public communication of science *very important/extremely important* to build public trust in scientific research and promote the use of research in decision-making. Circa 80 per cent considered that getting the public excited about science was also *very important/extremely important*. Few respondents (20 per cent) relied on parascientific genres such as crowd science projects and citizen science projects or online popularisation genres such as TED Talks or YouTube videos. Rather, to target non-specialist audiences and achieve such goals, approximately 75 per cent of the respondents referred to parascientific multimodal genres such as research-group websites, research blogs and social networks such as Facebook, Reddit, Twitter and so on, supporting Kirilenko and Stepchenkova's (2014) claim that there is growing blogging activity among researchers. It follows that engaging in these digital genres requires an awareness of the effects of the collapsing of contexts in Web 2.0 on the form and substance of the genres so as to satisfy the needs, interests and expectations of diverse audiences and virtual communities in public communication of science.

These considerations, along with the exploratory emic perspective provided by insiders, raise the question of how researchers actually go about multimodal composing and engage in semiotic remediation, that is to say, in the process of 'taking up the materials at hand, putting them to present use, and thereby producing altered conditions for future action' (Prior and Hengst, 2010: 1; see also Bolter and Grusin, 1999). As Prior (2013: 527) concludes, 'situated activity routinely involves semiotic performances that are re-represented and re-used across chains of activity'.

5.5.2 Multimodal semiotics

The genre and communication studies that have analysed the use of intertwined modes – the verbal and the (audio)visual – in expert and public communication of science have mainly been inspired by Kress's social semiotics theory (Kress, 2003, 2010; Kress and Van Leeuwen, 2001). As noted earlier in this chapter, these studies have highlighted the interdependence of verbal and visual meaning-making in written scientific communication in the STEMM fields, as well as in other disciplines such as the social sciences (Desnoyers, 2011; Mogull and

Stanfield, 2015; Wilcox, 2014). Using Kress's framework, Hafner (2018) contends that the function of multimodality in the Demonstration section of video methods articles in experimental biology is to construct an informative, fully explanatory visual and aural narrative. Sancho-Guinda (2019) examines the expression of emotions in graphical abstracts of high-impact factor journals and conceptualises them as 'promoemotional' because of the merge of semiotic codes – the linguistic (or verbal) and the visual.

For Porter (1986: 41), both verbal and visual are 'different modes of the same conceptual process' and therefore should not be treated independently. This author further distinguishes the following categories to conceptualise the dependence between visual and verbal: (i) image as visual, (ii) image and text as parallel arguments and (iii) joint arguments (intertwined) and contrasting arguments (p. 42). It is concluded that images can play a twofold function: argumentative and persuasive (p. 43). Another interesting view of multimodal composing is Roque's (2017), who rejects the hegemony of the verbal over the visual by claiming that both modes interact, influencing the rhetoric and argumentation of the text. His main arguments are, first, that argumentation and persuasion in a text are not exclusive and, therefore, visual figures such as syllepsis, prolepsis and metonymy may both influence the audience and/or produce a given effect on them and, secondly, that it cannot be assumed that verbal figures are transposed to visual ones (Roque, 2017: 36–37). Other studies have underlined the value of integrating visuals into scientific texts. It is argued that in activating the audiences' multicognitive skills (visual, aural), visuals elements enhance the persuasive appeal of the texts (Ostergren, 2013). Nieman (2000: 91) underscores the strategic use of colours for aesthetic purposes and the creation of eye-catching images and 'pretty pictures'. Visuals are likewise described as crucial elements to create an emotional appeal in crowdsourcing science (Mehlenbacher, 2017, 2019b; Paulus and Roberts, 2018) and in YouTube science vlogs created by young scientists (Riboni, 2020). Because multimodality in public communication of science is one of the aspects that has attracted the most attention in the scholarly literature, we can deduce that skills in engaging in different modes of the same conceptual process, as Porter puts it, are necessary for composing multimodal genres. The insiders' views corroborate the need to develop such skills given the multiple functionalities of this emerging genre. The small-scale survey administered to corresponding authors of *JoVE* for the purposes of this book (with a 16 per cent response rate) showed that VMAs were considered *important/very important/extremely important* for increasing the visibility of the researcher's work and building up professional reputation (scoring 90 per cent of all responses). Furthermore, 80 per cent of the respondents noted other communicative goals for this genre, namely, enhancing the STEM students' learning (as also claimed by Hafner, 2018) and engaging in responsible research. For 70 per cent, this genre helps to build public trust and for 60 per cent to ensure science reproducibility. Interestingly, for 90 per cent composing this genre requires skills in informing both other experts involved in similar research and a wider interdisciplinary readership. Also, almost unanimously (90 per cent), the respondents associated this genre with skills in constructing a detailed narrative on methodological procedures and skills in a good visual narrative. For 80 per cent, argumentation skills to persuade the readership of the value of the methods were necessary. Their responses also pointed to the importance of prior genre knowledge of schemata as a way to scaffold the composing process of this genre. A total of 80 per cent used their previous writing experience in writing methods for journal articles. Being skilled in video editing was only considered necessary by half of the respondents. Intersecting with these various skills, the survey respondents also indicated the need for digital skills to disseminate VMAs via their research-group websites, research blogs and personal blogs (as noted by 80 per cent of the respondents), prepublication repositories and ASNSs (arXiv.org, PMC, RePEc, ResearchGate, Academia.edu) (50 per cent) and social media networks (Facebook, LinkedIn, Twitter, Reddit, etc.) (40 per cent). Regarding these latter options we can further assume that disseminating this generic hybrid requires skills and strategies for knowledge transformation and transmedial gradation (Engberg and Maier, 2015; Gimenez et al., 2020).

If we adopt Kress's (2003: 36) approach to literacy and multimodality, both in writing for expert and public communication, a crucial skill is the ability to distinguish meaning as representation and meaning as interpretation. As we see increasing reliance on digital circulation knowledge dissemination, we can expect the integration of different semiotic resources in the same genre or in a genre assemblage to become a common practice, hence the need to pay attention in terms of pedagogy.

5.6 Intercultural literacy

Doubtless, intercultural communication is an inherent aspect of language socialisation across local and global academic and research settings (Canagarajah, 2018; Mauranen, Pérez-Llantada and Swales, 2020; Prior, 1998). In engaging in research genres, individuals' linguistic repertoires intersect with those used by each disciplinary community and the community (-ies) each individual belongs to. Given that at the interface between multilingualism and academic literacy there lies an ecology of genres that supports local and global communication, the aim of this section is to critically reflect on aspects of intercultural competence. The purpose is to propose ways of developing a good trade-off between the aforementioned literacies and intercultural literacy.

5.6.1 Big and small cultures

In addressing issues of language and identity, Collins and Blot (2003: 65) underline the cultural specificity of literacy practices by affirming that literacies 'are manifested in different ways in different contexts'. Likewise, Pennycook's (2010b: 130) critical enquiry into language as a local practice draws on the claim that when locality comes into play, variation in language use results from different social, cultural and geographical contexts. Barton and Hamilton (2012) emphasise the importance of examining the different cultural expressions imbricated in social action in literacy development. These claims lead us to assume that in using academic and research language(s) to fulfil communicative intentions, researchers 'engage in complex ecologies of language practices' (Pennycook, 2010b: 131). Therefore, developing skills to anticipate cultural and cross-cultural misunderstandings would be part of interculture, defined as 'the individual's degree of cultural competence' (Glaser et al., 2007: 37). This is, for example, a key skill in professional mobility and cross-cultural collaboration. From this perspective, 'interculture would not be the native-like command of the target cultural patterns, but rather the development of an optimal distance from each of these two cultures that allows both the relativisation of the first culture and personal growth' (Glaser et al., 2007: 37). By analogy, we can argue that in addition to the importance of developing the various skills in composing genres discussed earlier, developing intercultural competence is likewise important. To be fully effective, research communication should ensure that readers' reception and interpretation of meanings does not lead to cultural misunderstandings.

In contrastive rhetoric research and in genre and academic writing studies we find several arguments that can be linked to different aspects of intercultural literacy. The first argument is Cumming's (2013: 130) assertion that '[l]anguage, literacy, and culture intersect almost everywhere...intersections occur between cognitive skills, personal attitudes, social practices, and macro-societal structures'. Cumming explains that in situations of cultural and linguistic diversity, writers '[switch] for choices of words and phrases while composing' and select 'expressions of personal identity when writing for specific discourse communities'. Research on second-language writing also postulates the view of language and writing as cultural phenomena (Atkinson, 2003, 2004; Connor, 1996, 2011; Kaplan, 1966). The past decades have seen a very comprehensive characterisation of culture-specific linguistic and rhetorical styles in academic writing, one of the main conclusions being the existence of linguistic universals and cultural particulars in specialised language use (Mauranen, 1993; Mauranen, Pérez-Llantada and Swales, 2020; Shaw and Vassileva, 2009; Yakhontova, 2006). Devitt (2004) further claims that because they have social functions and are used for social action, genres work within the values, epistemology and social relationships of each particular community (see also Chapter 2). In discussing the transformation of genres in the digital era, Claridge (2016: 305) specifically refers to genres as 'cultural constructs (i.e., the conventionalized habits and expectations of people acting within certain sociohistorical context(s)'. A further point here is Atkinson's (2004: 278) proposed conceptualisation of 'culture' as one that encompasses different 'rhetorics and genres across cultures and languages'. For Atkinson, the process of writing and the product of writing (written texts) may reflect various types of culture, for example, the influence of 'received culture' (i.e., the culture of the society the writer belongs to), larger cultures (e.g., Western versus Eastern cultural thought and ways of being), culture as a way of engaging in the process of writing taking into account social constraints and culture that 'exists co-constitutively in the world and in the head' (p. 284). From Atkinson's insightful conceptualisation, it can be deduced that written texts embed not only specific cultural thought patterns that are reflected in the texts produced within each community and transferred across communities but also other sorts of cultural traits. Because genres are ascribed to the practices of specific socio-historic contexts, awareness of the implications of culture in writing processes and written texts becomes necessary.

   The view of genres as cultural constructs necessarily invites us to ponder whether genres really mean the same in all contexts. I tend to think that in many ways they do, which may explain the existence of genre conventions and the specific social value attached to each of them by existing structures and agents, as discussed in Chapter 2. However, genres may also have different meanings if we assume, as Cumming underlines, that each individual learns literacies in a particular individual and community setting. On the one hand, if we assent to Cumming's assertion, we could further claim that communicating scientific research, especially to the broader publics, requires sensitivity to the diverse linguacultural backgrounds the consumers of science today may come from. On the other hand, because genres are inherently attached to the value an individual and/or a community of practice attaches to them, awareness of language as a local practice seems necessary to communicate science effectively to those publics.

In the context of undergraduate L2 writing, and taking the genre of the application letter to illustrate her point, Tardy's work *Beyond Convention* is particularly revealing. While she notes that individuals can draw on genre knowledge acquired in a language to use the same genre in other languages, there exist interdependencies of locally acquired literacies and socially, community-acquired literacies. These interdependencies can be supported by Tardy's (2016) claim that both genre constraints and genre innovations are constructs shaped in different ways by the individual writer's genre expectations and the genre knowledge such individual has acquired in one language. Tardy further argues that differences in writing are not then only to be found at a discourse and rhetorical level, as research in contrastive rhetoric concludes. As Tardy explains, they are found in the way writers draw on genre expectations and apply prior genre knowledge across languages and, specifically, in the language and rhetorical choices they make to fulfil the particular communicative goals of a given genre. Tardy further refers to correlationalist models of multilingual writing such as that of Canagarajah (2007), according to which meaning-making is negotiated in such a way that it takes on board possible culturally bound interpretations. Based on those models, Tardy concludes that in the expression of authorial voice, writers can use similar, but not identical, strategies when writing the same genre text in different languages. Considering Tardy's claims, one might further deduce that interculture-savvy multilingual writers may be those perceptive of the specificities of the cultural background of their audience or interactants and/or those who may have a disposition to effectively address cultural differences when disseminating their research work to plurilingual, culturally diverse audiences without infringing genre conventions.

5.6.2 Intersecting continua

Rapidly changing social dynamics and technological developments make culture – in the senses described previously – and the disciplinary cultures of science crucial aspects of meaning-making processes when communicating scientific facts. Here, the emic perspective again sheds further light on the import of genres being different in different cultural contexts in the research world. If we go back to the exploratory survey of Experiment.com project launchers discussed in Chapter 4, the respondents unanimously agreed that the main functions of multimodal elements were to illustrate and to clarify the information, confirming that in the context of digital science communication visuals and images can be considered semiotic forms of languaging (Shohamy, 2006). Intersecting with multimodal composing skills, interculture awareness also came to light, as circa 80 per cent of the respondents reported that they used visuals, first, to attract the interest of a local community or networked audience along with the interest of the global community and, secondly, to reach communities from different cultural backgrounds. It can therefore be surmised that the collapsing of social contexts (Davis and Jurgenson, 2014) in the digital medium makes intercultural skills much needed. This is possibly the reason why the construction of narratives and the selection of images in the proposals were not associated with a shared culture. Rather, they were related to the idiosyncrasies of the very topic investigated (see also Luzón and Pérez-Llantada, forthcoming, for a similar claim with regard to citizen science projects). In other words, what Trench (2008) conceptualises as the 'erosion of boundaries' in online communication may explain the use of multisemiotic codes when composing rhetorical hybrids – overly simple images and familiar stereotypes of people, animals and landscapes on the one hand, along with texts that entail a low level of explanatory depth, that is, no complexity of knowledge to 'fulfil the requirements of explanation in non-expert situations' (Maier and Engberg, 2019: 134) on the other hand. This is precisely how the intersection of small and big cultures reflects at a textual level the impact of the context collapse on the Internet.

Drawing on Pauwels's (2006) notion of 'visual cultures of science', Ostergren (2013) explains that competence in visual communication includes an understanding of the communicative goals of science visuals and the skills and knowledge needed to create effective visuals and learning experiences. Ostergren's (2013: 54–58) framework for composing effective visuals is very discerning. It is based on the view that visuals '[m]aximize reliance on visual perception' and that a visual can minimise both 'the amount of information that must be stored in short-term memory' and 'demands on working memory by excluding redundant information' while 'maximiz[ing] retention and recall'. Therefore, in order to support researchers' advanced visual literacy skills, it seems germane to attend pedagogically to the aforementioned aspects of this framework for triggering 'the acquisition of these forms of skill and knowledge' (Ostergren, 2013: 68).

Considering the project launchers' responses to the survey, it also appears that in writing the same genre in two languages, the respondents were perceptive of possible rhetorical divergences, specifically, of the fact that adherence to disciplinary conventions does not exclude adherence to features of the language system of the local (physical) setting. As discussed earlier in this book, the way these writers establish proximity, define identity positions or handle the pragmatics of the language, including the role of humour, are aspects researchers need to take into account in online genre-mediated practices that target audiences with different languages and cultures. One further issue that explains why genres may convey different meaning in different local worlds relates to what Becher and Trowler (2001: 41) define as 'the cultural elements of disciplinary communities: their traditions, customs and practices, transmitted knowledge, beliefs, morals and rules of conduct, as well as their linguistic and symbolic forms of communication and the meaning they share'. We can find in the interdisciplinary literature a convincing argument to support Becher and Trowler's definition of cultural elements of disciplinary communities. In their analysis of narratives in climate-change communication, Lejano, Tavares-Reager and Berkes (2013: 63) conclude that '[n]-arratives are no doubt best appreciated by people who are intimate with the culture that produced them'.

If the understanding of the social action in a particular small culture differs across local settings, divergences may therefore be generic. From the responses of the multilingual project launchers in Experiment.com, the influence of actors, agents, structures and values attached to genres appears to be related to the individual's personal ways of approaching them. Here, then, there might be a conflation between 'culture' attached to the individual's language, language values and attitudes and 'culture' associated with disciplinary values, methods of enquiry, reasoning, approaches to the subject matter and other established practices within the community. At this point we could ask, what is the import in writing practices and the repertoires of genres? The small culture may actually have much greater impact than the disciplinary culture in genres that are not at the top of the genre hierarchy. What Atkinson (2003) conceptualises as the 'big culture' – associated with disciplinary values, methods of enquiry, reasoning and approach to the subject matter and other established practices within the community – seems to be more dominant than the small culture when genres perform social actions exclusively bounded to the expert scientific community. In this latter case, it is more an issue of meaning-making and contributing to the disciplinary field than an issue of maximising intercomprehensiveness and expressing an identity, possibly to be socially credible and raise trust, aspects that were rated as very important to the respondents. We can speculate further and say that through parascientific genres, the web enables researchers to localise global concerns, convey different information levels (and layers) through hypertextual extensions and integrate multiple modes (visual and verbal) and channels for communicating science. Their responses suggest that plurilingual competence exhibits strong inter-dependencies not only with interculture literacy but also with academic literacy, above all rhetorical (argumentative) skills, and digital (multimodal and visual rhetoric) literacy. This does not seem too far-fetched if one recalls that Larry Selinker (1972) proposed a unified account of interlanguage so as to *integrate* this concept with the concepts of interdialect, interculture and interliteracy (see Glaser et al., 2007: 36–37 for further explanation). How much interculture is acquired and learned within the disciplinary community (and within virtual communities) and how much it can be attributed to each individual's own sensitivity towards language and cultural diversity are possible areas for future research.

5.7 Chapter summary

This chapter has provided an overview of intersecting skills required to compose a wide repertoire of research genres today. It has underlined some of the main facets of writing research genres in online contexts. By this means I hope to have addressed the different dimensions of literacy, namely, sociohistorical, sociocultural, socially situated and cognitive. The emic perspective has tentatively suggested that we might be moving beyond LAP territory and entering Communication training, in which the main role of the genre practitioner is to 'raise students' awareness, give them a variety of experiences and exposures, encourage their analyses and critique of texts and contexts' (Johns and Swales, 2002: 26). Possible ways of doing so are proposed in Chapter 6.

6 Innovation and Change in Genre-Based Pedagogies

In light of the literature reviewed in the previous chapters, the corpus data and the views of insiders, it seems reasonable to argue that communicating science effectively in today's research world requires mastery in the use of an increasingly diverse repertoire of genres. This chapter takes a pedagogical standpoint and illustrates several tasks for developing skills in both expert-to-expert and public communication of science. To date, important pedagogical developments have already taken place to cater to early-career researchers' needs in written communication, as can be seen in authoritative textbooks for graduate students (e.g., Feak and Swales, 2009, 2011; Harwood, 2010; Swales and Feak, 2012) and in dissertation guides for PhD supervisors (e.g., Paltridge and Starfield, 2007). Doubtless, thesis and dissertation writing and writing for research publication purposes have both received the most attention in higher-education settings. Approaches in support of researchers at advanced literacy development stages, for example as part of their professional development, are comparatively less frequent. Thus, what follows is a rough outline of possible (guided prompts of) tasks that may be helpful to postgraduate and early-career researchers. They might also support experienced scientists who need or wish to engage in new forms and media to communicate their work.

Considering the emerging knowledge dissemination practices that result from the technological affordances for open-access publishing and science democratisation, we can identify three central challenges in learning and mastering online science communication. The first is ensuring clarity in the messages conveyed so that they are understood clearly. The second is coping with possible knowledge asymmetries when communicating science to audiences that may have different knowledge backgrounds, viewpoints and perceptions. The third is building trust and credibility with lay audiences who may not always perceive the scope and value of scientific research (Ch. E. Ball, 2016;

Besley, Dudo and Storksdieck, 2015; Bonney et al., 2009; Gross and Harmon, 2016; Lejano, Tavares-Reager and Berkes, 2013). Besley, Dudo and Storksdieck (2015) provide an insightful source of information on researchers' perceptions of the kind of training they need to communicate science effectively. Using a survey administered to members of the American Association for the Advancement of Science to identify scientists' 'perceived value of communication training' (p. 201) (with 9 per cent of responses and a margin of sampling error of ±5 per cent, i.e., 95 per cent confidence level), these authors report that engaging in online communication with non-expert audiences demands 'ensuring that audiences understand scientific facts and concepts ("message understanding")'. In the science communication literature, both building trust with audiences and framing specialised contents in ways that allow for effective processing of the information and better understanding are also perceived as important training goals (Loroño-Leturiondo and Davies, 2018). The exploratory survey to the Experiment.com project launchers carried out for the present book revealed similar perceived needs, namely, mastering ways of avoiding specialist jargon (90 per cent of all responses), adapting expert knowledge to a diversified audience (72.2 per cent), creating empathy with their intended audience (63.6 per cent), using visuals to illustrate or clarify information (100 per cent) and attracting the interest of the global community (72.7 per cent). Their perceptions hence recall the contextual model of science (not the deficit model), as defined by Gross (1994), one that targets at making science more trustable for some science stakeholders (see also Kirilenko and Stepchenkova, 2014; Loroño-Leturiondo and Davies, 2018; Smart, 2011).

Developing the range of literacies described in Chapter 5 requires meaningful pedagogies that 'should help students sharpen their ability to analyse language (written or spoken texts), become more aware of language uses and choices, and acquire new knowledge and skills so as to facilitate implementation' (Feak, 2011: 242). The approach I propose, consisting of four interrelated modules (Figure 6.1), is not new, as it builds on the cycle of rhetorical consciousness-raising (i.e., involving analysis → awareness → acquisition → achievement) (Feak, 2011; Swales and Feak, 2009). Although in the following sections I will present these modules sequentially, the order and possible starting point are not fixed. Rather, the starting point is subject to the specific language and communication needs of each learning group or individual. Likewise, the time devoted to each module should be adjusted to the learning group (or the individual's) knowledge background and priorities. Because the approach is intended to offer

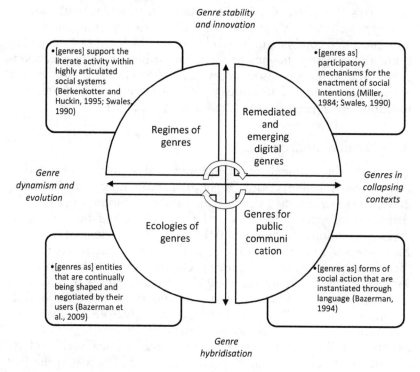

Figure 6.1 Facets of genres in RGaL pedagogy

individualised learning itineraries, independent learners can decide for themselves to skip a section or module if they are already familiarised with it.

This approach aims to raise awareness and bring about knowledge of the genres valued in genre regimes, such as the journal article, the abstract and the grant proposal. These genres have highly standard-ised conventions and, most likely, are those that researchers have access to and/or are familiarised with. This knowledge background can inform and pave the way for raising awareness of both remediated or repurposed genres and emerging genres, bringing about innovation and change. Eliciting critical reflection on 'potentials and constraints' (Puschmann, 2014) can prepare the ground for the acquisition and development of skills for engaging in expert and public communica-tion of science. Gaining such genre knowledge and developing a critical approach to aspects of genre evolution and change or even genre disappearance and death can be a proactive way for critically assessing what is gained and lost in old and new genres on the Internet.

In terms of cognitive development, the main reasoning underpinning this approach is the Vygotskian view of the role of consciousness as awareness in second-language development, which can be extended to genre and academic literacy learning and to bi/multiliteracy development. The approach also adopts Schmidt's (1993) views on the importance of input and noticing and awareness of the forms and functions of language in language-learning processes.

6.1 A critical approach

The underlying rationale for the genre-based approach presented in this chapter is 'be[ing] critical rather than accommodationist' (Swales, 2004: 241) towards the existing norms and conventions of genres, the rhetorical exigences of genres and the overt – and the covert, or 'hidden intentions' as Bhatia (2004) puts it – in professional practices. Moreover, every section or module of Figure 6.1 underscores the fact that the dynamic nature of genres is closely linked to the changes in social activity, based on the view that 'genres evolve over time in reciprocal interaction between institutionalized practices and individual human actions' (Yates and Orlikowski, 1992: 485). Lastly, but importantly, the approach connects to 'real life experience'. At the twenty-fifth ECML conference, Terry Lamb defined such real-life experience as one that builds on two principles. The first is the fact that it addresses not only challenges but also opportunities. The second is the fact that it includes all languages that are part of each individual's linguistic capital and that the knowledge gained in one language can be applied to any other of the languages of science. All the facets of genres summarised in Figure 6.1 draw on these two language-related principles.

I also advocate a research-informed pedagogy of writing, based both on data-driven learning (DDL) (Cheng, 2007; Chen and Flowerdew, 2018) and the use of small-scale exemplar corpora for language teaching or learning purposes (Tribble, 2001). DDL has proved to be an effective teaching and learning approach. As argued in the EAP literature (Charles, 2007; Feak, 2011; Pérez-Llantada and Swales, 2017), corpora can be used as a reference source of texts in a discipline and as a pedagogical resource for understanding the expectations of the disciplinary community. Feak (2011: 244) recommends that students put together a small collection of examples (ten to fifteen texts) that they can use as a reference source for consciousness-raising of the forms and functions of language and rhetorical aspects. This combination of sources provides enriched input and 'real' models that can be later taken into account when engaging in text composing tasks. A needs analysis conducted with the target group of individuals to be taught or trained can be helpful to determine the specific selection of genres to aim at (see Bocanegra-Valle, 2016, for further discussion). This means that the selection of genres illustrated in the following tasks are by no means the only genres worth targeting. Lastly, and more importantly, it is worth noting that in all four modules, both input and practice should be informed by Devitt's (2009) theorisation on inter-genre-ality (as defined in Chapter 2), Salö and Hanell's (2014) discussion of strategies of interdiscursivity in writing and Gentil's (2011, 2017) arguments on biliteracy transfer (both discussed in Chapter 5). In other words, the tasks proposed in one language can likewise be used to reflect on texts and produce texts in other academic and research languages.

6.1.1 Regimes and related innovations

In the context of writing in a foreign language, Tribble (2001) states that '[w]riters need at least four kinds of knowledge in a writing task: knowledge of content, writing process, context and language system'. A critical approach to expert-to-expert communication of science assumes that researchers have knowledge of content and knowledge of, or at least familiarity with, writing processes. In this first module, Task 1 thus illustrates a critical approach to the other two kinds of knowledge, context and language system. This task is centred on genres constrained by regimes and systems of research assessment. Here, a reference collection (i.e., a small corpus of texts compiled by the researcher) can effectively work to examine aspects of the language system, to reflect on communicative purposes and language use and to assess the dynamics of research publishing and its textualisation. Task 1 draws on data from a small-scale corpus of *eLife* and *PLoS* articles.[1] The design of this task is based on work by Cheng (2007) and Simpson-Vlach and Ellis (2010) and its goal is to raise awareness of the high lexical density of these genre texts, the systematicity in the use of recurring formulaic language and their communicative purposes, putting the emphasis on the stability of the research article genre and the social action it enacts. Task 2 focuses on language identification (awareness) and language production in order to focus on the utilisation of metalinguistic – that is, referential and reflexive – features of

---

[1] Extracts from these journals are distributed under the terms of the Creative Commons Attribution License, which permits unrestricted use and redistribution provided that the original author and source are credited. They are therefore a useful source of information for pedagogical purposes.

writing. This task aims to underline how both types of features can maximise message understanding in different ways. The reasoning behind this task is research on the functional roles of formulaicity 'in language acquisition, processing, fluency, idiomaticity, and instruction' (O'Donnell, Römer and Ellis, 2013: 83) and research on the discourse functions of phraseology and self-reflexivity in texts (i.e., text talking about text) (Ädel, 2006; Mauranen, 1993; Pérez-Llantada, 2010). In this task it is important to raise awareness that these formulas might be learnable incidentally. Task 3 seeks to elicit awareness of the use of interpersonal – or metalinguistic – discourse to build arguments, establish proximity or distance with the imagined readership ('display both authority as an expert and a personal position towards issues in an unfolding text' (Hyland, 2010: 116)) and pave the way for subsequent written production practice. This guided writing task is informed by theories of move analysis (Swales, 1990, 2004) and thus circumscribed to move identification and writing a sequence of moves in an article introduction. Lastly, Task 4 invites reflection on how a 'regime genre' can be enhanced by an emerging genre, introducing generic innovation. The task also places the focus on persuasion and argumentation, seeking to elicit audience awareness through the analysis of a genre set (an article and its associated podcast).

Prompts for Task 1

Let us consider one type of writing you may be familiar with, writing journal article abstracts. Read the abstract below and underline the subject-matter vocabulary in order to identify what we call the 'lexical density' of the text.

Interspecies interactions can impact antibiotic activity through many mechanisms, including alterations to bacterial physiology. Here, we studied synthetic communities constructed from the core members of the fruit fly gut microbiota. Co-culturing of Lactobacillus plantarum with Acetobacter species altered its tolerance to the transcriptional inhibitor rifampin. By measuring key metabolites and environmental pH, we determined that Acetobacter species counter the acidification driven by L. plantarum production of lactate. Shifts in pH were sufficient to modulate L. plantarum tolerance to rifampin and the translational inhibitor erythromycin. A reduction in lag time exiting stationary phase was linked to L. plantarum tolerance to rifampicin, opposite to a previously identified mode of tolerance to ampicillin in E. coli. This mechanistic understanding of the coupling among interspecies interactions, environmental pH, and antibiotic tolerance enables future predictions of growth and the effects of antibiotics in more complex communities.

Source: Aranda-Díaz, A., Obadia, B., Dodge, R., Thomsen, T., Hallberg, Z. F., Zehra Tüzün Güvener, Ludington, W. B., Huang, K. C. (2020). Bacterial interspecies interactions modulate pH-mediated antibiotic tolerance. *eLife* 2020;9:e51493. DOI: https://doi.org/10.7554/eLife.51493 1–26.

Why do you think 'nounness' is so frequent? Is this genre text therefore appropriate for a specialist or a non-specialist readership?

Prompts for Task 2

Now look at some recurring word combinations (phraseological expressions) in journal articles. Can you identify the functions of these expressions (e.g., to define subject-specific concepts, to introduce the purpose of the text, to indicate reason-result and so forth)?

○ *In the present study*, we used several type/size of nanoparticles, that is gold nanoparticles, latex beads and dextrans to characterize ...
○ The species is *one of the* most widely distributed ...
○ We *demonstrate that* Hfq CLASH robustly captures *bona fide* RNA-RNA interactions.
○ *As a result, the* bundle tension is given by the average ...

What other recurring word combinations do you use when you write journal articles? How did you learn them?

Now it is time to write. Improve the draft of an abstract or article introduction that you are writing at the moment. Use the metalinguistic (referential and reflexive) features. Make sure that the readers find it easy to understand the text.

Prompts for Task 3

Imagine that an audience of experts in your discipline is going to read the Discussion section of your journal article. Can you predict the possible arguments this audience may raise for and/or against your research findings?

Write a 200-word paragraph describing the significance of your current research. Once you have finished, think about how your imagined audience (i.e., audience awareness) has determined your choice of language features and the way you have expressed your ideas.

Prompts for Task 4

Read the following abstract from *Nature* and, afterwards, listen to its associated podcast (available at *related innovations* https://www.nature.com/articles/d41586-018-05568-1#MO0). In this podcast (00:53), one of the authors of the abstract (Jen Burney) discusses with the reporter about the human cost of unclean air. Identify similarities and differences in terms of contents, communicative purpose, target audience and language choice. What makes these two texts different?

Abstract

Poor air quality is thought to be an important mortality risk factor globally, but there is little direct evidence from the developing world on how mortality risk varies with changing exposure to ambient particulate matter. Current global estimates apply exposure–response relationships that have been derived mostly from wealthy, mid-latitude countries to spatial population data, and these estimates remain unvalidated across large portions of the globe. Here we combine household survey-based information on the location and timing of nearly 1 million births across sub-Saharan Africa with satellite-based estimates of exposure to ambient respirable particulate matter with an aerodynamic diameter less than 2.5 µm ($PM_{2.5}$) to estimate the impact of air quality on mortality rates among infants in Africa. We find that a $10\,\mu g\,m^{-3}$ increase in $PM_{2.5}$ concentration is associated with a 9% (95% confidence interval, 4–14%) rise in infant mortality across the dataset. This effect has not declined over the last 15 years and does not diminish with higher levels of household wealth. Our estimates suggest that $PM_{2.5}$ concentrations above minimum exposure levels were responsible for 22% (95% confidence interval, 9–35%) of infant deaths in our 30 study countries and led to 449,000 (95% confidence interval, 194,000–709,000) additional deaths of infants in 2015, an estimate that is more than three times higher than existing estimates that attribute death of infants to poor air quality for these countries. Upward revision of disease-burden estimates in the studied countries in Africa alone would result in a doubling of current estimates of global deaths of infants that are associated with air pollution, and modest reductions in African $PM_{2.5}$ exposures are predicted to have health benefits to infants that are larger than most known health interventions.

Source: Heft-Neal, S., Burney, J., Bendavid, E. et al. Robust relationship between air quality and infant mortality in Africa. *Nature* 559, 254–258 (2018). https://doi.org/10.1038/s41586-018-0263-3 (Permission to reproduce this abstract has been granted by Springer Nature.)

Lastly, reflect on the opportunities and difficulties that you come across in formal academic writing, as discussed in this module.

6.1.2 Remediated and emerging digital genres

Having addressed some key aspects of language and writing conventions for research publication purposes and having reflected upon the perspective of the audience, the tasks of the second module focus on aspects of genre innovation in the broader contexts of Open Science (Science 2.0) and OA publishing. The aim is to raise awareness of genre change in processes of genre remediation and, above all, of the creation of genre assemblages that combine both traditional and emerging genres drawing on the technological affordances of the Internet (i.e., enhanced publications). In placing the emphasis on the 'digital environment', this set of tasks addresses aspects of multimodality, hypertextuality and intertextuality, as described in Chapter 5. Witte, Latham and Gross's (2019) ways of 'critiquing, resisting, and remixing promotional peritextual elements' to develop literacy is analogous to the critical approach to genre innovation and evolution this task involves. Task 5 explores navigational and intra-textual elements in different 'sub-texts' by looking at the online texts accompanying journal articles in enhanced publications. This task also seeks to prompt familiarisation with the forms and functions of the informational and evaluative elements at a text-linguistic level of online interconnected genres. Task 6 is designed to invite multimodal composing of a short text for an audioslide presentation on the assumption that, as Swales (1990: 86) notes, 'both content and formal schemata can contribute to a recognition of genres and so guide the production of exemplars'. Assuming prior knowledge of the genre schemata and of the IMRaD organisation pattern, the audioslide template can be a pedagogically effective way of engaging in multimodal text-composing. A further rationale for proposing this task is Johns and Swales's (2002: 13) observation that the proposed writing is 'real', that its audience is clearly identifiable and that there is space for a personal voice. Task 7 analyses a genre chain to prompt critical reflection on the logical sequencing of the genre texts forming this chain, as well as on the various agents participating in them. One advantage of creating materials and tasks based on free open-access texts is the possibility of putting together text exemplars that are real models that can later be used to compose similar texts. Exemplars from open-access journals such as *PLoS* can be used to raise awareness of how the social agents involved in this chain – editors, reviewers, diversified audiences shape the texts in various ways at both linguistic and rhetorical levels. Reflections on texts and contexts can be prompted by considering issues of style conventions and language choice (e.g., the use of metadiscourse strategies of hedging and boosting in open-access peer-review processes). Broader issues such as ways of addressing a diversified audience and the collapsing of contexts (boyd, 2002; Davis and Jurgenson, 2014) in online research writing can also be raised in this task. For example, to further reflect on the effects of context collapse, this task can be expanded by adding a task comparing a small corpus of traditional peer reviews (an occluded genre), if available, with a small corpus of open-access peer reviews. Lastly, informed by the literature, Task 8 is intended to raise awareness of the possibilities offered by academic social networking sites and elicit critical reflection on their functionalities. The task closes by inviting self-assessment on the ease and difficulties of composing the repertoire of genres (formal, evaluative, informal) included in the task. Such self-assessment can become part of a reflective portfolio (or electronic portfolio), a valuable tool for the instructor to assist each individual.

Prompts for Task 5

Explore the following journal website. What are the affordances of modularity in the way information is presented? And the affordances of hypertextuality?

Identifying underlying medical causes of pediatric obesity: Results of a systematic diagnostic approach in a pediatric obesity center

Lotte Kleinendorst ⬚, Ozair Abawi ⬚, Bibian van der Voorn, Mieke H. T. M. Jongejan, Annelies E. Brandsma, Jenny A. Visser, Elisabeth F. C. van Rossum, Bert van der Zwaag, Mariëlle Alders, Elles M. J. Boon, Mieke M. van Haelst ⬚, Erica L. T. van den Akker ⬚ ⬚

Published: May 8, 2020 • https://doi.org/10.1371/journal.pone.0232990

Article	Authors	Metrics	Comments	Media Coverage	Peer Review
⌄					

Abstract
Introduction
Methods
Results
Discussion
Conclusion
Supporting information
Acknowledgments
References

Reader Comments (1)
Media Coverage (1)
Figures

Abstract

Background

Underlying medical causes of obesity (endocrine disorders, genetic obesity disorders, cerebral or medication-induced obesities) are thought to be rare. Even in specialized pediatric endocrinology clinics, low diagnostic yield is reported, but evidence is limited. Identifying these causes is vital for patient-tailored treatment.

Objectives

To present the results of a systematic diagnostic workup in children and adolescents referred to a specialized pediatric obesity center.

Methods

This is a prospective observational study. Prevalence of underlying medical causes was determined after a multidisciplinary, systematic diagnostic workup including growth charts

Screenshot (retrieved from https://journals.plos.org/plosone/article?id=10.1371/ journal.pone.0232990 [last accessed on 15 May 2020])

Consider the impact that open-access publishing can have on your publications record. Reflect on how publishing open access may affect the way you write and your writing practices or activity.

Take a look at the Peer Review Tab, where you can find the Decision letter and the Authors' response to the reviewers. How effective is the use of informational and evaluative language in the Authors' response to reviewers? Consider the following extract from the Authors' response:

○ *Reviewer 1 has brought up a good point* about the longevity of negshell-produced soft robots. We agree that the fragments <u>can cause</u> issues if cross-hatch is designed improperly. Blockage <u>can be mitigated</u> by making the pattern smaller than the smallest orifice in the design thus even if a fragment is lodged in an orifice, <u>the fragment will have</u> perforations to allow fluids to travel through. As for the sharpness of the fragments, <u>we argue that</u> as the fragments are created while physically crushing the negshell cores during the fabrication process, the soft material used <u>must be able to</u> mechanically withstand them anyways. Our fabrication process <u>would be invalidated</u> if they were *in fact* causing damage to the structure, which our prototypes and experiments show *otherwise*.

Consider the opening and closing sentences of the review. Are they appropriate? Is this the way you open and close a response letter? Why or why not?

○ First of all, we would like to thank the editors and all reviewers for their valuable input for our paper.
○ We hope that the revisions satisfy the reviewers' concerns and are welcome to any additional comments.

Prompts for Task 6

Create an audioslide presentation for a journal article you have recently written. A template is available on the publisher's website. What opportunities have you found in composing this audiovisual genre? And difficulties?

Think of the textual material that you have borrowed from the journal article and explain why you used it (or why you didn't use it).

How important is your 'personal voice' in the audioslides? Compare this genre with an author video abstract, a multimodal text in which the author explains the information visually. In Cell Press video abstracts library you will find some examples that you can consider to answer the question.

Cell Press video abstracts library:

www.cell.com/video/video-abstracts?startPage=24

Prompts for Task 7

This is a genre chain that involves both 'producers' and 'consumers' of scientific texts. What genre text do you find most difficult to write? What are the main difficulties you find in writing the submitted manuscript, the response to reviewers and the final draft?

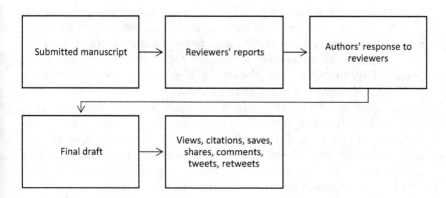

What aspects of your final draft determine the number of responses (views, citations, saves, etc.)?

Prompts for Task 8

Virtual communities. How do you initiate the role of reviewer?

Use ResearchGate to start a scientific discussion with peers. Post the question 'How do you initiate the role of reviewer?' and wait for replies. Once you have some replies, analyse the Discussion thread. Is there something new that you have learned? If so, what? In what ways will this new knowledge help you in your future academic career?

6.1.3 Genres for public communication of science

Along with add-on genres and the use of web affordances in enhanced publications, attention can be drawn to remediated genres (open laboratory notes), generic hybrids (graphical abstracts, video abstracts, etc.) and parascientific or trans-scientific genres (blogs, citizen science projects, etc.) used to engage the public (Kelly and Miller, 2016; Mehlenbacher, 2019b). Module 3 includes tasks that introduce aspects of digital genres for professional and public communication of science. Task 9 aims to raise awareness of new genres that have emerged and adopted features of traditional genres. Some exemplars that can be used to critically reflect on an expanding repertoire of genres are graphical and video abstracts, registered reports and open laboratory notebooks. These genres exemplify how a traditional genre acts as an antecedent from which the new genre borrows certain features. In Task 10, an analysis of two genre exemplars, crowdfunding projects and citizen science projects demonstrates the similarities and differences (in terms of depth of contents, language and style) between these project types and their genre antecedents, the latter characterised by features of formal academic writing (i.e., the grant proposal and the journal article). The cross-generic comparison can raise awareness of how features of the traditional genres have been reused and repurposed and, more broadly, how genre innovation and evolution are realised. Because grant proposal writing may not always be a genre addressed in writing pedagogy and early-career researchers may not be thoroughly familiarised with it, or perhaps only to a limited extent, these rhetorical hybrids become pedagogically appropriate. Both citizen science and crowdfunding science projects involve composing short hyperlinked texts arranged in different tabs in the main menu of the interface (Luzón and Pérez-Llantada, forthcoming; see also Chapter 3). Task 10 also aims to raise awareness of the extent to which the rhetorical moves for organising the information in these multimodal genres resemble the traditional CARS model for writing article introductions (Mehlenbacher, 2019b: 59). It is also a task for raising awareness of the modularity' (Hafner and Miller, 2011) or non-linearity of these genres and for reflecting on the advantages of modular writing in composing them. For this task, a small-scale corpus is used to show how the language of these projects adheres to the Gricean maxims of clarity, brevity and simplicity, how elements of persuasion and aspects of proximity are textualised and how a personal voice is constructed to convey a professional identity while appealing to the audience. In addition to learning proposal-writing strategies, the task can also be helpful for examining functions of grammar and discourse style and strategies of recontextualisation of specialist knowledge, that is, transmedial gradation processes (as described in Engberg and Maier, 2015; Maier and Engberg, 2019; Pérez-Llantada, 2021a). Concgrams and concordance lines can be used for better understanding language in context and context-sensitive features of discourse and register. Task 11 involves further practice of strategies for constructing credibility and authority and for creating a persuasive appeal. This task can thus be a useful composing exercise bearing in mind audiences and the effects of context collapse. It can help gain skills in compressing essential information, expressing *logos* and *pathos* and conveying credibility (*ethos*). Lastly, because this genre involves an ensemble of modes (photographs, author videos, vimeo animations), aspects of visual rhetoric are addressed. Highlighting the coequal or supplementary relation between the texts and visual elements, attention can be paid to the different types of multimodal elements and the rhetorical effects of visual or audiovisual material. Lastly, Task 12 focuses on the analysis of images and multimodal elements to reflect on how they combine and complement one another in digital genres. This task involves writing an informal text, which can be either a blog post or a 280-character tweet. It also seeks to raise awareness of the linguistic, discourse and rhetorical features of genres for public communication of science, such as blogs and social media networks. The task can be reinforced by prompting critical reflection on the role of public communication of science, the rewards and risks of social media for researchers (Britton, Jackson and Wade, 2019) and the agendas that promote this type of communication for the democratisation of science and for enhancing scientific literacy among citizens (Fujun, 2013; Gunnarsson and Elam, 2012).

Prompt for Task 9

Access the *eLife* journal website (https://elifesciences.org/) and find an abstract and its associated graphical abstract. Discuss similarities and differences between the abstract (the graphical abstract's antecedent genre) and the graphical abstract (an emerging genre) in terms of communicative goals, use of language and persuasion.

Prompts for Task 10

This is the structure of a crowdfunding project proposal, a genre for public communication of science. What information do you expect to find in each section? Do any of these part genres recall part(s) of other genres you may be familiarised with? Which one(s)?

| Overview | Methods | Labnotes | Discussion |

Explore the modular structure of these projects (https://experiment.com/). Click on each Tab section and analyse the use of specialised vocabulary, the language and the style used by the project launcher. Compare these features with the typical features of a journal article. What similarities and differences do you find?

Discuss the communicative functions of each section in relation to language use.

The Overview texts of the crowdfunding proposals contain hyperlinks. Where do hyperlinks take readers to? What is the functionality of these hyperlinks?

Prompts for Task 11

In this task you are going to practice language mediation skills, that is, skills involving the transformation of specialist contents into non-specialist contents. Here is a list of citizen science and crowdfunding science project platforms. Google these platforms and pick up a project of your speciality.

- ○ Consano
- ○ MedStartr
- ○ Kickstarter
- ○ Experiment.com
- ○ EU-Citizen.Science
- ○ Zooniverse

Imagine you are going to launch a similar project. Write a 300-word presentation of your project. It is important that you keep in mind that you are addressing a diversified audience.

Once you have finished, use the CEFR language mediation descriptors rubric to self-assess your skills in what you have written. Reflect on your writing strengths and on areas, if any, for improving your writing.

Prompts for Task 12

Explore this science blog titled 'Climate change could cause abrupt biodiversity losses this century', available at https://theconversation.com/climate-change-could-cause-abrupt-biodiversity-losses-this-century-135968.

Consider how the bloggers use the language. What language do they use to

o appeal to the audience
o highlight the topic
o construct credibility and authority
o construct persuasive arguments
o engage the audience

Blogs are multimodal genres. In blogs, language (text) is often accompanied by images. Have a look at the visual elements accompanying the text. What are the functions of these visuals?

6.1.4 Ecologies of genres

The goal of the set of tasks in Module 4 is to raise awareness of how and why genres in digital environments create interrelationships among them to address rhetorical exigences, as Casper (2016) explains for the case of the online research article. Links can be made both with Modules 1–2 focusing on genre remediation and enhanced publications and with Module 3 on parascientific genres for public communication of science. Task 13 is centred on two genre sets – first, video methods articles and their associated verbal texts and, secondly, data articles and their associated articles – to target the aforementioned pedagogical goal. This task is once again assisted by DDL analysis to elicit critical reflection about the degree of genre stabilisation of remediated genres (i.e., articles) and the degree of genre innovation of their add-ons or extensions. The analysis of corpus data at both linguistic and rhetorical level can draw the focus to the identification of language choice, for example, the choice of textual features that reflect the rhetorical exigences that account for the emergence of these genre sets – the need for greater transparency of research results and reproducibility of scientific research (Schulson, 2018). Two important ideas that need to be underlined in this task are, first, that the focus of these add-on genres is on the research process and the procedures followed to obtain results and, secondly, the fact that these interrelated genres instantiate different degrees of genre standardisation and stabilisation that can be identified through the analysis of aspects of genre, register and style. Task 14 intends to provide exposure to interrelated genres forming part of the ecology of the journal article, for example, an abstract and a lay summary accompanying the article or a short text accompanying an article abstract. The specific aim of the task is to raise awareness of the level of explanatory depth in each genre exemplar, their complementarity and their functionality as thresholds of interpretation in relation to hypertextual affordances. This task also elicits awareness of the function of intertextuality in genre assemblages. In reflecting on the possibilities and difficulties that composing these add-on texts entail, critical comments can be elicited on how much is actually 'innovation' or merely 'trial and error' attempts to enhance the ecology of the journal article. The underlying theoretical rationale for proposing this 'ecological' task is Giltrow and Stein's (2009: 10) claim that 'genres are notable not only for their irrepressible capacity for reproducing themselves but also for their capacity to arrive on the scene – to answer newly defined exigence – and also to disappear with the scene'.

Prompts for Task 13

Compare the extracts below from the beginning of a video methods article and its associated verbal text. To what extent are they 'parallel texts'? What is the added value of the video methods article?

Video methods article (beginning of Protocol section)	Associated text Protocol section
[Caption in video: Designing and Preparing the Peptides]	1. Designing and Preparing the Peptides
The first step in peptide design is to acquire the sequence of the fusion protein of interest from a public database such as NCBI or the Virus Pathogen Database. Choose the protease recognition site preceding the fusion peptide and include 2–3 amino acids upstream and downstream of this sequence.	1. Acquire the sequence of the fusion protein of interest from a public database such as NCBI (www.ncbi.nlm.nih.gov/) or the virus pathogen database (www.viprbrc.org). Choose the protease recognition site preceding the fusion peptide and include 2–3 amino acids upstream and downstream of this sequence.
	2. When ordering the peptides, modify them with the FRET pair 7-methoxycoumarin-4-yl acetyl (MCA) at the N-terminus and N-2,4-dinitrophenyl (DNP) at the C-terminus.
	NOTE: Several suppliers provide these modifications. Price and delivery time depend on the supplier of choice. However, alternative modifications exist, which vary in sensitivity and require adjustments of the plate reader in terms of wavelengths.

[Caption in video: Preparing the Fluorescence Plate Reader]

Begin this procedure by turning on the plate reader and waiting until the cell test is finished. Next, open the operating software on the attached computer and make sure it is connected with the plate reader...

[Caption in video: Preparing the Assay]

Prepare the appropriate assay buffers for the proteases as described in the test protocol...

2. Preparing the Fluorescence Plate Reader

1. Turn on the plate reader and wait until the cell test is finished.
2. Open the operating software on the attached computer and make sure it is connected with the plate reader....

3. Preparing the Assay

1. Prepare the assay buffer by calculating the appropriate quantities for each ingredient and adding it. For furin, make buffer consisting of 100 mM HEPES, 1 mM $CaCl_2$, 1 mM 2-mercaptoethanol, 5% Triton X-100. For trypsin, use standard phosphate buffered saline (PBS) solution.

NOTE: Volumes of 10 mL or less are sufficient. Depending on the protease(s) used in the assay, the buffer varies.

Source: Jaimes, J. A., Millet, J. K., Goldstein, M. E., Whittaker, G. R. and Straus, M. R. A Fluorogenic Peptide Cleavage Assay to Screen for Proteolytic Activity: Applications for coronavirus spike protein activation. *Journal of Visualised Experiments* (143), e58892, DOI: 10.3791/58892 (2019). www.jove.com/video/ 58892/a-fluorogenic-peptide-cleavage-assay-to-screen-for-proteolytic) [last accessed on 24 March 2020].

Discuss the possibilities and difficulties that you find in composing these two genre texts (the verbal and the visual). Use the following list to agree (A) or disagree (D) with the statements.

1. ____ I have a clear idea of the conventions for composing a video methods article and writing its associated verbal text.
2. ____ The article methods section expands on the information of the visualised experiment methods section.
3. ____ Data from the article methods section can be (re)used for writing the visualised experiment methods section.

Let's now look at a different emerging genre, the data article. Read the Value of the data section of a *DiB* article and its associated abstract. What value does this section add to the article abstract and the abstract of the *DiB* article?

Value of the Data	Article abstract
• These data point to the fact that several plant species are used by herbalists to boost immunity in people living with HIV/AIDS. • These data can be of benefit to other researchers and policy makers. • These data can be useful in understanding the use patterns and dynamics of herbal medicines and antiretroviral drugs among people living with HIV/AIDS. • The data provide a basis for further investigation of these plant species as potential drug candidates for modulating the immune system in people who are immunocompromised.	This Data in Brief article provides supplementary information to our earlier Ethnobotanical survey on medicinal plants used by traditional medicine practitioners to boost the immune system in people living with HIV/AIDS in Uganda [1]. We identified 71 medicinal plant species from 37 families and 64 genera. The data were analysed using descriptive statistics such as frequencies and percentages. Most of the plant species used were trees (27) and herbs (25) from the Fabaceae (15.7%) Asteraceae Phyllanthaceae (8.6%), Rubiaceae (5.7%) and Rubiaceae (5.7%) families. Additionally, we conducted a detailed literature review of the documented species to justify their use as immunostimulants. This data is derived from a larger survey to document the use of medicinal plant species in treating opportunistic infections in Uganda by Anywar et al. [2].

Source: Anywar, G., Kakudidi, E., Byamukama, R., Mukonzo, J., Schubert, A. and Oryem-Origa, H. (2020). Data on medicinal plants used by herbalists for boosting immunity in people living with HIV/AIDS in Uganda. *Data in Brief*, *29*, 105097. https://doi.org/10.1016/j.dib.2019.105097 [last accessed on 31 May 2020].

Discuss the possibilities and difficulties that you would find in composing this section and other sections of a data article.

Prompts for Task 14
Read the following extract of a short summary and its corresponding article from *Nature*. Think of the communicative purposes and audiences of these texts. In what ways do these genre texts complement one another?

Short text	Abstract
Climate velocity reveals increasing exposure of deep-ocean biodiversity to future warming	Slower warming in the deep ocean encourages a perception that its biodiversity is less exposed to

Marine biodiversity is at risk as the ocean warms, but currently the focus has been at the surface as the deep ocean has warmed less. Climate velocity – the speed and direction of isotherm displacement – is calculated to be faster in the deep ocean, and projections show this difference will grow.

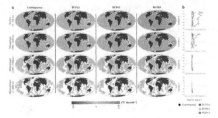

climate change than that of surface waters. We challenge this notion by analysing climate velocity, which provides expectations for species' range shifts. We find that contemporary (1955–2005) climate velocities are faster in the deep ocean than at the surface. Moreover, projected climate velocities in the future (2050–2100) are faster for all depth layers, except at the surface, under the most aggressive GHG mitigation pathway considered (representative concentration pathway, RCP 2.6). This suggests that while mitigation could limit climate change threats for surface biodiversity, deep-ocean biodiversity faces an unavoidable escalation in climate velocities, most prominently in the mesopelagic (200–1,000 m). To optimize opportunities for climate adaptation among deep-ocean communities, future open-ocean protected areas must be designed to retain species moving at different speeds at different depths under climate change while managing non-climate threats, such as fishing and mining.

Retrieved from https://www.nature.com/nclimate/volumes/10/issues/6 [last accessed on 31 May 2020].

Retrieved from www.nature.com/articles/s41558-020-0773-5 [last accessed on 31 May 2020].

Do you agree (A) or disagree (D) with the following statements?

1. ____ These texts fulfil different communicative purposes.
2. ____ They target different audiences.
3. ____ The short text clarifies the specialist content of the other.
4. ____ The short text expands on the information of the abstract.
5. ____ The abstract has a greater amount of commentary.
6. ____ They have different levels of explanatory depth (or complexity of contents), as seen in the use of grammar, discourse style and register.

These sets of tasks sketch out some ideas to create tailor-made materials and what to consider when developing materials. As such, they ought to be taken as a starting point for the creation of learning or training materials that assist the development of the range of literacies discussed in Chapter 5. The tasks are based solely on the corpus data and survey-based data collected for the present book. As Feak (2011) recommends, good materials need to be tested and improved in order to ensure quality standards, timeliness and, above all, effectiveness.

This genre-based approach can also draw on the individuals' experiences accumulated in writing practices. Tasks can be proposed putting into practice 'strategies of interdiscursive connectivity' (Salö, 2015; Salö and Hanell, 2014) based on the assumption that prior knowledge of languages, genres, modes and semiotic elements can scaffold the composing process of other genres, both written, spoken and mixed (written and spoken). The materials designer should take into account the progression of task complexity in terms of length, depth of analysis and skills development when creating materials based on operational genre transferability.

The genre-based approach described previously is designed to offer rich input and exposure to authentic data through DDL, based on both large- and small-scale specialised corpora (T. Johns, 1991; Tribble, 2001). In doing so, the tasks aim to prompt an understanding of how genres enact social actions and to elicit reflection on the challenges and opportunities of each individual's multilingual repertoire, as I noted in the first section of this chapter. This means that all the tasks can be approached in one or more languages to best cater to the individuals' plurilingual research communication needs. Multilingual genre learning widens the perspective of how languages and language repertoires intersect with genred activity and can raise awareness of the dynamic model of bilingualism, according to which prior knowledge of the rhetorical form of genres is transposable to different languages and hence assists researchers when composing texts (Gentil, 2011, 2017; Linares, 2019). A further argument to support multilingual genre learning is North and Piccardo's (2016) claim that the relevance of mediation 'is not confined to the teaching of foreign/second languages. Rather, an interpretation of mediation more in line with educational literature within and beyond the language field leads to a definition of mediation competencies that are potentially relevant to all types and contexts of language use' (North and Piccardo, 2016: 13).

6.2 Digital learning

Online learning environments seem apposite for several reasons. First, by relying on sophisticated technological platforms and other affordances on the Internet, the aforementioned modules can be implemented and further developed to support different stages and aspects of multilingual genre learning. These platforms also enable personalised learning itineraries that should be conveniently monitored and assisted by an LAP instructor or coach. Secondly, they pose no fixed learning or training time constraints. Massive Open Online Courses (MOOCs), Open Course Ware (OCW) courses and open-source learning platforms such as Moodle and Blackboard enable flexible timetables, foster independence and provide specific targets to cater to each individual's needs and preferences (Crawford Camiciottoli, 2018). Thirdly, online learning sites and educational technologies also offer the possibility to network with other participants in the virtual learning community, as illustrated further. Moreover, the technological architectures make it possible to expand the tasks in terms of content, approach and meaningful activities. By way of illustration, I provide a list of extended tasks that can be implemented in these platforms to support classroom learning and independent, self-directed learning processes (Table 6.1).

Up to this point, I have sought to illustrate some corpus-informed and DDL learning tasks – analysis of corpus extracts, analysis of concordance lines – that can prepare the ground for developing analytical and critical thinking and engage those interested in subsequent text-composing practice. Creative use of technologies seems germane considering that digital competence is one of the crucial skills to engage in online research communication, both for professional – above all, research publication – purposes and public understanding of science.

6.2.1 Hands-on learning

In the past decades, the literature has reported the use of several technological applications that support genre-based pedagogies in educational platforms. As I argue elsewhere (2017: 51), while indirect applications of corpora are employed by materials writers, direct applications provide 'hands-on corpus experiences for language learners and language instructors so that both groups experience direct interactions with corpora findings'. The DDL approach described by Johns (1991) nowadays relies on sophisticated technology-learning tools that bring with them important benefits. From the perspective of SLA theory, Chapelle (2001) underlines the language-learning potential of computer applications by noting that they enable teachers and/or instructors to focus on form and to adapt the level of difficulties to individual characteristics and dominant learning styles. Like Chapelle (2001: 37), I would argue here that another important learning benefit is their utility in identifying systematic patterns of language use and register variation.

Table 6.1 Extended tasks for assisting online multilingual genre learning

Proposed genre(s) under focus	Aim of extended tasks	Proposed tasks
Genres and regimes of research assessment	To further develop and reinforce the dynamics of genres in contexts of research assessment policies favouring certain genres and places for publication (Tusting, 2018). To raise further awareness of social action of genres.	• Tasks eliciting practice on manuscript editing (as a reference source, see Mišák, Marušić and Marušić, 2005)[a] • Analytical tasks on peer-review genres (reviewers' reports and responses to reviewers' reports)[a] • Critical-thinking tasks based on analysis of alternative metrics (annotations, views metrics, downloads, likes, comments, etc.)
Remediated and emerging digital genres	To recognise the plurality of semiotic codes for meaning making. To further raise awareness of research process-oriented genres and on the exigences of scientific research practice. To practice strategies of genre transmediality, for example, recontextualisation of specialist contents. To practice mediation strategies (North and Piccardo, 2016: 22). This can include 'linking to previous knowledge, amplifying text, streamlining text, restructuring text in appropriate discourse culture, breaking down complicated information, visually representing information, adjusting language' (cf. also Maier and Engberg, 2019).	• Tasks involving text-composing of remediated genres incorporating multimodal elements (e.g., embedded videos, video abstracts, visualised experiments) • Analytical tasks on remediated genres related to research practice (e.g., open laboratory notebooks) • Tasks involving the creation of a podcast or videocast accompanying an online journal article[a] • Tasks involving text-composing of three-minute thesis dissertations[a] • Critical-thinking tasks on registered reports (e.g., those freely available in Zotero library www.zotero.org/groups/479248/osf/collections/KEJP68G9)

Genres for public communication of science	• To raise further awareness of the use of visuals for making complex information more comprehensible (Ostergren, 2013: 37–45). • To develop skills by creating effective visuals, that is, maximising reliance on visual perception and minimising demands on working memory by excluding redundant information and maximising retention and recall (Ostergren, 2013: 54–57). • To further increase awareness of and engage in 'co-construction of meaning in interaction' in social-media interactions.	• Analytical and text-composing tasks involving multimodal composing of digital science documentaries (Jones and Hafner, 2012), approaching content, interactivity, multimedia, hyperlinking aspects • Analytical and critical-thinking tasks involving text-composing of microblogs or blog posts[a] • Analytical and critical-thinking tasks on promotional videos for research-group websites[a] • Analytical and critical-thinking tasks on academic social networking sites • Critical-thinking tasks on TED-talks and Google talks
Ecologies of genres	• To further practice language and register features (e.g., discourse features such as active or passive verbs, negation, parentheticals and hedges for speculation, boosters for conveying promotion, etc.) across genre assemblages. • To reflect further on the role of a personal voice in relation to the degree of explanatory depth. • To further practice skills in visual rhetoric and 'visual cultures of science' (Pauwels, 2006). The ecological view offers possibilities to address critically issues of language choice, language loss and disappearance, as well as polylanguaging in digital genre assemblages.	• Analytical and critical-thinking tasks involving proposal-writing strategies (Ding, 2008) • Tasks involving critical analysis of hyperlinked genres in citizen science platforms[a] • Tasks involving critical analysis of hyperlinked genres in research-group blogs[a] • Critical-thinking task on journal policies www .enago.com/academy/exploring-video-journals-an-interview-with-latest-thinking/ • Critical-thinking tasks on research dissemination practices using academic and social-media networking sites (cf. Luzón and Pérez-Llantada, forthcoming)[a] • Tasks involving analysis of storytelling techniques, use of narrative focalisers (Hyland, 2018; Mehlenbacher, 2017) and ways of constructing strong identities in crowdsourcing science projects (Paulus and Roberts, 2018)[a]

[a] Can involve multilingual production practice.

Some of the awareness-raising and critical-thinking tasks described earlier in this chapter illustrate this point. Tribble (2001: 391) proposes tasks based on keyword analysis and concordance lines to examine different levels of linguistic analysis, namely, lexico-grammatical features, analysis of text-pattern and structural interpretation of the text-genre. 'Concgramming,' a computer-driven approach proposed by Greaves and Warren (2007), can be done through computer-assisted hands-on tasks that involve the automatic identification of the phraseological profile to identify the 'aboutness' of a text or sets of texts. Yoon (2011: 30) also notes that the use of concordancing for LAP writing development enhances learner autonomy. Some of the aforementioned tasks displayed the use of corpus-driven data of phraseology and collocations to raise awareness of features of expert discourse such as lexical density (e.g., the 'nounness' of the texts) and syntactic complexity in expert-to-expert research genres. Römer (2011) advocates this approach for direct classroom applications of specialised language corpora. Free software like *Antconc* (Anthony, 2019), *FireAnt* (Anthony and Hardaker, 2017) and *KfNgram* (Fletcher, 2002–2007) are useful electronic tools for n-gram analysis and for keyword and concordance analysis.

Further benefits of instructional intervention using web-based tools can be found in the literature. For example, regarding blended learning environments, that is, environments involving online learning and face-to-face interaction, Shih (2011: 832) proposes collaborative learning requiring students 'to post their writing assignments on Facebook, assess the writings of other group members, and then provide them feedback and comments on Facebook weekly'. This author highlights the positive effect of integrating Facebook and peer assessment to improve skills and knowledge aspects of content, text organisation and genre in L2 essay writing at an undergraduate level. Using genre-based online pedagogy, Mort and Drury (2012) report positive responses from students' participation in a writing module-based course that provided online support (examples, reinforcement exercises and teacher feedback) as well as guidelines to raise awareness and develop skills in report writing. In addition, it has been argued that hands-on corpus compilation tasks for EAP students provide handy exemplars of the repertoire of genres specific to each individual's disciplinary field. For example, Charles (2018: 16, see also 2012, 2015) emphasises the value of corpus compilation for PhD thesis editing purposes, both to better grasp aspects of content and reinforce knowledge of text organisation as well as to become acquainted with discipline-specific phraseology and its functionality at a discourse level.

6.2.2 Computer-supported collaborative learning

In previous chapters I underlined the crucial role of collaborative work and networked communication in the research world. For example, in the introduction, I mentioned the role of collaboration in relation to the mobility of skilled populations (Guthrie et al., 2017). We have also seen in previous chapters that collaborative work has privileged English as the main lingua franca of science among researchers worldwide (Pérez-Llantada, 2012) and that professional networking related, for instance, to the production of international co-authorship in journal articles is highly valued (e.g., the International collaboration index, National Science Foundation. Science and engineering indicators 2016). In Chapter 2 we have seen that one of the main bibliometric indicators for international collaboration is cross-border co-authorship, and Chapter 3 has introduced Web 2.0 as a major driver of physical and virtual research networking, collaboration and distribution of scientific knowledge. Moving beyond expert-to-expert communication, Chapter 3 has also underlined the importance of collaboration between researchers and the broad publics in citizen science projects as a response to social exigences such as the democratisation of science (Follett and Strezov, 2015). Chapter 4 has delved into the language dynamics of collaborative work to raise issues of language contact, language diversity and language variation and change, while in Chapter 5 we have seen how disciplines are engaging more and more in collaborative work to solve global challenges. Moreover, I noted earlier that transdisciplinary research sustains collaboration among researchers, businesses and companies (Trachtenberg et al., 2016). At present, there is unprecedented collaboration at the time of the Covid-19 pandemic to face one of the world's biggest health challenges: to understand the rapid spread of the virus and its 'ferocious rampage through the body' (Wadman et al., 2020) and to find an effective vaccine in the shortest possible timeline.

Therefore, it seems germane to support learning or training experiences with collaborative opportunities that can enhance professional development. Some inspiring strategies for developing teamwork skills can be found in the EAP literature. For example, the use of an online forum is highly valued as a pedagogical tool to construct knowledge collaboratively in an undergraduate student class (Kuteeva, 2007). The wiki and the blog, both described by Myers (2010) as digital genres that support new and easily publishable forms of conversation on the web, also prove helpful in learning environments to engage multicultural classes in collaborative work. In an exploratory case study, Kuteeva (2016) reports that a task involving the creation of wiki pages, in the undergraduates' view, helped them in organising the contents and structuring the text, in handling audiovisual elements and hyperlinks and in identifying the functionality of reader-oriented metadiscourse resources for constructing effective arguments. McGrath (2016) reports on the use of interactive tools – namely, thread comments posted by blog participants – to collaboratively draft and revise an open-access co-authored research article. Hafner and Miller (2011) and Jones and Hafner (2012) also propose collaborative tasks to develop digital literacies through multimodal composing of science documentaries in an undergraduate science course. As these authors put it, collaborative learning activities involving the creation of digital stories develop the students' digital literacies and their autonomy as learners. They further note that they raise their awareness of features of the genre, a blend of 'rhetorical and linguistic features characteristic of highly authoritative scientific genres such as the research article or dissertation...with those more typical of popularizations of science' (p. 72) as well as their awareness of peer collaboration as a way of addressing complex projects, in this case, creating a science documentary. I do not know to what extent these experiences can be fruitful for expert researchers at advanced stages of literacy development, but they may indeed be helpful for PhD students and novice researchers who may find technological tools for multimodal composing effective and, at the same time, motivating.

6.2.3 Cloud-based learning

In investigating communication in social networks, Buck (2012: 10) contends that 'digital literacy practices must be seen within larger systems of literate activity and larger literacy ecologies'. Buck's claim also applies to genre-based approaches, as these need to convey the view of genres as mechanisms embedded in literate activity and constructs that entail multiliteracies (see Chapter 5). Cloud-based learning environments can be very supportive of genre-based approaches seeking to implement DDL, hands-on learning and computer-based collaborative learning. All of them are types of learning that can be easily embedded in the web environment. Cloud-based platforms such as Moodle and Blackboard (widely used in educational settings) or Grovo (a widely used staff-training platform for delivering professional development courses) can keep learning on the go in a flexible way. Moreover, the architecture of these platforms is dynamic in the sense that new and/or supplementary course contents can be designed and options for individualised learning can be set while the course is running. These platforms also contain various educational tools to host virtual training sessions, forums and links to social media. They can also be the most suitable option for researchers in advanced stages of their careers who can opt for self-directed, independent learning. An added advantage of these platforms is the possibility to create templates, for example, for illustrating points and for text-composing practices. The use of tools such as programmes, templates and rubrics, links to resources and so on should always be assisted by the course instructor or supervisor. Increasingly popular technologies in learning (e.g., MOOCs and OCW courses) afford similar possibilities, including embedding of video tutorials, exercises for practising genre identification and genre composing and online chats for interacting with the tutor(s) and other course participants.

In the case of research communication learning or training, our main target populations are groups of researchers (with specific genre learning or training needs) and individuals who need or want to engage in self-directed learning (see the following section). Personalised learning itineraries carefully designed by the LAP instructor and recommended entry points to access the course materials should be based on a previous language and communication needs analysis. Again, it is the role of the LAP instructor to conduct this analysis before the start of the course. It should also be noted that the tasks sketched out earlier address only written communication. However, given the increasing reliance on digital multimodal genres and social media for expert and public communication of science, the spoken mode, not addressed in this book for reasons of space, should gain ground in pedagogical or training endeavours. Cloud-based technologies can facilitate ways of supplementing the aforementioned tasks with extended tasks and further contents and materials to enhance spoken communication needs.

6.3 Self-directed learning

As an alternative form of training, self-directed learning is one type of learning in which the individual can set his or her own learning goals. In the self-directed learning approach, the individual is also involved in the process of materials selection, in the decision-making process of the lesson (stages, methodological procedures and learning outcomes) and in the evaluation of learning (Quality Improvement Scheme).[2]

---

[2] www.europeansharedtreasure.eu/detail.php?id_project_base=2011-1-BG1-GRU06-04962 [last accessed on 20 June 2020].

This form of learning is suitable for supporting adult language education and, in the research world, to support an individual's interests, needs, strengths and challenges in using languages for communicating science. Evaluation of learning can be done through regular self-assessment of the individual's language and communicative performance. Self-assessment tools such as writing guidelines, rubrics, competence descriptors, self-assessment grids, individual (e-)portfolios and learning diaries, to name a few, can be useful for supporting the independent learning process (Hafner and Miller, 2011). Because they enable to check one's progress, they are key in independent study. The assessment methods that I would propose for LAP formal instruction, namely, e-portfolios of multiliteracies and plurilingual e-portfolios of genre assemblages (including a variety of tasks showcasing an individual's genre knowledge, rhetorical, multimodal and intercultural competences in two or more languages, as well as reflections on the degree of achievement in those tasks), can also be used as self-assessment tools in self-directed learning as long as detailed rubrics are provided. Moreover, effective self-directed learning approaches draw on tools such as regular feedback questionnaires with which learners can give their opinion on the usefulness of the materials, tasks, tools and self-assessment tools on the management of the learning programme, on the human resources (specialised support staff, i.e., instructors or advisers giving assistance with learning) and on material resources, specifically, their availability and adaptability to the potential users.

In e-learning contexts, both the individual and the instructor are co-participants in the design and development of a personalised learning itinerary. With the appropriate monitoring and assistance of the LAP instructor, self-directed learning experiences based on DDL using small-scale specialised corpora can cater to each individual's communication training needs. As advocated by Yoon (2011: 130) and others (Charles, 2012, 2018; T. Johns, 1991), corpora as reference tools and concordancing for identification and critical analysis of language use are 'tools' with significant potential to 'increase learner autonomy'. As explained in the literature, self-directed learning not only fosters the individual's autonomy but also triggers metacognition, that is, an individual's understanding of the way he or she learns (Bazerman, 1994; Beaufort, 2007), as well as self-efficacy in writing processes and self-regulation of learning and performance. For Rounsaville, Goldberg and Bawarshi (2008: 98), metacognition is defined as

the ability to seek and reflect on connections between contexts, to abstract from skills and knowledge, to know what prior resources to draw on and what new resources to seek, and to be rhetorically astute and agile are all hallmark strategies that effective writers bring with them to any new writing context.

If we recall the concepts of inter-genre-ality (Devitt, 2004, 2009) and interdiscursivity (Salö and Hanell, 2014), we see that both actually relate to strategies of metacognition and self-efficacy (i.e., the individual's approach to different communicative scenarios). Negretti and McGrath (2018) convincingly demonstrate that, through appropriate learning tasks, a genre-based approach can scaffold both genre knowledge and metacognition.

6.4 Becoming ethnographers

In Chapter 5 I discussed some possible scenarios for situated learning in today's research world. In a world of changing genres and constantly evolving and emerging forms of communication, lifelong learning becomes a necessity. In this sense, informal learning of genre knowledge through participation and observation of the communicative situations that occur within the community can be an important source of information on researchers' genred activity. In my view, it is essential to encourage novice researchers to assume the role of ethnographers so as to explore conventions, writing processes and motivations behind genre uptake. As the seminal literature reports (Berkenkotter and Huckin, 1995; Johns, 1997), participating in the community group can provide many opportunities to become acquainted with the repertoire of genres and the established genre hierarchies and to understand the mediatory role of genres and languages in the researchers' professional activity.

Further, a perceptive 'ethnographer' can find opportunities to identify the communicative goals and target audiences of genre assemblages or aggregates of genres that are formed in online environments. Through observation of literate action, it is possible to become perceptive of different ways of using language, genre and discourse conventions. Becoming an ethnographer can also offer opportunities to become acquainted with language varieties and aspects of register variation according to situational contexts, as defined in Hallidayan linguistics (Halliday and Martin, 1993). Awareness of register variation in relation to translingual practices is a useful way of thinking about diversity in languaging and language diversities (Shohamy, 2017) and the use of multisemiotic resources (Pennycook, 2018) when using digital genres to target multilingual audiences.

In observing the world of research genres at the level of the community of practice, an individual ethnographer can also become aware of the specific 'repertoires', that is, sets of genres used by a community to fulfil all its communication needs (Devitt, 2009; Orlikowski and Yates, 1994). Becoming acquainted with the opportunities and challenges Web 2.0 communication poses to peers and other members of an individual's disciplinary community can prompt awareness of one's strengths and challenges posed by online communication. As an example, regarding online social-media practices, Buck (2012: 10) notes that doctoral students find it challenging to construct their writer's identity and self-representation in blogging practices (see also Mewburn and Thomson, 2013). Additionally, the web itself offers myriad opportunities to learn from other researchers and from their practices, views and values regarding research communication. Earlier, for instance, we discussed participating in ASNSs as an informal way of learning about the dynamic nature of digital genres (see, e.g., Jeng et al., 2017) and 'the functional versatility of genres' for research communication (Giltrow and Stein, 2009: 9).

Berkenkotter and Huckin (1995), Johns (1997) and Swales (2004) also point out that a way of becoming acquainted with disciplinary genres is through engagement in collaborative research projects and cooperation with peers. This can be done both in the local setting and with peers cross-nationally. Observation of senior researchers' discipline-specific practices can give indications of, for example, what they publish and what language choices they make, what their influential publications mean to them and what collaboration networks they are involved in and why. Specifically, it would be useful for novice researchers to keep a diary or a record of observed practices in context and become critical towards aspects of genre-mediated multilingual practices. Johns (1997) encouraged students 'to investigate and reflect upon the academic texts, roles and contexts they encounter'. Observation of literate action can help understand 'the tremendous power of the typification processes and the specific role of written genres in forming our modern way of life and our modern systems of knowledge' (Bazerman, 2015: 83).

6.5 LAP teacher professional development

Following Feak (2011), in this chapter I have tried to explain my reasoning behind the proposed tasks and the theoretical considerations that lie beneath them, first and foremost, the cycle of rhetorical consciousness-raising (Feak and Swales, 2010; Swales and Feak, 2009a). That said, underpinning any effective learning or training in the competences and skills defined previously, there lies the role of the language professionals and LAP practitioners. With some exceptions (e.g., Trappes-Lomax and Ferguson, 2002), this is a role that is not always sufficiently discussed in the literature with regard to teacher training and professional development.

The critical roles of LAP teachers discussed in, for example, Casanave and Vandrick (2002), Feak and Swales (2010), Johns (1991) and Swales (1990, 2004) remain, to date, very much the same. What seems to have changed with the current and fast-changing social, technological and educational scenarios is the greater depth of knowledge and skills required for teaching or training research communication. In this last section, I provide some thoughts along these lines by adapting the Eaquals Framework for Language Teacher Training and Development (TD Framework hereafter) (Eaquals, 2016[3]) to LAP in the STEMM areas. The aim of the TD Framework is to provide 'an overview of the main training and experience, competences, and professionalism of language teachers at six successive phases in their [professional] development' (Eaquals, 2016: 4). The TDFram covers course and materials design (planning teaching and learning), implementation of pedagogical intervention (teaching and supporting learning), assessment of effectiveness of the intervention (assessment of learning), teacher knowledge and skills in intercultural communication (language, communication and culture) and LAP teachers' professional development (the teacher as a professional). Although this framework distinguishes three developmental phases (beginner, intermediate and expert), here I make no distinction, as I just propose a preliminary framework for teacher training in languages for research communication purposes. Table 6.2 summarises the main areas and key knowledge and skills that, in my experience and considering the evidence given in this book, would be required to support LAP teachers' professional development, both in their role of instructors in formal teaching or learning contexts and in their role of advisers in self-directed learning processes.[4] Although this table mainly draws on the TD Framework descriptors, I include some additional descriptors considering the specificity of teaching or learning professional and public communication of science using a genre-based approach.

---

[3] Available online at www.eaquals.org/our-expertise/teacher-development/the-eaquals-framework-for-teacher-training-and-development/ [last accessed on 21 September 2020].

[4] See also BALEAP Competency Framework for Teachers of English for Academic Purposes, which offers very useful guidelines for EAP teacher professional development available at https://www.baleap.org/wp-content/uploads/2016/04/teap-competency-framework.pdf [last accessed on 21 September 2020].

Table 6.2 Descriptors of LAP teacher competences

Main area	Sub-section	Knowledge of	Skills in
Planning teaching and learning	Learner needs and learning processes	• Possible language and communication needs and ways of making learners aware of them	• Designing procedures to find out about learners' genre-learning needs and setting relevant learning objectives • Helping less-experienced teachers to anticipate and take learners' needs into account in designing the course tasks
	Lesson aims and outcomes	• A wide range of aspects of genre, rhetoric and communication: text types and genres; levels of language (phraseology, discourse and register); aspects of rhetoric; genre as social action • The way academic and research languages work at different levels of formality across cultural settings	• Linking language and communication skills development with real-life needs • Analysing and developing plans for teaching all aspects of genres for academic and research communication • Providing guidance to less-experienced teachers in developing lesson aims that match the learners' needs
	The lesson tasks and materials	• Techniques to raise awareness and critical-thinking skills and to prompt writing practice activities, interaction patterns • The cognitive demands of the task • A wide range of strategies for lifelong learning	• Selecting and creating materials based on authentic genre exemplars • Assisting less-experienced teachers in selecting materials and resources and planning tasks and activities

Teaching and supporting learning	Teaching methodology	• Theories and applications of genre and task-based learning and the rhetorical consciousness-raising cycle	• Evaluating the effectiveness of the methodology and creatively deploying and combining task-based genre learning with other techniques (group work)
	Resources and materials	• The theories and rationale(s) behind the design and sequencing of the tasks, including digital and web-based media • The functionality of genres and text types	• Adapting published materials and resources, including digital resources • Evaluating the suitability of the materials, taking into account changing language and communication needs • Mentoring and guiding colleagues in selecting, adapting and designing materials • Developing and managing online learning management platforms (e.g., Moodle) in a blended learning context
	Interacting with learners	• Applications of classroom discourse analysis in observation and self-observation • The appropriate metalanguage relevant to providing explanations and clarifications	• Writing clear instructions and teacher's notes for tasks to be managed by other colleagues • Guiding them in ways of familiarising learners with the essential metalanguage
	Using digital media	• Theories of corpus linguistics and applications of corpora (e.g., DDL) • Multimodal texts and visual rhetoric • Academic and social media networks	• Creating tasks from corpus data • Using corpus linguistics tools (e.g., concordancing) and software for multimodal text-composing

(continued)

Table 6.2 (*cont.*)

Main area	Sub-section	Knowledge of	Skills in
		• Learning management systems (LMS) that support independent and self-directed learning	• Showing colleagues how to exploit large- and small-scale corpora. • Designing blended learning modules using an LMS (e.g., Moodle).
	Monitoring learning	• Research in the acquisition of genre and academic literacy • Main conclusions from research on second-language writing and biliteracy genre-based learning	• Listening actively to learners and advising them on difficulties and ways of addressing them • Advising colleagues on techniques for monitoring learning, giving feedback and assisting learners in their difficulties
Assessment of learning	Impact of assessment on learning	• Ways of giving useful feedback and giving support to individual genre and literacy development processes	• Analysing and evaluating the most effective approach to feedback for individualized learning
Language, communication and culture	Giving models and guidance	• Bi/multilingual literacy development theories	• Providing exposure to bi/multilingual genre exemplars and eliciting comparison of genres across languages and academic writing cultures
	Handling cultural issues	• Similarities and differences among academic writing cultures • Relevant theories and approaches to big and small cultures	• Prompting critical reflection of academic cultures and cultural issues • Prompting critical reflection on issues of culture in relation to digital genres and context collapse

The teacher as a professional	Collaborative development		• Contributing to the professional development of other teachers through coaching or mentoring • Providing informed views when consulted on professional and institutional policies, processes, etc.
	Conducting applied linguistics research (new)	• Relevant theories on applied linguistics and SLA research (e.g., action research and the like) • Software for quantitative and qualitative research	• Collecting, analysing and interpreting data for applied linguistics research[a] • Designing tools and protocols for data collection • Using software
	Conducting genre analysis research (new)	• Relevant theories on genres as social structures, specialised discourse and register, rhetoric and multimodal communication • Relevant theories on genres and digital communication • Software for quantitative and qualitative research	• Collecting, analysing and interpreting (through relevant frameworks) data for applied linguistics research[a] • Designing tools and protocols for data collection • Using software

[a] Exactly as in the Eaquals TD Framework.
Source: Adapted from general language teacher descriptors of the Eaquals Framework for Language Teacher Training & Development (Eaquals, 2016).

As shown in Table 6.2, the descriptors are mainly associated with an expert LAP teacher profile, as well as with knowledge of theories and skills in planning materials design, managing learning, monitoring learning processes and assessing learning outcomes. In fact, these areas have been extensively discussed in EAP/LAP fora. It is also worth noting in Table 6.2 one facet that has been much less often described in the literature and that, in my experience as an LAP practitioner for over thirty years, has proved to be very valuable. It is competence in research. Empirically grounded research data are always useful to inform the creation of tasks and the selection and creation of learning materials and resources to best cater to the researchers' specific language and communication needs. Information from research data provides a solid base from which to assess the scope of tasks, the effectiveness of learning materials, resources and assessment types and the quality of the teacher's explanations and individual feedback along the way. This approach is, in my view, most relevant, since the world of genres is subject to ongoing social changes and technological developments. Chen and Flowerdew (2018: 43) sagely observe that while this area of research inquiry provides insights useful for gaining knowledge of genres and taking this knowledge on board to design materials and resources, often these studies offer 'concrete pedagogical suggestions that do not seem to have been driven by pedagogical needs or grounded in pedagogical realities'. Some exceptions can be found in research published in *English for Specific Purposes, Journal of English for Academic Purposes, Journal of Second Language Writing, Language Learning and Technology* and *ELT Journal* and works mentioned in this chapter to illustrate SLA-related action and empirical classroom-based research. Another area for further enquiry, as hinted elsewhere (Pérez-Llantada and Swales, 2017: 52), is the extent to which handling multilingual specialised corpora outside of the classroom 'has potential to develop independent learning and life-long learning skills – e.g., researching skills, preparation of essays, manuscripts, revision and self-assessment of one's own writing' and leads to 'an enhanced consciousness of and sensitivity to the forms and functions of language' (Carter, 2003: 64).

In closing, it remains to be said that at the core of a genre-based pedagogy should be the teachers' 'commitment to promoting linguistic diversity, plurilingualism and pluriculturalism, and respect for varieties of language' (Eaquals, 2016: 8). I tend to think that such a commitment can trigger awareness of language forms, functions and varieties characterising today's research communication.

6.6 Chapter summary

In this chapter I have sought to illustrate how findings from both corpus research and exploratory qualitative research can help inform and develop teaching proposals. I have also proposed a pedagogical approach that takes on board genres and languages, the fluidity of both and ongoing evolution, innovation and change. I have also illustrated how Web 2.0 can support researchers and LAP practitioners to cater to diversified learning or training needs in both formal and self-directed types of learning.

7 *The Way Ahead*

The broad aim of this book has been to discuss the development of genres associated with unprecedented technological advances and echoing Blommaert, Collins and Slembrouck (2005) with spaces for multilingualism. Specifically, the book has provided a descriptive and critical account of genre evolution and innovation in multilingual genre-mediated activity, highlighting the intersection of digital discourses and multilingual practices in local and global science communication. One important remark that should be made is that global genre diversity in today's research world is very hard to capture. In this book I have only looked at a small part of it, the world of STEMM disciplines. Its fast-evolving nature is intrinsically related to the complex agendas underpinning global and local research knowledge production and dissemination. It should also be noted that although such global diversity has been approached from the perspective of ecologies of genres, there are ostensible divergences in the academic and research ecosystem. I have also used the term 'ecologies' of genres, in the plural, to refer to genre assemblages formed by extensions of genres interrelated to remediated genres, reflecting increasing generification and the rich diversity of literate action across communities of practice. In this last chapter, I draw several conclusions, propose some areas for future research and, in closing, offer some final reflections on research methods that can support more methodologically robust enquiry into research genres across languages.

7.1 The evolutionary nature of genres

In the opening remarks of this book, I declared my intention to provide an updated view of the research world in a broader context, discuss emerging constellations of genres and bring genre analysis closer to contemporary issues while taking on board issues of multilingualism and linguistic diversity. Accordingly, I have aimed to

provide a general view of genred-activity in rapidly changing sociological and technological contexts and to start an empirically informed
scholarly conversation on genres and multilingual science
communication, putting the focus on facets of genre exemplars beyond
the sentence level and tracing uses of language, issues of lingua franca,
languaging phenomena and multiliterate practices. This section wraps
up the main theoretical and methodological arguments raised in the
previous chapters concerning the evolutionary nature of genres. It also
sets up an agenda for future joint research on research genres and
languages of science.

In identifying some core issues and crucial gaps in accounts of
genres and languages, I have demonstrated how genre theory can
cover a broad spectrum of text exemplars, textual dimensions, social
contexts and agendas. The theoretical considerations on genre evolution and change, along with corpus and ethnomethodological data,
lend support to Bakhtin's (1986b: 61) claim that the entire repertoire
of genres '*grows* as the particular sphere [of human activity] develops
and becomes *more complex*' (my emphasis). Moving the Swalesian
tradition forward, I hope I have been able to illustrate the social
demands that motivate the remediation of traditional genres and that
have triggered the emergence of add-on genres, parascientific genres
and other genre innovations. Throughout, I have emphasised how
internet affordances support the formation of complex genre assemblages of various types (genre sets, systems, repertoires and ecologies)
that combine different systems of meaning (visual, verbal and aural).
I have also discussed the functionalities of the intertextual and hypermodal (hypertextual and multimodal) linkages in genre assemblages.
The previous chapters have showcased that even if traditional genres,
now remediated genres, are relatively stable, being 'a conventional
category of discourse based in large-scale typification of rhetorical
action' (Miller, 1984: 161), they may further evolve to a certain extent
as a result of new social demands, such as a greater need for science
reproducibility and transparency (Schulson, 2018). Besides, I have
argued that large-scale characterisation of new online genres remains,
to date, problematic. These genres have not fully stabilised and have
not yet become completely sedimented within the STEMM scientific
community – at least not as much as traditional genres such as journal
articles, abstracts, PhD dissertations and research grants have done.
Besides, I have shown that while some of the genres that have emerged
and expanded the existing ecology of genres have proved transient
(e.g., audioslides), others have eventually stabilised (e.g., research
blogs). As Miller (1984: 161) puts it, a genre only 'acquires meaning
from situation and from the social context in which that situation

arose'. For this reason, I have aimed to provide descriptive, and not prescriptive, characterisations of genres, trying to emphasise their dynamic nature and openness to innovation and ongoing evolution.

The empirically grounded perspective taken in this book lends credence to the idea that genre analytical approaches, either top-down or bottom-up (Swales, 2004: 72–73), allow us to identify the main textual features that characterise today's research genres. Several genre exemplars have been described by looking at different text-linguistic dimensions (e.g., indices of lexical density and diversity, syntactic complexity, recurring phraseology and grammar features) for the identification of registers and discourse styles. A genre analytical approach has also proved insightful for determining the discourse organisation of these exemplars at both meso (i.e., rhetorical move analysis) and macro levels (i.e., overall rhetorical organisation of the information conveyed in the text). Analogies and concepts borrowed from literary criticism have proved helpful to understand how reme- diated genres and their associated genres are interrelated. We have also seen that genres often work in conjunction to fulfil multiple communicative goals (e.g., articles and their associated short texts, abstracts, graphical abstracts and author summaries or methodology articles and their corresponding video methods articles, to name a few). I have given evidence that the world of research genres has changed as a result of the way researchers can access, share infor- mation and interact with their audiences using Web 2.0. Additionally, the genre lens has also allowed us to address multisemiotic meaning- making in online texts supplemented with web-mediated extensions of science reporting (e.g., enhanced publications, as described in Gross and Buehl, 2016). Lastly, I have critically discussed multimodal digital genres for professional and public communication of science (e.g., graphical abstracts and citizen science projects) and explored recurrent patterns of language(s) use, discourse strategies and rhetoric, covering a wide range of written practices ranging from registered reports (Mehlenbacher, 2019a) to blog posting and microblogging (Büchi, 2016; Mauranen, 2013).

In addition to enquiring into 'end-products', in this book I have also tentatively explored the processes of composing genre texts and offered several considerations regarding, for example, the creation of digital generic hybrids from antecedent genres in both high-stakes science, expert-to-expert science and public communication of science (e.g., the case of graphical abstracts, registered reports and crowd- funding projects). I have also aimed to approach the analysis of aspects of generic hybridisation by considering processes of genre transmedi- ality (Engberg and Maier, 2015; Maier and Engberg, 2019). Lastly, in addition to end-texts and processes, I have addressed transformative practice to contend that the traditional view of genres as mechanisms that act within highly articulated social systems (Berkenkotter and Huckin, 1995) can be applied to the emerging forms of communication in the STEMM fields. Notwithstanding the limitations of the small-scale exploratory surveys conducted for the present book, the insiders' perspective has proved supportive of Miller's (1984: 161) claim that 'a genre is a rhetorical means for mediating private intentions and social exigence; it motivates by connecting the private with the public, the singular with the recurrent'. In this respect, the emic approach tentatively suggested that researchers' choice of genres and languages is constrained by socioeconomic, geolinguistic and policy (institutional, national and supranational) agendas, as well as by individuals' interests and motivations. Because these multifaceted agendas may change over time, we can expect to witness further expansion of the genre repertoire and evolution of the ecology (and ecologies) of research genres.

7.2 Ecological diversity

In Chapter 2 and throughout this book, I have contended that genres, even prototypical ones, are open to change because they are highly context-based and situated constructs. The corpus-informed discussions of the previous chapters have also highlighted the dynamism of genres and, in Giltrow and Stein's (2009) words, their capacity to arrive on the scene in response to new social demands. Analyses of remediated genres, add-on genres, open-access genres and parascientific genres have illustrated such openness and dynamism in various ways and exemplified the range of linguistic and rhetorical resources that these genres deploy in response to the collapsing of contexts on the web. In the era of growing interconnectivity and, assuming a plausible deflation rather than conflation of mobility in the current troublesome times, with voices from economists suggesting an upcoming process of deglobalisation (Irwin, 2020), the inevitable conclusion is that genres and Web 2.0 will become the prevailing means to share, exchange, disseminate and advance scientific knowledge. A 'notable quotable' posted on 22 April 2020 in a *Nature* briefing by research-policy manager Elizabeth Gadd exemplifies the functionality of the web in this respect, specifically the recognition for open and more shareable and transparent science: 'The virus is reminding us that the purpose of scholarly communication is not to allocate credit for career advancement, and neither is it to keep publishers afloat'. It would be naive to believe that credit and merit are unimportant to scientists today when we see that scientific journals have created a space in their websites with open-access articles and shareable data on Covid-19 and when we witness an extremely competitive race for a vaccine on a global scale. Notwithstanding personal satisfaction and love for science, whether we like it or not, credit and merit lead to academic rewards and recognition and, above all, greater possibilities for funding.

Given the aforementioned considerations, one could predict that the journal article, the research genre par excellence, together with other genres such as abstracts, grant proposals and related occluded genres (reviewer reports, response to reviewers, etc.) will remain core genres in the existing ecology, with open-access gaining much more ground. Constellating around these major genres, genre innovations enhancing contents and 'asset-value' will possibly remain on the scene (short summaries, author summaries or graphical abstracts, to name a few). In effect, new ecologies of genres will be created, forming complex genre networks or macrogenres that should be looked at in future research. At the same time, we can anticipate if not greater, then at least sustained, use of preprint repositories and archives along with use of other media options – for example, personal home pages, research-group websites, Facebook pages and Twitter accounts – for achieving greater visibility and impact. Considering the emic perspective discussed in previous chapters, we can also expect that collaboration and formal or informal discussions among expert-to-expert researchers will continue to be assisted by electronic communication and academic social networking sites. While, surely, more sophisticated technologies will be developed and take up the existing technological affordances, digital genres and media will keep on playing a key facilitating role for sharing data and maintaining both formal and informal discussions. For example, science transparency and reproducibility of research will likely support the maintenance of research-process genres and prompt the emergence of genres that will borrow features of already existing genres. In previous chapters we have seen some examples of hybrid genres illustrating such ecological development (e.g., registered reports, electronic laboratory notebooks and video methods articles). Lastly, with the affordances of Web 2.0, in particular the multicognitive effects of multimodality (Ostergren, 2013) and the impact of visual rhetoric, one could foresee that multi-semiotic (visual/audiovisual and verbal) digital genres will soon take over monomodal genres. This, I believe, is more likely to occur in the case of genres that target non-specialist audiences and that, as the insiders surveyed for this book stated, aim to get others excited about science and to build public trust in scientific research.

7.2.1 Endangered genres, endangered languages

From the corpus evidence given in this book, it can be inferred that digital genres are not and will not be used – or will not keep on being used – to the same extent across the STEMM fields. While focusing interest in citizen science and crowdsourcing science may remain important for raising funds in the biomedical field, it is likely that certain generic innovations such as graphical abstracts will keep on being circumscribed to what Becher and Trowler (2001: 36) conceptualise as hard-pure and hard-applied disciplinary groupings (e.g., chemistry and engineering, respectively), showing little spread in non-STEMM disciplines and subfields. This, however, creates tensions between the practices of distinct disciplinary cultures and the practices resulting from increasing interdisciplinarity and cooperation in the research world, the latter showing potential for cross-fertilisation among various disciplinary tribes. It is unlikely that some discipline-specific practices will be adopted beyond the STEMM fields, and here the nature of knowledge and the epistemology of each discipline concur with the contexts and agendas ruling the STEMM disciplines. As noted earlier, these are characterised by fiercer competition and, in many ways, stronger social and economic impact than the humanities and the social sciences disciplines. The upsurge of digital genres is not unconnected with genre loss. I stated previously that audioslide presentations associated with online journal articles have lost momentum as a result of having an unclear rhetorical action. On the other hand, the decreasing use of (and interest in) some traditional genres such as the monograph, still a very important genre in the humanities and social sciences disciplines, may be an indication of the eventual loss of this genre in the STEMM fields (see Pérez-Llantada, 2021b, for further evidence). Turning to genres of public understanding of science, citizen science genres that, at present, are making the research of some STEMM fields more visible, are highly dependent on social agendas and to date are not valued according to research assessment regulations of the genre regimes, which might cause their gradual disappearance. The surveys of corresponding authors (*Cell, Nature, eLife* and *PLoS*) revealed much less interest in these genres for disseminating research work compared to social media genres.

The previous chapters have also addressed where and how languages, languaging practices and language ecologies intersect with genre-mediated literate activity. I would propose the following future genres and languages scenarios. In the context of knowledge-intensive economies, the circulation of scientific knowledge will necessarily draw on a lingua franca, possibly English, but in this case the different

English varieties produced by both native and non-native English speakers worldwide. It would be very impractical to change this well-established social interaction dynamic, above all if we consider the massive amount of global science produced and communicated in this language and the size of the multilingual community participating in such dynamic. Rather than thinking in terms of 'endangered' languages, we should rather envisage a likely divide between monolingual (English mainly, but also other languages of science) genres coexisting with multilingual genres for science in and for society, above all, if the latter genre types are appropriately fuelled by policies promoting the democratisation of science and the enhancement of society's scientific literacy. A different future scenario, and a far-reaching one because it goes beyond the academic community as an ecosystem, can be depicted by aligning with Skutnabb-Kangas and Phillipson's (2011: 190) assertion that '[l]anguages do not in fact "spread" without agents, just as language "death" and "attrition" are not "natural" processes, analogous to biological processes'. As global and local knowledge of science mutually benefit one another (Amano, González-Varo and Sutherland, 2016), endangered languages and language loss will possibly lead to loss of local knowledge of science. This will have a truly negative impact on the research world and on the advancement of knowledge. At present, language diversity surfaces as a major global challenge, the more so if our aim is to strive for sustainable development goals through strategic alliances between scientists, educators and public policymakers (UNESCO, 2015; see, e.g., the AIMS project for agriculture in Africa, briefly discussed in Chapter 5).

7.2.2 Multilingualisation of science

In this book the metaphors of 'ecology of genres' and 'ecology of languages' have sought to represent complex sets of relationships between genres and languages and their environment(s). Moreover, they have aimed to capture the multilingual nature of constellations of genres that draw on hypertextual linkages to connect multimodal and multilingual genres. By this means, these constellations support both local and international communication of science and reach multilingual audiences. And while the centrality of English in some research genres appears to be indisputable, such centrality nonetheless instantiates the existence of different similects – conceptualised as ELF lects (Mauranen, 2018), academic Englishes (Mauranen, Pérez-Llantada and Swales, 2010, 2020) and lingua franca Englishes (Guillén-Galve and Vázquez, 2018), as explained in Chapter 4. Acknowledging this diversity not only contests assumptions of monolingual (English-only) scientific communication but also manifests language variation and patterns of visible participation of plurilingual researchers. Additionally, in the light of the findings reported in this book, we can also conclude that Web 2.0 offers a wide range of affordances. The web makes available different channels for sharing new knowledge and for participating in formal dialogic encounters via online genres reporting both research outcomes and research processes or methodological protocols. The web also supports informal discussion among peers in the virtual space, for example, via ASNSs, and provides possibilities for telling, sharing and disseminating science with expert and non-specialist audiences. Moreover, it provides technological tools and resources for interacting with interested audiences, such as those provided by crowdfunding platforms, Ask Me Anything sessions on Reddit r/science (Hara, Abbazio and Perkins, 2019) and replies to posts and comments in research-group blogs (Luzón, 2011).

The insights gained from the ecological view of genres also enable us to affirm that in the domain of research communication, the written mode will likely be more dominant than the spoken mode. The impinging socioeconomic agendas and established genre regimes, both of them imposing a hierarchical order in research outputs, point in this direction. Nevertheless, this will only be to some extent given that with the Internet, multimodal forms and visual cultures are gradually permeating the domain of science communication. In this respect, whether the balance tilts towards literacy and not towards orality is a moving target, subject to the various and fluctuating interests of the different science stakeholders. What is indeed certain is that multimodal genres have arrived on the scene to offer the producers of science possibilities for composing multilayered texts. In combining visual and verbal messages and different levels of explanatory depth (e.g., journal articles and their associated podcasts, video abstracts or embedded author videos), these texts make available different information access paths that can satisfy the interests of audiences. In sum, the technological innovations and the interactivity of Web 2.0 ensure the development of the ecology of genres.

As explained in the following subsection, a number of language-related implications derive from the ongoing change and evolution of the existing repertoire (and repertoires) of research genres. A key concern is how to best manage and preserve linguistic diversity through institutional, national, regional and global agendas.

7.2.3 Language management

Recurring emphasis throughout this book has been put on the various intersections of genres and languages, and language(s) use across multilingual users. Language users rely on the stability of prototypical genres to enact social action and on the capacity of genres to emerge when non-routine situational contexts occur. As social structures change, so do genres adapt and evolve in response to new rhetorical exigences. As Bazerman (2011: 226) explains, a genre starts to recur and its rhetorical action becomes typified only when language users identify it:

Language users. . .in the course of interaction call upon the resources of language that are socially and culturally available and that have been *typified through histories of social circulation*; nonetheless, individuals *construct meanings and consequentiality* from their perception of particular novel situations and their participant action in those situations. (My emphasis)

In this book I have critically discussed the social contexts of genres, especially the socioeconomic, geolinguistic and geopolitical agendas (Lillis and Curry, 2010; Linn, 2016; Tusting, 2018) to show how these agendas impact on researchers' choice of language(s) and strategic use of linguistic repertoires, at times determining such choice and, at other times, constraining it. From a language-policy perspective, the increasingly mobile and polyglot population of researchers worldwide, noted earlier in the Introduction and Chapter 4, inevitably requires a shared lingua franca to be operational. But, along with this lingua franca, researchers need to become acquainted with and sensitised towards the rich linguistic and cultural diversity of today's research world.

The present book has also studied multilingualism from a genre analytical perspective and has offered a new understanding of genres across local and global plurilingual communities. A feasible means to enhance the 'multilingualisation of science' (Amano, González-Varo and Sutherland, 2016) is by gradually pluralising professional and public communication of science at both local and global levels. Maintaining high-stakes genres in one single lingua franca is a taken-for-granted option, not just for the sake of researchers' recognition and promotion but also for international cooperation purposes. But this, then, needs to be counterbalanced by effective multilingual policymaking in science communication online. The affordances of the Internet offer a myriad of possibilities to do this (multilingual websites, translation tools and use of multilingual genre sets, as discussed in previous chapters). It is in science and social policymakers' hands to support polylanguaging phenomena in and outside of the academic and research ecosystem.

Multilingual education is a second and perhaps more practical and feasible way of managing linguistic diversity in the research world so that it has an impact on society and social well-being. Here, language management, a discipline sensitive to issues of migration, globalisation and cultural diversity as Ferguson (2006) explains, can inspire us in finding ways for promoting multilingualism in science communication online. One of the book's main contributions has been to bring to the fore multilingual genres and languaging practices of various kinds in genre-mediated activity for the practitioner. In particular, Chapter 6 has described the main aims and rationales for possible approaches to multilingual, genre-based pedagogical intervention. This new understanding of the contexts and agendas of genres across languages should not only guide formal instruction and/or training but also invite us to ask ourselves important questions that need addressing in terms of language planning. Echoing Giddens, the first questions relate to the social structures: How effectively are institutions (university and research centres) addressing language planning for their research staff in their mission and vision? Do institutions have explicit policy formulations? If language planning is already in place, how are the processes and outcomes assessed according to quality benchmarks? Other further questions we can pose revolve around the social agents, for example, to what extent do the research workforce in those institutions and the LAP teachers or practitioners have a voice in planning and enhancing instructional programmes? Addressing these questions will give us important hints as to how successfully language diversity is actually managed.

7.3 Future agendas for genres and languages research

This book has covered a reasonable part of the existing repertoire of research genres, tackling issues of interdependence between old and new genres, processes of knowledge remediation and the effects of polycontextuality and context collapse. By this means, I have sought to expand and update the repertoire of research genres described in Swales (2004), the same year that Web 2.0 officially began. Therefore, for reasons of space limitations, I have not examined spoken genres, neither old genres (e.g., lectures, conference presentations, poster presentations, dissertation defences, etc.) nor new genres (e.g., scientific monologues, TED Talks, research pitches, three-minute thesis presentations, to name a few). Indeed, this could have captured a more comprehensive view of research genres in the contemporary world. One crucial point that should be included on the future research agenda is, therefore, the world of spoken genres. We need to examine further their nature and functionality within the ecology and their interdependence with other spoken and written genres. We also need to assess their evolutionary development. Possibly, enquiry into spoken genres will trigger further critical debates on AEs, ELF lects or Lingua Franca Englishes on the one hand and bi/multilingual practices on the other. It goes without saying that the two strands, the written and the spoken, 'are reciprocally supportive and leading in the same direction' (Rubin and Kang, 2008: 220).

It should readily be acknowledged that this book has placed the focus only on the STEMM sciences. My main reasons were, first, to narrow down the scope of the book and, secondly, to have sufficient space to dig deep into the written communication dynamics of these disciplines. Obviously, this opens a major (and much needed) avenue for future research on genre texts, contexts and practices across the disciplines. The digital turn is also dramatically impacting them, but creating different language dynamics (see, e.g., Luzón and Pérez-Llantada, forthcoming). Research and social agendas are also gearing towards open-access options that allow researchers to gain visibility and trust. These changing agendas may make the repertoires of genres and languages evolve and may cause, as stated previously, genre disappearance and eventual loss. Monolingual and multilingual genres used across the disciplines could give us a more profound understanding of research communication across languages.

In delving into written (verbal) texts, I have mentioned very briefly the use of visuals accompanying some genre exemplars and the role of visual rhetoric. Both are key aspects in the formation of genres in Web 2.0, and, therefore, future research could shed further light on the intersemiotic modes at play within a single macrogenre or within a given genre set, genre system or genre ecology. The complementarity of text and visual or imagery thus emerges as an essential aspect for further enquiry. This is particularly important at a time in which multimodal (verbal and visual) genres are proliferating in both expert and non-specialist public communication of science (e.g., graphical abstracts, author videos, tweets with pinned images or citizen science projects and crowdfunding projects with catchy images that immediately attract volunteers and funders). How much '(inter)culture' and 'cultural differences' are taken on board when researchers use visuals for public communication of science is also a worthwhile path for future research enquiry.

Moving on to text-linguistic aspects, in this book corpus-informed genre analysis has confirmed that the rhetorical structures of some digital hybrid genres are highly predictable, as they adopt the structures of already existing genres (e.g., crowdfunding and citizen science projects). Further investigative efforts, then, need to revolve around genre hybridisation at both lexical and grammatical levels and, above all, hybridisation of discourse styles so as to track the extent to which their specific linguistic features are associated with one or more registers. In the EAP literature, recurring formulaic language has been considered a distinct feature of L1 and L2 academic writing (Hyland, 2009; Simpson-Vlach and Ellis, 2010). An important strand of literature has pointed out that these formulas make writing more systematic and, in the case of multilingual writers, can scaffold L2 (or L*n*) writing processes (Ädel, 2006; Cortes, 2004). Building on this previous literature, we could get a much better grasp of how writers perform interdiscursive connectivity (Salö and Hanell, 2014) and rely on bi/multiliteracy transfer (Gentil, 2011) when composing genre texts.

Turning to issues of genres and professional practices, I would say that a productive line of future enquiry would be examining interdiscursivity, or the appropriation of features of professional discourses, especially features from the discourse of journalism, in the discourse in or about science. These have already been traced in corporate discourses (Bhatia, 2004) and science popularisations (Motta-Roth and Scherer, 2016). Regarding genre and register, it will be of particular interest in future research to trace whether academic writing is becoming more informal, experiencing a shift towards orality, as contended by Biber and Gray (2016).

In this book, the only attempt to gather disciplinary insiders' views and perceptions – what I have referred to as the emic perspective – has been through small-scale exploratory surveys of different groups of researchers. The results are reported in Chapters 3–5 (involving an overall total target population of 800 researchers, with 15 per cent to 20 per cent response rates, and almost all with a 95 per cent level of significance and a 10 per cent margin of error). Although the survey data has been insightful and confirmatory of previous assumptions, a much more in-depth approach could be more revealing for engaging in materials design and planning formal instruction and self-directed learning. There is still a lot we need to know about the processes of composing verbal and audiovisual genre texts and about the challenges of delivering planned and unplanned speech in multimodal genres such as audioslides or video methods articles. To date, there are not many 'thick descriptions' (Lillis, 2008) and not much information is available regarding, for example, the strategies and resources researchers deploy and the challenges they face in composing digital texts. How and why they do so could make genre-based approaches more focused and guide LAP instructors in supporting researchers' difficulties in composing texts. The exploratory surveys to authors of graphical abstracts, *JoVE* authors and Experiment.com project launchers, for instance, suggested that aspects such as prior genre

210 Research Genres Across Languages

knowledge, knowledge of recurring phraseology and intertextual borrowing at the lexical and phraseological levels, along with rhetorical skills and a sound understanding of visual and multimodal rhetoric, need particular attention.

The perspective of situated learning offers ample opportunities for researching genre-based activity, recurring social interaction practices, language choice in those practices and hierarchies of genres and occluded genres, among other aspects of academic enculturation. Important points on the future research agenda are the rationales (both personal and institutional) for moving towards open-access publishing options, as there is already a huge movement within digital publishing. Understanding the motives and agendas of Science 2.0, which benefits from networked technologies for supporting information-sharing and collaboration, and basing such understanding on longitudinal studies could reveal more accurately the true impact of social and research agendas and the implications that ensue regarding the representativeness and maintenance of linguistic diversity in the research world. Future studies nurturing from the emic perspective can also be helpful to identify researchers' current and prospective interests in engaging in transformative practice. These studies could trace the existence of overt (and covert) 'hierarchical orders' ranking not only old and new genres but also academic languages across communities of practice. The scope of this research should not be limited to the physical community (or communities) of practice but should also be extended to the virtual communities of multilingual researchers that are supported by the affordances of the Internet, as I explained in Chapter 5.

Future research on the effects of context collapse on genre texts can also draw on the perspective of reception theory. This is an area of enquiry that has been under-researched in the fields of EAP and LAP, but it is a crucial approach to evaluate the effectiveness of processes of genre remediation, recontextualisation and transformation of specialised knowledge, or the use of features of grammatical compression and, in the case of multimodal genres, the use of visual rhetoric. Studies need to be carried out to know what exactly attracts the attention of the readership and audiences and what prompts their response.

One important theoretical and empirical endeavour of this book has been to bring to the fore the diversity of languages in science communication, as illustrated in translanguaging practices in research blogs, in citizen science projects with multilingual websites and in the use of formal conversations and informal virtual discussions among users of English as a Lingua Franca. Cutting across aspects of genre evolution and innovation, issues of language ecology, languages in contact and languages and socialisation need addressing in future research. The future agenda for languages should also address whether genres mean the same in all languages. Tardy (2016: 2–4) explains that while genres may be perceived 'as templates or formulas' and 'the conventions may be interpreted as rules', disciplinary novices may perceive 'the heteroglossic nature of written communication' in different ways for various reasons. These can be the individual's past experiences or his or her linguistic repertoire and culture-specific beliefs and expectations. Therefore, further research should be undertaken to examine whether a given writer's stylistic choices are similar when he or she composes the same genre in different languages or whether he or she transgresses the conventions of a particular genre in one language but not in another language.

Lastly, like Giltrow (1994: 148), I would stress 'the utility of genre study in cultural inquiry' and recommend further work to capture the plurality of global and local discourses beyond native norms and to investigate whether research genres are different in different cultural contexts.

7.4 What research methods afford

In the previous chapters of this book, I have sought to illustrate several possibilities to analyse genre exemplars and gain insights into the ways contexts shape their form and substance and the actions they perform (Miller, 1984). Corpus analytical methods and both large- and small-scale specialised corpora have been used to explore lexical, phraseological, discourse, rhetorical and register features. Using the analytical approach proposed in theories of intertextuality in the field of literary criticism (Bakhtin, 1981, 1986a), I have also pointed at, but not actually conducted, the analysis of features of intertextuality and hypertextuality in interdependent genres forming genre assemblages in web environments. An area that falls outside the scope of this book has been the analysis of multisemiotic texts and visual rhetoric.

For reasons of space constraints, this book cannot capture all possible analytical approaches from which genre analysis nurtures. Therefore, in the following subsections, I only outline some major analytical and interpretative approaches that can be used to obtain a precise view of how research genres operate in response to new realities and how languages best support the functionalities of genres.

7.4.1 Rhetorical genre analysis

This type of analysis draws on close reading of genre exemplars to trace formal regularities in the way arguments are constructed to create the intended rhetorical effects through rhetorical moves and steps. It can be used to track the effects of context collapse in remediated genres, open-access genres, hybrid genres and parascientific genres. Rhetorical analysis can also be employed to assess the evolution of genres and dynamic systems of genres in relation to their sociorhetorical contexts. Analyses of multimodal and visual rhetoric facilitate the examination of multisemiotic (audiovisual and verbal) genres and intersemiotic meaning-making processes. Cross-linguistic rhetorical analysis can be used to identify how the same writers negotiate meanings in a given genre written in different languages or in genre ecologies supporting translanguaging and polylanguaging practices.

7.4.2 Register analysis

Register analysis can be a welcome addition to understanding aspects of genre and discourse. It can offer empirical descriptive accounts of language varieties and language variation and change through the identification of grammar features that characterise different discourse styles. Register analysis can yield a better understanding of the impact of computer-mediated communication in formal academic discourse in different genres and languages. Using register analysis, the genre analyst can track the lexical, grammatical and syntactic realisations of different levels of explanatory depth in multilingual genre networks. This can give a more precise view of processes of transmedial gradation in knowledge transformation and remediation (Bolter and Grusin 1999; Engberg and Maier, 2015). Corpus data from register analysis can also help us better understand authors' awareness of the effects of context collapse on digital text composing and language use.

7.4.3 Critical genre analysis

This type of analysis is apposite for the study of language and social structures in relation to digital genres and genre assemblages and to digital genres that embed multimodal (audiovisual) elements (e.g., author videos, video methods articles, academic home pages or research-group blogs, among others). It is helpful to those genre analysts concerned with examining 'genre colonisation', that is to say, the appropriation of professional discourses from different domains of language use, in particular, professional discourses (Bhatia, 2004, 2017). In addition, critical genre analysis can be applied in studies on aspects of intertextuality and interdiscursivity, for example, in scifotainment or edutainment genres and citizen science genres, and on features of dialogism and multilanguagedness. It is also an appropriate analytical approach to explore intergeneric hybridisation or the non-conventional use of linguistic resources for promotional purposes, a language phenomenon that we take for granted considering 'the invasion of promotional values in most forms of discourse' in recent years (Bhatia, 2005: 213).

7.4.4 Ethnographic analysis

When conducted systematically, ethnographies of academic writing contexts become robust analytical methodologies to examine literate activity and the skills needed to engage successfully in genre recognition and genre use. This analytical approach is close to the sociocultural and analytical framework of activity theory applied to professional communication (Spinuzzi, 2003; Spinuzzi and Guile, 2019). It enables qualitative exploration of texts in situated contexts (conceptualised as 'textographies', Swales, 1998), as well as insiders' perceptions and views of genres and writing activity. Possible data-collection tools range from semi-structured interviews, focus groups and think-aloud protocols to self-reflective narratives and journey plots (Creswell, 2013; Guillén-Galve and Bocanegra-Valle, 2021). This analysis also enables researchers to look more closely at the intersections of genre and language use (e.g., aspects of bi/multiliteracy development in writing), both as part of experiential learning and in text-composing tasks.

7.4.5 Reader-response analysis

Lastly, it is worth mentioning reader-response analysis and the framework of reception theory, a theory that takes up literary reader-response criticism (Fish, 1980). This can be done using quantitative – bibliometrics, webometrics and altmetrics – data, which reveals the online activity surrounding a given genre exemplar. Swales and Leeder's (2012) reception study of the most highly cited papers in the *English for Specific Purposes* journal from 1990 to 1999 is a good start to enquire into the reception of online genre texts by tracing their sequential uptake. For example, this analysis can inform us about what makes a given monolingual and/or multilingual genre exemplar (e.g., an article, a blog post or a tweet) highly citable and/or mentioned, shared, commented and (re)tweeted in one, two or more languages.

In his inspiring analysis of stories and styles of two molecular biologists' review articles, Greg Myers (1990: 70) concluded as follows:

Literary critics have begun to look beyond the 'original form' of artistic communications to the 'stream of knowledge' of which they are a part. Analysts of scientific texts, too, need to look more closely at the textual forms in which the original communication is modified, amplified, fused, and melted.

I shall close by reaffirming that genre theory and genre analysis can capture a comprehensive picture of the intersecting dynamics of genres and languages. It can unveil the various ways in which knowledge is constructed and, echoing Myers, modified, amplified, fused and melted in response to the current social contexts and agendas. Continuing enquiry into evolutionary developments of genres and ongoing generic innovation (on the web) will bring with it a more informed understanding of genres across linguistically diverse academic and research settings.

References

Aalbersberg, I. J., Heeman, F., Koers, H. and Zudilova-Seinstra, E. (2012). Elsevier's Article of the Future. Enhancing the user experience and integrating data through applications. *Insights: The UKSG Journal*, 25(1), 33–43.

Abt, H. A. (2007). Changing sources for research literature. In A. Heck and L. Houziaux, eds., *Future Professional Communication in Astronomy*. Bruxelles: Académie Royale de Belgique, pp. 151–160.

Ädel, A. (2006). *Metadiscourse in L1 and L2 English*. Amsterdam and Philadelphia: John Benjamins.

Ai, H. (2010–2017a). Web-based L2 Syntactic Complexity Analyzer. Available at https://aihaiyang.com/software/ [last accessed 5 June 2020].

Ai, H. (2010–2017b). Web-based Lexical Complexity Analyzer. Available at https://aihaiyang.com/software/lca/ [last accessed 5 June 2020].

Altbach, P. G. (2004). Globalisation and the university: Myths and realities in an unequal world. *Tertiary Education and Management*, 10(1), 3–25.

Altbach, P. G. (2007). The imperial tongue: English as the dominating academic language. *Economic and Political Weekly*, 42(36), 3608–3611.

Amano, T., González-Varo, J. P. and Sutherland, W. J. (2016). Languages are still a major barrier to global science. *PLoS Biology*, 14(12), e2000933.

Ammon, U. (2001). English as a future language of science at German universities? A question of difficult consequences, posed by the decline of German as a language of science. In U. Ammon, ed., *The Dominance of English as a Language of Science*. Berlin: Mouton de Gruyter, pp. 343–361.

Ammon, U. (2006). Language planning for international scientific communication: An overview of questions and potential solutions. *Current Issues in Language Planning*, 7(1), 1–30.

Anderson, K. (2009). The 'Article of the Future' – Just lipstick again? Available at https://scholarlykitchen.sspnet.org/2009/07/21/the-article-of-the-future-lipstick-on-a-pig/ [last accessed on 16 April 2019].

Anthony, L. (2019). AntConc (Version 3.5.8) [Computer Software]. Tokyo: Waseda University. Available at www.laurenceanthony.net/software/antconc/ [last accessed on 7 July 2020].

Anthony, L. and Hardaker, C. (2017). FireAnt (Version 1.1.4) [Computer Software]. Tokyo: Waseda University. Available at www.laurenceanthony .net/software [last accessed on 7 July 2020].

Askehave, I. and Swales, J. M. (2001). Genre identification and communicative purpose: A problem and a possible solution. *Applied Linguistics*, 22(2), 195–212.

Atkinson, D. (2003). Writing and culture in the post-process era. *Journal of Second Language Writing*, 12, 49–63.

Atkinson, D. (2004). Contrasting rhetorics/contrasting cultures: Why contrastive rhetoric needs a better conceptualization of culture. *Journal of English for Academic Purposes*, 3(4), 277–289.

Aydinli, E. and Mathews, J. (2000). Are the core and periphery irreconcilable? The curious world of publishing in contemporary international relations. *International Studies Perspectives*, 1, 289–303.

Ayers, G. (2008). The evolutionary nature of genre: An investigation of the short texts accompanying research articles in the scientific journal *Nature*. *English for Specific Purposes*, 27, 22–41.

Bak, T. H. and Mehmedbegovic, D. (2017). Healthy linguistic diet: The value of linguistic diversity and language learning across the lifespan. *Languages, Society & Policy*, DOI: https://doi.org/10.17863/CAM.9854.

Bakhtin, M. M. (1981). *The Dialogic Imagination. Four Essays*. C. Emerson and M. Holquist (trans.), M. Holquist, ed. Austin: University of Texas Press.

Bakhtin, M. M. (1986a). Discourse in the novel. In M. Holquist, ed., *The Dialogic Imagination* (trans. C. Emerson and M. Holquist). Austin: University of Texas Press, pp. 259–422.

Bakhtin, M. M. (1986b). *Speech Genres and Other Late Essays*. V. W. McGee (trans.), C. Emerson and M. Holquist, eds. Austin: University of Texas Press.

Ball, Ch. E. (2016). The shifting genres of scholarly multimedia: Webtexts as innovation. *The Journal of Media Innovations*, 3(2), 52–71.

Ball, D. (2016). *The Impact of Open Science*. Available at www.fosteropenscience.eu/content/impact-open-science [last accessed 1 July 2020].

Barbieri, F. (2018). I don't want to and don't get me wrong: Lexical bundles as a window to subjectivity and intersubjectivity in American blogs. In J. Kopaczyk and J. Tyrkkö, eds., *Applications of Pattern-Driven Methods in Corpus Linguistics*. Amsterdam and Philadelphia: John Benjamins, pp. 251–276.

Baron, N. S. (2016). The impact of electronically-mediated communication on language standards and style. In T. Nevalainen and E. C. Traugott, eds., *The Oxford Handbook of the History of English*. Oxford: Oxford University Press, pp. 329–340.

Barras, R. (1978). *Scientists Must Write. A Guide to Better Writing for Scientists, Engineers and Students*. London and New York: Chapman & Hall.

Barton, D. (2001). Directions for literacy research: Analysing language and social practices in a textually mediated world. *Language and Education*, 15(2), 92–104.

Barton, D. (2007). *Literacy. An Introduction to the Ecology of Written Language*. Malden: Blackwell Publishing.

Barton, D. and Hamilton, M. (2012). *Local Literacies. Reading and Writing in One Community*. 2nd ed. London and New York: Routledge.

Barton, D., Hamilton, M. and Ivanič, R., eds. (2000). *Situated Literacies. Reading and Writing in Context*. 1st ed. London and New York: Routledge.

Bateman, J. A. (2017). Triangulating transmediality: A multimodal semiotic framework relating media, modes and genres. *Discourse, Context and Media*, 20, 160–174. DOI: https://doi.org/10.1016/j.dcm.2017.06.009.

Bauman, Z. (2000). *Liquid Modernity*. Cambridge: Polity Press.

Bawarshi, A. (2001). The ecology of genre. In S. I. Dobrin and C. R. Weisser, eds., *Ecocomposition: Theoretical and Pedagogical Approaches*. New York: University of New York Press, pp. 69–80.

Bawarshi, A. (2016). Accounting for genre performances: Why uptake matters. In N. Artemeva and A. Freedman, eds., *Trends and Traditions in Genre Studies*. Edmonton: Inkshed Publications, pp. 186–206.

Bawarshi, A. S. and Reiff, M. J. (2010). *Genre. An Introduction to History, Theory, Research and Pedagogy*. 1st ed. West Lafayette, IN: Parlor Press.

Bazerman, C. (1994). Systems of genres and the enactment of social intentions. In A. Freedman and P. Medway, eds., *Genre and the New Rhetoric*. London: Taylor & Francis, pp. 79–101.

Bazerman, C. (2004a). Speech acts, genres, and activity systems: How texts organize activity and people. In C. Bazerman and P. Prior, eds., *What Writing Does and How It Does It: An Introduction to Analysing Texts and Textual Practices*. New York: Taylor & Francis, pp. 309–339.

Bazerman, C. (2004b). Intertextuality: How texts rely on other texts. In C. Bazerman and P. Prior, eds., *What Writing Does and How It Does It: An Introduction to Analysing Texts and Textual Practices*. New York: Taylor & Francis, pp. 83–96.

Bazerman, C. (2011). Genre as social action. In J. P. Gee and M. Handford, eds., *Routledge Handbook of Discourse Analysis*. London and New York: Routledge, pp. 226–238.

Bazerman, C. (2015). A genre-based theory of literate action. In N. Artemeva and A. Freedman, eds., *Genre Studies around the Globe: Beyond the Three Traditions*. Edmonton: Inkshed Publications, pp. 80–94.

Bazerman, C. and Prior, P., eds. (2004). *What Writing Does and How It Does It: An Introduction to Analysing Texts and Textual Practices*. New York: Taylor & Francis.

Beaufort, A. (2007). *College Writing and Beyond: A New Framework for University Writing Instruction*. Logan: Utah State University Press.

Becher, T. (1981). Towards a definition of disciplinary cultures. *Studies in Higher Education*, 6(2), 109–122.

Becher, T. and Trowler, P. (2001). *Academic Tribes and Territories. Intellectual Enquiry and the Culture of Disciplines*. Buckingham: The Society of Research into Higher Education and Open University Press.

Belcher, D. (2009). How research space is created in a diverse research world. *Journal of Second Language Writing*, 18(4), 221–234.

Bennett, K., ed. (2014). *The Semiperiphery of Academic Writing: Discourses, Communities and Practices*. Basingstoke: Palgrave Macmillan.

Berkenkotter, C. and Huckin, T. N. (1995). *Genre Knowledge in Disciplinary Communication: Cognition/Culture/Power*. Hillsdale: Lawrence Erlbaum Associates.

Besley, J. C., Dudo, A. and Storksdieck, M. (2015). Scientists' views about communication training. *Journal of Research in Science Teaching*, 52(2), 199–220.

Bhatia, V. K. (2004). *Worlds of Written Discourse*. London: Continuum.

Bhatia, V. K. (2005). Generic patterns in promotional discourse. In H. Halmari and T. Virtanen, eds., *Persuasion across Genres: A Linguistic Approach*. Amsterdam and Philadelphia: John Benjamins, pp. 213–225.

Bhatia, V. K. (2017). *Critical Genre Analysis: Investigating Interdiscursive Performance in Professional Practice*. London and New York: Routledge.

Biber, D. and Gray, B. (2010). Challenging stereotypes about academic writing: Complexity, elaboration, explicitness. *Journal of English for Academic Purposes*, 9, 2–20.

Biber, D. and Gray, B. (2016). The competing demands of popularisation vs. economy: Written language in the age of mass literacy. In T. Nevalainen and E. C. Traugott, eds., *The Oxford Handbook of the History of English*. Oxford: Oxford University Press, pp. 314–328.

Biber, D., Johansson, S., Leech, G., Conrad, S. and Finegan, E., eds. (1999). *Longman Grammar of Spoken and Written English*. Harlow: Pearson Education Limited.

Blommaert, J. (2010). *The Sociolinguistics of Globalization*. Cambridge: Cambridge University Press.

Blommaert, J. and Dong, J. (2010). *Ethnographic Fieldwork. A Beginner's Guide*. Bristol: Multilingual Matters.

Blommaert, J., Collins, J. and Slembrouck, S. (2005). Spaces for multilingualism. *Language and Communication*, 25, 197–216.

Bocanegra-Valle, A. (2015). Peer reviewers' recommendations for language improvements in research writing. In R. Plo Alastrué and C. Pérez-Llantada, eds., *English as a Scientific and Research Language. Debates and Discourses*. Berlin: De Gruyter Mouton, pp. 207–230.

Bocanegra-Valle, A. (2016). Needs analysis for curriculum design. In K. Hyland and P. Shaw, eds., *The Routledge Handbook of English for Academic Purposes*. Abingdon, Oxford: Routledge, pp. 560–576.

Boekholt, P., Edler, J., Cunningham, P. and Flanagan, K. (2009). Drivers of International collaboration in research Final Report. Retrieved from https://ec.europa.eu/research/evaluations/pdf/archive/other_reports_studies_and_documents/drivers_of_international_cooperation_in_research.pdf [last accessed on 6 July 2020].

Bolter, J. D. and Grusin, R. (1999). *Remediation – Understanding New Media*. Cambridge: The MIT Press.

Bondi, M., Cacchiani, S. and Mazzi, D. (2015). Discourse in and through the media: Recontextualizing and reconceptualizing expert discourse. In M. Bondi, S. Cacchiani and D. Mazzi, eds., *Discourse In and Through the Media: Recontextualizing and Reconceptualizing Expert Discourse*. Newcastle upon Tyne: Cambridge Scholars Publishing, pp. 1–21.

Bonney, R., Cooper, C. B., Dickinson, J., Kelling, S., Phillips, T., Rosenberg, K. V. and Shirk, J. (2009). Citizen science: A developing tool for expanding science knowledge and scientific literacy. *BioScience*, 59(11), 977–984.

Bosch, T. (2012). Blogging and tweeting climate change in South Africa. *Ecquid Novi: African Journalism Studies*, 33(1), 44–53.

boyd, D. M. (2002). *Faceted Identity: Managing Representation in a Digital World.* Unpublished master's thesis. Cambridge, Massachusetts Institute of Technology.

Breeze, R. (2016). Tracing the development of an emergent part-genre: The author summary. *English for Specific Purposes*, 42, 50–65.

Breeze, R. (2019). Continuity and change. Negotiating relationships in traditional and online peer review genres. In M.-J. Luzón and C. Pérez-Llantada, eds., *Science Communication on the Internet: Old Genres Meet New Genres.* Amsterdam and Philadelphia: John Benjamins, pp. 107–129.

Breiteneder, A. (2009). English as a lingua franca in Europe: An empirical perspective. *World Englishes*, 28(2), 256–269.

Briggs, C. L. and Bauman, R. (1992). Genre, intertextuality and social power. *Journal of Linguistic Anthropology*, 2(2), 131–172.

Britton, B., Jackson, C. and Wade, J. (2019). The reward and risk of social media for academics. *Nature Reviews Chemistry*, 3(8), 459–461.

Brutt-Griffler, J. (2002). *World English. A Study of Its Development.* Bristol: Multilingual Matters.

Büchi, M. (2016). Microblogging as an extension of science reporting. *Public Understanding of Science*, 26(8), 953–968.

Buck, A. (2012). Examining digital literacy practices on social network sites. *Research in the Teaching of English*, 47(1), 9–38.

Buckingham, L. (2014). Building a career in English: Users of English as an Additional Language in academia in the Arabian Gulf. *TESOL Quarterly*, 48, 6–33.

Buehl, J. (2016). *Assembling Arguments: Multimodal Rhetoric and Scientific Discourse.* Columbia: University of South Carolina Press.

Burrough-Boenisch, J. (2002). *Culture and Conventions: Writing and Reading Dutch Scientific English.* Utrecht, LOT dissertation series 59, Utrecht.

Caliendo, G. (2012). The popularisation of science in web-based genres. In G. Caliendo and G. Bongo, eds., *The Language of Popularisation: Theoretical and Descriptive Models.* Bern: Peter Lang, pp. 101–132.

Canagarajah, S. (1996). Non-discursive requirements in academic publishing, material resources of periphery scholars, and the politics of knowledge production. *Written Communication*, 13(4), 435–472.

Canagarajah, S. (2002a). *A Geopolitics of Academic Writing.* Pittsburgh: University of Pittsburgh Press.

Canagarajah, S. (2002b). Multilingual writers and the academic community: Towards a critical relationship. *Journal of English for Academic Purposes*, 1(1), 29–44.

Canagarajah, S. (2007). Lingua franca English, multilingual communities, and language acquisition. *The Modern Language Journal*, 91, 923–939.

Canagarajah, S. (2013). *Translingual Practice. Global Englishes and Cosmopolitan Relations.* London and New York: Routledge.

Canagarajah, S. (2018). Translingual practice as spatial repertoires: Expanding the paradigm beyond structuralist orientations. *Applied Linguistics*, 39(1), 31–54.

Canagarajah, S. and Said, S. (2011). Linguistic imperialism. In J. Simpson, ed., *The Routledge Handbook of Applied Linguistics*. London and New York: Routledge, pp. 388–400.

Carli, A. and Ammon, U., eds. (2007). Linguistic inequality in scientific communication today. What can future applied linguistics do to mitigate disadvantages for non-Anglophones? *AILA Review*, 20.

Carter, R. (2003). Language awareness. *ELT Journal*, 57(1), 64–65.

Casanave, C. P. (2008). The stigmatizing effect of Goffman's stigma label: A response to John Flowerdew. *Journal of English for Academic Purposes*, 7, 264–267.

Casanave, C. P. and Vandrick, S., eds. (2002). *Writing for Scholarly Publication: Behind the Scenes in Language Education*. Mahwah: Lawrence Erlbaum.

Casper, C. F. (2016). The online research article and the ecological basis of new digital genres. In A. G. Gross and J. Buehl, eds., *Science and the Internet: Communicating Knowledge in a Digital Age*. Amityville: Baywood's Technical Communications Series, pp. 77–98.

Chapelle, C. A. (2001). *Computer Applications in Second Language Acquisition. Foundations for Teaching, Testing and Research*. 1st ed. Cambridge: Cambridge University Press.

Charles, M. (2007). Reconciling top-down and bottom-up approaches to graduate writing: Using a corpus to teach rhetorical functions. *Journal of English for Academic Purposes*, 6(4), 289–302.

Charles, M. (2012). 'Proper vocabulary and juicy collocations': EAP students evaluate do-it-yourself corpus-building. *English for Specific Purposes*, 31(2), 93–102.

Charles, M. (2015). Same task, different corpus: The role of personal corpora in EAP classes. In A. Leńko-Szymańka and A. Boulton, eds., *Multiple Affordances of Language Corpora for Data-driven Learning*. Amsterdam and Philadelphia: John Benjamins, pp. 131–154.

Charles, M. (2018). Corpus-assisted editing for doctoral students: More than just concordancing. *Journal of English for Academic Purposes*, 36, 15–25.

Chen, M. and Flowerdew, J. (2018). A critical review of research and practice in data-driven learning (DDL) in the academic writing classroom. *International Journal of Corpus Linguistics*, 23(3), 335–369.

Cheng, A. (2016). EAP at the tertiary level in China. In K. Hyland and P. Shaw, eds., *The Routledge Handbook of English for Academic Purposes*. London: Routledge, pp. 97–108.

Cheng, A. (2019). Examining the "applied aspirations" in the ESP genre analysis of published journal articles. *Journal of English for Academic Purposes*, 38, 36–47. DOI: https://doi.org/10.1016/j.jeap.2018.12.005.

Cheng, W. (2007). Concgramming: A corpus-driven approach to learning the phraseology of discipline-specific texts. *CORELL: Computer Resources for Language Learning*, 1, 22–35.

Claridge, C. (2016). From manuscript to printing. Transformation of genres in the history of English. In T. Nevalainen and E. C. Traugott, eds., *The Oxford*

Handbook of the History of English. Oxford: Oxford University Press, pp. 304–313.

Cody, E. M., Reagan, A. J., Mitchell, L., Dodds, P. S. and Danforth, C. M. (2015). Climate change sentiment on Twitter: An unsolicited public opinion poll. *PLoS ONE*, **10**(8), e0136092. https://dx.plos.org/10.1371/journal.pone.0136092

Cogo, A. and Dewey, M. (2006). Efficiency in ELF communication: From pragmatic motives to lexico-grammatical innovation. *Nordic Journal of English Studies*, **5**(2), 59–93.

Collins, J. and Blot, R. (2003). *Literacy and Literacies. Texts, Power, and Identity*. Cambridge: Cambridge University Press.

Connor, U. (1996). *Contrastive Rhetoric. Cross-cultural Aspects of Second Language Writing*. Cambridge: Cambridge University Press.

Connor, U. (2011). *Intercultural Rhetoric in the Writing Classroom*. Ann Arbor: University of Michigan Press.

Cook, V. (2013). ELF: Central or atypical second language acquisition? In D. Singleton, J. A. Fishman, L. Aronin and M. O. Laoire, eds., *Current Multilingualism: A New Linguistic Dispensation*. Berlin: De Gruyter, pp. 27–44.

Cook, V. and Singleton, D. (2014). *Key Topics in Second Language Acquisition*. Bristol: Multilingual Matters.

Corcoran, J. N., Englander, K. and Muresan, L.-M. (2019). Diverse global perspectives on scholarly writing for publication. In J. N. Corcoran, K. Englander and L.-M. Muresan, eds., *Pedagogies and Policies on Publishing Research in English: Local Initiatives Supporting International Scholars*. New York: Routledge, pp. 1–16.

Cortes, V. (2004). Lexical bundles in published and student disciplinary writing: Examples from history and biology. *English for Specific Purposes*, **23**(4), 397–423.

Cortes, V. (2013). 'The purpose of this study is to': Connecting lexical bundles and moves in research article introductions. *Journal of English for Academic Purposes*, **12**, 33–43.

Council of Europe (2018). *Common European Framework of Reference for Languages: Learning, Teaching, Assessment*. Companion Volume with New Descriptors. Strasbourg: Council of Europe. https://rm.coe.int/cefr-companion-volume-with-new-descriptors-2018/1680787989 [last accessed on 7 February 2020].

Coupland, N., ed. (2010). *Handbook of Language and Globalization*. Malden: Wiley-Blackwell.

Cox, L. (2015). Are Graphical Abstracts Changing the Way We Publish? https://www.wiley.com/network/researchers/promoting-your-article/are-graphical-abstracts-changing-the-way-we-publish [last accessed 20 June 2020].

Crawford Camiciottoli, B. (2018). OpenCourseWare lectures: A new genre for knowledge dissemination?. Paper presented at the CERLIS Conference 2018, Bergamo, *Italy*, 21–23 June 2018.

Creswell, J. W. (2013). *Research Design: Qualitative, Quantitative, and Mixed Methods Approaches*. 4th ed. Thousand Oaks: SAGE Publications, Inc.

Crystal, D. (2003). *The Cambridge Encyclopaedia of the English Language*. 2nd ed. Cambridge: Cambridge University Press.

Cumming, A. (2013). Multiple dimensions of academic language and literacy development. *Language Learning*, 63(1), 130–152.

Curry, M. J. and Lillis, T. (2019). Unpacking the lore on multilingual scholars publishing in English: A discussion paper. *Publications*, 7, 1–27.

Davis, J. L. and Jurgenson, N. (2014). Context collapse: Theorizing context collusions and collisions. *Information, Communication and Society*, 17(4), 476–485.

Demarest, B. and Sugimoto, C. S. (2014). Argue, observe, assess: Measuring disciplinary identities and differences through socio-epistemic discourse dissertations. *Journal of the Association for Information Science and Technology*, 66 (7), 1374–1387.

Desnoyers, L. (2011). Visuals and text in scientific articles. *Information Design Journal*, 19(2), 155–171.

Devitt, A. J. (2004). *Writing Genres*. Carbondale: Southern Illinois University.

Devitt, A. J. (2009). Re-fusing form in genre study. In J. Giltrow and D. Stein, eds., *Genres in the Internet: Issues in the Theory of Genre*. Philadelphia: John Benjamins Publishing Company, pp. 27–47.

Ding, H. (2008). The use of cognitive and social apprenticeship to teach a disciplinary genre: Initiation of graduate students into NIH grant writing. *Written Communication*, 25(1), 3–52.

Duszak, A. and Lewkowicz, J. (2008). Publishing academic texts in English: A Polish perspective. *Journal of English for Academic Purposes*, 7, 108–120.

Eaquals (2016). *The Eaquals Framework for Language Teacher Training and Development*. https://www.eaquals.org/wp-content/uploads/The-Eaquals-Framework-for-Language-Teacher-Training-and-Development-Online.pdf

Edminster, J. and Moxley, J. (2002). Graduate education and the evolving genre of electronic theses and dissertations. *Computers and Composition*, 19(1), 89–104.

Eitzel, M. V., Cappadonna, J. L., Santos-Lang, C., Duerr, R. E., Virapongse, A., West, S. E. et al. (2017). Citizen science terminology matters: Exploring key terms. *Citizen Science: Theory and Practice*, 2(1), 1.

Engberg, J. and Maier, C. D. (2015). Exploring the hypermodal communication of academic knowledge beyond generic structures. In M. Bondi, S. Cacchiani and D. Mazzi, eds., *Discourse In and Through the Media: Recontextualising and Reconceptualising Expert Discourse*. Newcastle upon Tyne: Cambridge Scholars, pp. 46–65.

Engeström, Y., Engeström, R. and Kärkkäinen, M. (1995). Polycontextuality and boundary crossing in expert cognition: Learning and problem solving in complex work activities. *Learning and Instruction*, 5(4), 319–336.

Erickson, T. (2000). Making sense of computer-mediated communication (CMC): Conversations as genres, CMC systems as genre ecologies. In Ralph H. Sprague Jr., ed., *33rd Hawaii International Conference on System Sciences*, vol. 2. Maui, HI: IEEE Computer Society Press.

Fahnestock, J. (1986). Accommodating science: The rhetorical life of scientific facts. *Written Communication*, 3(3), 275–296.

Fairclough, N. (1992). *Discourse and Social Change*. Cambridge: Polity Press.

Feak, C. B. (2011). Putting strategy into ESP materials development. In C. Pérez-Llantada and M. Watson, eds., *Specialized Languages in the Global Village*. Newcastle: Cambridge Scholars Publishing, pp. 239–260.

Feak, C. B. and Swales, J. M. (2009). *Telling a Research Story. Writing a Literature Review*. Ann Arbor: Michigan University Press.

Feak, C. B. and Swales, J. M. (2010). Writing for publication: Corpus-informed materials for post-doctoral fellows in perinatology. In N. Harwood, ed., *English Language Teaching Materials: Theory and Practice*. Cambridge: Cambridge University Press, pp. 279–300.

Feak, C. B. and Swales, J. M. (2011). *Creating Contexts. Writing Introductions across Genres*. Ann Arbor: Michigan University Press.

Fecher, B. and Friesike, S. (2014). Open science: One term, five schools of thought. In S. Bartling and S. Friesike, eds., *Opening Science*. Cham: Springer, pp. 17–47.

Ferguson, G. R. (2006). *Language Planning and Education*. Amsterdam and Philadelphia: John Benjamins.

Ferguson, G. R. (2007). The global spread of English, scientific communication and ESP: Questions of equity, access and domain loss. *Iberica, Journal of the European Association of Languages for Specific Purposes*, 13, 7–38.

Ferguson, G. R. (2012). English in language policy and management. In B. Spolsky, ed., *Cambridge Handbook of Language Policy*. Cambridge: Cambridge University Press, pp. 475–498.

Ferguson, G. R., Pérez-Llantada, C. and Plo, R. (2011). English as an international language of scientific publication: A study of attitudes. *World Englishes*, 29(3), 41–59.

Fill, A. and Mühlhäusler, P. (2001). *The Ecolinguistics Reader*. London: Continuum.

de Fina, A., Ikizoglu, D. and Wegner, J., eds. (2017). *Diversity and Superdiversity*. Washington, DC: Georgetown University Press.

Fish, S. (1980). *Is There a Text in This Class? The Authority of Interpretive Communities*. Cambridge: Harvard University Press.

Fishelov, D. (1993). *Metaphors of Genre. The Role of Analogies in Genre Theory*. University Park: Penn State University Press.

Fletcher, W. H. (2002–2007). *KfNgram*. Annapolis: USNA.

Flowerdew, J. (1999). Writing for scholarly publication in English: The case of Hong Kong. *Journal of Second Language Writing*, 8, 123–146.

Flowerdew, L. (2004). The argument for using English specialized corpora to understand academic professional language. In U. Connor and T. A. Upton, eds., *Discourse in the Professions: Perspectives from Corpus Linguistics*. Amsterdam and Philadelphia: John Benjamins, pp. 11–33.

Flowerdew, J. (2008). Scholarly writers who use English as an additional language: What can Goffman's *stigma* tell us? *Journal of English for Academic Purposes*, 7(4), 77–86.

Follett R. and Strezov, V. (2015). An analysis of citizen science based research: Usage and publication patterns. *PLoS ONE* 10(11), e0143687. https://doi.org/10.1371/journal.pone.0143687.

Fujun, R. (2013). The connotation and goal of science popularisation in modern China. *Journal of Scientific Temper*, 1, 29–45.

Gates, D. (1968). Energy exchange and ecology. *BioScience*, 18(2), 90–95.

Gee, J. P. (1996). *Social Linguistics and Literacies: Ideologies in Discourse*. London: Taylor & Francis.

Geertz, C. (1983). *Local Knowledge: Further Essays in Interpretive Anthropology*. New York: Basic Books.

Genette, G. (1997). *Paratexts. Thresholds of Interpretation*. Foreword by Richard Macksey. Translated by Jane E. Lewin. Cambridge: Cambridge University Press DOI: https://doi.org/10.1017/CBO9780511549373

Geng, Y. and Wharton, S. (2016). Evaluative language in discussion sections of doctoral theses: Similarities and differences between L1 Chinese and L1 English writers. *Journal of English for Academic Purposes*, 22, 80–91.

Gentil, G. (2011). A biliteracy agenda for genre research. *Journal of Second Language Writing*, 20(1), 6–23.

Gentil, G. (2017). Afterword: Moving forward with academic biliteracy research. In D. Palfreyman and C. van der Walt, eds., *Academic Biliteracies: Translanguaging and Multilingual Repertoires in Higher Education Settings*. Clevendon: Multilingual Matters, pp. 206–220.

Gentil, G. and Séror, J. (2014). Canada has two official languages – or does it? Case studies of Canadian scholars' language choices and practices in disseminating knowledge. *Journal of English for Academic Purposes*, 13 (1), 17–30.

Geuna, A. (2015). *Global Mobility of Research Scientists. The Economics of Who Goes Where and Why*. San Diego: Academic Press.

Giampapa, F. and Canagarajah, S. (2017). Skilled migration and global English. *Globalisation, Societies and Education*, 15(1), 1–4.

Giannoni, D. (2008). Medical writing at the periphery: The case of Italian journal editorials. *Journal of English for Academic Purposes*, 7(2), 97–107.

Giddens, A. (1986). *The Constitution of Society. Outline of the Theory of Structuration*. Cambridge: Polity Press.

Giddens, A. (1990). *The Consequences of Modernity*. Cambridge: Cambridge Polity Press.

Giddens, A. (1999). *Runaway World: How Globalization is Reshaping our Lives*. London: Profile Books.

Gilbert, J. (2005). *Catching the Knowledge Wave? The Knowledge Society and the Future of Education*. Wellington: NZGER Press.

Gilquin, G., Granger, S. and Paquot, M. (2007). Learner corpora: The missing link in EAP pedagogy. *Journal of English for Academic Purposes*, 6(4), 319–335.

Giltrow, J. (1994). Genre and the pragmatic concept of background knowledge. In A. Freedman and P. Medway, eds., *Genre and the New Rhetoric. Critical*

Perspectives on Literacy and Education. London: Taylor & Francis, pp. 155–178.

Giltrow, J. (2017). Bridge to genre: Spanning technological change. In C. R. Miller and A. R. Kelly, eds., *Emerging Genres in New Media Environments*. Baltimore: Palgrave Macmillan, pp. 39–61.

Giltrow, J. and Stein, D. (2009). *Genres in the Internet: Issues in the Theory of Genre*. Amsterdam and Philadelphia: John Benjamins.

Gimenez, J., Baldwin, M., Breen, P., Green, J., Gutierrez, E., Paterson, R. et al. (2020). Reproduced, reinterpreted, lost: Trajectories of scientific knowledge across contexts. *Text & Talk*, 40(3), 293–324.

Gladkova, O. L., DiMarco, C. and Harris, R. A. (2015). Argumentative meanings and their stylistic configurations in clinical research publications. *Argument and Computation*, 6(3), 310–346.

Glänzel, W., Debackere, K. and Meyer, M. (2007). Triad or tetrad? On global changes in a dynamic world. *Working Paper Series*, 1–17.

Glänzel, W. and Schubert, A. (2004). Analysing scientific networks through co-authorship. In H. F. Moed, W. Glänzel and U. Schmoch, eds., *Handbook of Quantitative Science and Technology Research*. Dordrecht: Kluwer Academic Publishers, pp. 257–276.

Glaser, E., Guilherme, M., Méndez García, M. C. and Mughan, T. (2007). *Intercultural Competence for Professional Mobility*. Graz: Council of Europe.

Goodrum, A. A., McCain, K. W., Lawrence, S. and Giles, C. L. (2001). Scholarly publishing in the Internet age: A citation analysis of computer science literature. *Information Processing and Management*, 37, 661–675.

Goodwin, S., Jeng, W. and He, D. (2014). Changing communication on ResearchGate through interface updates. *Proceedings of the American Society for Information Science and Technology*, 51(1), 1–4.

Gordin, M. F. (2015). *Scientific Babel: How Science Was Done Before and After Global English*. Chicago: The University of Chicago Press.

Gosden, H. (2001). Thank you for your critical comments and helpful suggestions: Compliance and conflict in authors' replies to referees' comments in peer reviews of scientific research papers. *Ibérica, Journal of the European Association of Languages for Specific Purposes*, 3, 3–17.

Gosden, H. (2003). 'Why not give us the full story?': Functions of referees' comments in peer reviews of scientific research papers. *Journal of English for Academic Purposes*, 2(2), 87–101.

Gotti, M. (2014). Reformulation and recontextualisation in popularisation discourse. *Ibérica, Journal of the European Association of Languages for Specific Purposes*, 27, 15–34.

Greaves, C. and Warren, M. (2007). Concgramming: A computer driven approach to learning the phraseology of English. *ReCALL*, 19(3), 287–306.

Greenbaum, S. (1996). *The Oxford English Grammar*. Oxford: Oxford University Press.

Gross, A. G. (1990). *The Rhetoric of Science: The Rhetorical Analysis of Scientific Texts*. Cambridge: Harvard University Press.

Gross, A. G. (1994). The roles of rhetoric in the public understanding of science. *Public Understanding of Science*, **3**, 3–23.

Gross, A. G. (2016). Why all scientists write in English. *Metascience*, **25**(1), 125–129.

Gross, A. G. and Buehl, J. (2016). *Science and the Internet: Communicating Knowledge in a Digital Age*. Amityville, NY: Baywood's Technical Communications Series.

Gross, A. G. and Harmon, J. E. (2016). *The Internet Revolution in the Sciences and Humanities*. Oxford: Oxford University Press.

Gross, A. G., Harmon, J. and Reidy, M. (2002). *Communicating Science: The Scientific Article from the 17th Century to the Present*. Oxford: Oxford University Press.

Guillén-Galve, I. and Vázquez, I., eds. (2018). *English as a Lingua Franca and Intercultural Communication: Implications and/or Applications to the Feld of English Language Teaching*. Bern: Peter Lang.

Guillén-Galve, I. and Bocanegra-Valle, A., eds. (2021). *Ethnographies of Academic Writing Research: Theory, Methods, and Interpretation*. Amsterdam and New York: John Benjamins.

Gunnarsson, A. and Elam, M. (2012). Food fight! The Swedish Low-Carb/High Fat (LCHF) movement and the turning of science popularisation against the scientists. *Science as Culture*, **21**(3), 315–334.

Guthrie, S., Lichten, C., Corbett, J. and Wooding, S. (2017a). *International Mobility of Researchers. A Review of the Literature*. Santa Monica, CA, and Cambridge, UK: RAND Corporation. www.rand.org/content/dam/rand/pubs/research_reports/RR1900/RR1991/RAND_RR1991z1.pdf [last accessed on 5 July 2020].

Guthrie, S., Lichten, C., Harte, E., Parks, S. and Wooding, S. (2017b). *International Mobility of Researchers. A Survey of Researchers in the UK*. Santa Monica, CA, and Cambridge, UK: RAND Corporation.

Haberland, H. (2005). Domains and domain loss. In B. Preisler, A. Fabricius, H. Haberland, S. Kjærbeck and K. Risager, eds., *The Consequences of Mobility*. Roskilde: Roskilde University, Department of Language and Culture, pp. 227–237.

Hafner, C. A. (2018). Genre innovation and multimodal expression in scholarly communication: Video methods articles in experimental biology. *Ibérica, Journal of the European Association of Languages for Specific Purposes*, **36**, 15–42.

Hafner, C. A. and Miller, L. (2011). Fostering learner autonomy in English for science: A collaborative digital video project in a technological learning environment. *Language Learning and Technology*, **15**(3), 68–86.

Halliday, M. A. K. and Martin, J. R., eds. (1993). *Writing Science: Literacy and Discursive Power*. London and Washington, DC: The Falmer Press.

Hamel, R. E. (2006a). The development of language empires. In U. Ammon, N. Dittmar, K. Mattheier and P. Trudgill, eds., *Sociolinguistics. An International Handbook of the Science of Language and Society*. Berlin: Walter de Gruyter, pp. 2240–2258.

Hamel, R. E. (2006b). Spanish in science and higher education: Perspectives for a plurilingual language policy in the Spanish-speaking world. *Current Issues in Language Planning*, 7(1), 95–125.

Hamel, R. E. (2007). The dominance of English in the international scientific periodical literature and the future of language use in science. *AILA Review*, 20, 53–71.

Hancioğlu, N., Neufeld, S. and Eldridge, J. (2008). Through the looking glass and into the land of lexico-grammar. *English for Specific Purposes*, 27, 459–479.

Hara, N., Abbazio, J. and Perkins, K. (2019). An emerging form of public engagement with science: Ask Me Anything (AMA) sessions on Reddit r/science. *PLoS ONE*. DOI: https://doi.org/10.1371/journal.pone.0216789

Harmon, J. E. (2019). At the frontiers of the online scientific article. In M.-J. Luzón and C. Pérez-Llantada, eds., *Genres and Science in the Digital Age: Connecting Traditional and New Genres*. Amsterdam and Philadelphia: John Benjamins, pp. 19–40.

Harwood, N., ed. (2010). *English Language Teaching Materials: Theory and Practice*. Cambridge: Cambridge University Press.

Harzing, A. W. K. and van der Wal, R. (2009). A Google Scholar H-Index for journals: An alternative metric to measure journal impact in economics and business? *Journal of the American Society for Information Science and Technology*, 60(1), 41–46.

Hendges, G. R. and Florek, C. S. (2019). The graphical abstract as a new genre in the promotion of science. In M.-J. Luzón and C. Pérez-Llantada, eds., *Science Communication on the Internet. Old Genres Meet New Genres*. Amsterdam and Philadelphia: John Benjamins, pp. 59–80.

Herdina, P. and Jessner, U. (2002). *A Dynamic Model of Multilingualism. Perspectives of Change in Psycholinguistics*. Amsterdam and Philadelphia: John Benjamins.

Herring, S. (2013). Discourse in Web 2.0: Familiar, reconfigured, and emergent. In D. Tannen and A. Trester, eds., *Discourse 2.0*. Georgetown: Georgetown University Press, pp. 1–25.

Hewings, A., Lillis, T. and Vladimirou, D. (2010). Who's citing whose writings? A corpus based study of citations as interpersonal resource in English medium national and English medium international journals. *Journal of English for Academic Purposes*, 9(2), 102–115.

Hirvela, A. and Belcher, D. (2001). Coming back to voice: The multiple voices and identities of mature multilingual writers. *Journal of Second Language Writing*, 10(1–2), 83–106.

Hoey, M. (1983). *On the Surface of Discourse*. London: George Allen and Unwin.

Hook, D. W., Porter, S. J. and Herzog, C. (2018). Dimensions: Building context for search and evaluation. *Frontiers in Research Metrics Analytics*, 3, 1–11, DOI: 10.3389/frma.2018.00023 (online).

House, J. (2003). English as a lingua franca. A threat to multilingualism? *Journal of Sociolinguistics*, 7(4), 556–578.

Huckin, T. (2001). Abstracting from abstracts. In M. Hewings, ed., *Academic Writing in Context. Implications and Applications*. Birmingham: The University of Birmingham Press, pp. 93–103.

Hultgren, A. K., Gregersen, F. and Thøgersen, J. (2014). *English in Nordic Universities: Ideologies and Practices*. Amsterdam and Philadelphia: John Benjamins, pp. 1–26.

Hyland, K. (1998). Persuasion and context. The pragmatics of academic metadiscourse. *Journal of Pragmatics*, 30, 437–455.

Hyland, K. (1999). Academic attribution: Citation and the construction of disciplinary knowledge. *Applied Linguistics*, 20(3), 341–367.

Hyland, K. (2005). Stance and engagement: A model of interaction in academic discourse. *Discourse Studies,* 6(2), 173–191.

Hyland, K. (2008). As can be seen: Lexical bundles and disciplinary variation. *English for Specific Purposes*, 27, 4–21.

Hyland, K. (2009). *Academic Discourse*. London: Continuum.

Hyland, K. (2010). Constructing proximity: Relating to readers in popular and professional science. *English for Academic Purposes*, 9(2), 116–127.

Hyland, K. (2012). *Disciplinary Identities. Individuality and Community in Academic Discourse*. Cambridge: Cambridge University Press.

Hyland, K. (2016). Academic publishing and the myth of linguistic injustice. *Journal of Second Language Writing*, 31, 58–69.

Hyland, K. (2018). Narrative, identity and academic storytelling. *ILCEA* (online), 31. DOI: http:///doi.org/10.4000/ilcea.4677

Hyland, K. and Jiang, F. (K.) (2019). *Academic Discourse and Global Publishing*. London and New York: Routledge.

Hyland, K. and Tse, P. (2005). Hooking the reader: A corpus study of evaluative that in abstracts. *English for Specific Purposes*, 24, 12–39.

Hynninen, N. (2018). Exploring regimes of academic writing: Introduction to the special issue. *Language and Education*, 32(6), 471–476.

Hynninen, N. and Kuteeva, M. (2017). 'Good' and 'acceptable' English in L2 research writing: Ideals and realities in history and computer science. *Journal of English for Academic Purposes*, 30, 53–65.

Irwin, D. (2020). The pandemic adds momentum to the deglobalisation trend. *VOX CEPR Policy Portal*. Retrieved from https://voxeu.org/article/pandemic-adds-momentum-deglobalisation-trend [last accessed on 1 July 2020].

Ivanič, R. (1998). *Writing and Identity. The Discoursal Construction of Identity in Academic Writing*. Amsterdam and Philadelphia: John Benjamins.

Jamieson, K. M. (1975). Antecedent genre as rhetorical constraint. *Quarterly Journal of Speech*, 61, 406–415.

Jamieson, K. H. and Campbell, K. K. (1982). Rhetorical hybrids: Fusions of generic elements. *Quarterly Journal of Speech*, 69, 146–157.

Jeng, W., Goodwin, S., He, D. and Li, L. (2017). Information exchange on an academic social networking site: A multidiscipline comparison on ResearchGate Q&A. *Journal of the Association for Information Science & Technology*, 68(3), 638–652.

Jenkins, J. (2000). *The Phonology of English as an International Language.* Oxford: Oxford University Press.

Jenkins, J. (2015). Repositioning English and multilingualism in English as a Lingua Franca. *Englishes in Practice*, 2(3), 49–85.

Johns, A. M. (1997). *Text, Role and Context: Developing Academic Literacies.* 1st ed. Cambridge: Cambridge University Press.

Johns, A. M., ed. (2002). *Genre in the Classroom: Multiple Perspectives.* Mahwah, NJ: Lawrence Erlbaum Associates.

Johns, A. M. and Swales, J. M. (2002). Literacy and disciplinary practices: Opening and closing perspectives. *Journal of English for Academic Purposes*, 1, 13–28.

Johns, T. (1991). Should you be persuaded: Two samples of data-driven learning. *English Language Research Journal*, 4, 1–16.

Jones, R. and Hafner, C. (2012) *Understanding Digital Literacies: A Practical Introduction.* 1st ed. Oxon: Routledge.

Jordan, K. (2014). Academics and their online networks: Exploring the role of academic social networking sites. *First Monday*, 19(11). DOI: http://doi.org/ http://dx.doi.org/10.5210/fm.v19i11.4937

Jørgensen, J. N. (2010). *Languaging. Nine Years of Poly-Lingual Development of Young Turkish-Danish Grade School Students.* Copenhagen: University of Copenhagen, Faculty of Humanities.

Jørgensen, J. N., Karrebæk, M. S., Madsen, L. M. and Møller, J. S. (2011). Polylanguaging in superdiversity. *Diversities*, 13(2), 23–38. Retrieved from www.unesco.org/shs/diversities/vol13/issue2/art2 [last accessed on 26 January 2020].

Kachru, B. B. (1985). Standards, codification and sociolinguistic realism: The English language in the outer circle. In R. Quirk and H. Widdowson, eds., *English in the World: Teaching and Learning the Language and the Literatures.* Cambridge: Cambridge University Press in Association with the British Council, pp. 11–30.

Kachru, B. B. (1986). The power and politics of English. *World Englishes*, 5(2–3), 121–140.

Kaplan, R. (1966). Cultural thought patterns in intercultural education. *Language Learning*, 16(1), 1–20.

Kelly, A. R. and Maddalena, K. (2016). Networks, genres, and complex wholes: Citizen science and how we act together through typified text. *Canadian Journal of Communication*, 41(2), 287–303.

Kelly, A. R. and Miller, C. R. (2016). Intersections: Scientific and parascientific communication on the Internet. In A. G. Gross and J. Buehl, eds., *Science and the Internet: Communicating Knowledge in a Digital Age.* Amityville, NY: Baywood, pp. 221–245.

Kim, L. C. and Lim, J. M. (2013). Metadiscourse in English and Chinese research article introductions. *Discourse Studies*, 15(2), 129–146.

Kirilenko, A. P. and Stepchenkova, S. O. (2014). Public microblogging on climate change: One year of Twitter worldwide. *Global Environmental Change*, 26, 171–182.

Kjellberg, S. (2009). Scholarly blogging practice as situated genre: An analytical framework based on genre theory. *Information Research*, **14**(3), paper 410. Retrieved from http://InformationR.net/ir/14-3/paper410.html [last accessed on 5 July 2020].

Knievel, M. (2009). What is humanistic about computers and writing? Historical patterns and contemporary possibilities for the field. *Computers and Composition*, **26**(2), 92–106.

Kravchenko, A. V. (2016). Two views on language ecology and ecolinguistics. *Language Sciences*, 54, 102–113.

Kress, G. and Van Leeuwen, T. (2001). *Multimodal Discourse: The Modes and Media of Contemporary Communication*. London: Arnold.

Kress, G. R. (2003). *Literacy in the New Media Age*. London: Routledge.

Kress, G. R. (2010). *Multimodality: A Social Semiotic Approach to Contemporary Communication*. London: Taylor & Francis, Routledge.

Kuteeva, M. (2007). The use of online forums in language teaching: The importance of task design. In M. B. Nunes, M. McPherson and P. Isaías, eds., *IADIS International Conference Proceedings: E-Learning*, 6–8 July, Lisbon, Portugal, IADIS, Lisbon (2007), pp. 305–308.

Kuteeva, M. (2016). Research blogs, tweets and wikis. In K. Hyland and P. Shaw, eds., *The Routledge Handbook of English for Academic Purposes*. London: Routledge, pp. 433–445.

Kuteeva, M. and Mauranen, A. K. (2018). Digital academic discourse: Texts and contexts. Introduction. *Discourse, Context and Media*, 24, 1–7.

Kuteeva, M. and McGrath, L. (2014). Taming tyrannosaurus rex: English use in the research and publication practices of humanities scholars in Sweden. *Multilingua: Journal of Cross-Cultural and Interlanguage Communication*, 33(3–4), 367–389.

Kwok, R. (2018). Lab notebooks go digital. *Nature*, **560**, 269–270.

Latour, B. and Woolgar, S. (1986). *Laboratory Life: The Construction of Scientific Facts*. Princeton: Princeton University Press.

Lave, J. and Wenger, E. (1991). *Situated Learning: Legitimate Peripheral Participation*. Cambridge: Cambridge University Press.

Lee, H. and Lee, K. (2013). Publish (in international indexed journals) or perish: Neoliberal ideology in a Korean university. *Language Policy*, **12**(3), 215–230.

Lejano, R. P., Tavares-Reager, J. and Berkes, F. (2013). Climate and narrative: Environmental knowledge in everyday life. *Environmental Science and Policy*, 31, 61–70.

Lillis, T. (2008). Ethnography as method, methodology, and 'deep theorizing': Closing the gap between text and context in academic writing research. *Written Communication*, **25**(3), 353–388.

Lillis, T. and Curry, M. J. (2010). *Academic Writing in a Global Context*. London: Routledge.

Lillis, T., Hewings, A., Vladimirou, D. and Curry, M. J. (2010). The geolinguistics of English as an academic lingua franca: Citation practices across English-medium national and English-medium international journals. *International Journal of Applied Linguistics*, **20**(1), 111–135.

Linares, E. (2019). Afterword: Socialization to the practice of multilingual research. *Critical Multilingualism Studies*, 7(1), 124–129.

Linn, A. (2016). *Investigating English in Europe: Contexts and Agendas*. Boston and Berlin: Walter de Gruyter.

Ljosland, R. (2007). English in Norwegian academia: A step towards diglossia? *World Englishes*, 26(4), 395–410.

Loroño-Leturiondo, M. and Davies, S. R. (2018). Responsibility and science communication: Scientists' experiences of and perspectives on public communication activities. *Journal of Responsible Innovation*, 5(2), 170–185.

Lu, X. (2010). Automatic analysis of syntactic complexity in second language writing. *International Journal of Corpus Linguistics*, 15(4), 474–496.

Luzón, M. J. (2011). Interesting post, but I disagree: Social presence and antisocial behaviour in academic weblogs. *Applied Linguistics*, 32(5), 517–540.

Luzón, M. J. (2013). Public communication of science in blogs: Recontextualizing scientific discourse for a diversified audience. *Written Communication*, 30(4), 428–457.

Luzón, M. J. (2017). Connecting genres and languages in online scholarly communication. *Written Communication*, 34(4), 441–471.

Luzón, M. J. (2018a). Features of online ELF in research group blogs written by multilingual scholars. *Discourse, Context and Media*, 24, 24–32.

Luzón, M. J. (2018b). English as a Lingua Franca in academic blogs: Its coexistence and interaction with other languages. In Z. Tatsioka, B. Seidlhofer, N. Sifakis and G. Ferguson, eds., *Using English as a Lingua Franca in education in Europe*. Berlin and Boston: de Gruyter Mouton, pp. 125–149.

Luzón, M. J. and Pérez-Llantada, C., eds. (2019). *Science Communication on the Internet: Old Genres Meet New Genres*. Amsterdam and Philadelphia: John Benjamins, pp. 131–152.

Luzón, M. J. and Pérez-Llantada, C. (forthcoming). *Digital Genres in Knowledge Production and Dissemination: Perspectives and Practices*. Bristol: Multilingual Matters.

Mackenzie Owen, J. (2007). *The Scientific Article in the Age of Digitization*. Dordrecht: Springer.

Maier, C. D. and Engberg, J. (2019). The multimodal bridge between academics and practitioners in the Harvard Business Review's digital context: A multilevelled qualitative analysis of knowledge construction. In M.-J. Luzón and C. Pérez-Llantada, eds., *Science Communication on the Internet: Old Genres Meet New Genres*. Amsterdam and Philadelphia: John Benjamins, pp. 131–152.

Major, J. (1969). Historical development of the ecosystem concept. In G. M. Van Dyne, ed., *The Ecosystem Concept in Natural Resource Management*. New York: Academic Press, pp. 9–22.

Marwick, A. and boyd, d. (2011). 'I tweet honestly, I tweet passionately': Twitter users, context collapse, and the imagined audience. *New Media and Society*, 13, 96–113.

Matsuda, P. K. and Tardy, C. M. (2007). Voice in academic writing: The rhetorical construction of author identity in blind manuscript review. *English for Specific Purposes*, 26(2), 235–249.

Mauranen, A. (1993). *Cultural Differences in Academic Rhetoric*. Frankfurt and Main: Peter Lang.

Mauranen. A. (2012). *Exploring ELF: Academic English Shaped by Non-Native Speakers*. 1st ed. Cambridge: Cambridge University Press.

Mauranen, A. (2013). Hybridism, edutainment, and doubt: Science blogging finding its feet. *Nordic Journal of English Studies*, 13(1), 7–36.

Mauranen, A. (2018). Second Language Acquisition, World Englishes, and English as a Lingua Franca (ELF). *World Englishes*, 37(1), 106–119.

Mauranen, A., Pérez-Llantada, C. and Swales, J. M. (2010). Academic Englishes: A standardised knowledge? In A. Kirkpatrick, ed., *The World Englishes Handbook*. 1st ed. Abingdon: Routledge, pp. 634–652.

Mauranen, A., Pérez-Llantada, C. and Swales, J. M. (2020). Academic Englishes: A standardised knowledge? In A. Kirkpatrick (ed.), *The World Englishes Handbook*. 2nd ed. Abingdon: Routledge, pp. 659–676.

McGrath, L. (2016). Open-access writing: An investigation into the online drafting and revision of a research article in pure mathematics. *English for Specific Purposes*, 43, 25–36.

McLuhan, M. (1987). *Understanding Media. The Extensions of Man*. London: Ark.

Mehlenbacher, A. R. (2017). Crowdfunding science: Exigencies and strategies in an emerging genre of science communication. *Technical Communication Quarterly*, 26(2), 127–144.

Mehlenbacher, A. R. (2019a). Registered reports: An emerging scientific research article genre. *Written Communication*, 36(1), 38–67.

Mehlenbacher, A. R. (2019b). *Science Communication Online. Engaging Experts and Publics on the Internet*. Columbus: The Ohio State University Press.

Mehlenbacher, A. R. and Mehlenbacher, B. (2019). The case of the scientific research article and lessons concerning genre change online. In M.-J. Luzón and C. Pérez-Llantada, eds., *Science Communication on the Internet. Old Genres Meet New Genres*. Amsterdam and Philadelphia: John Benjamins, pp. 41–58.

Meriläinen, S., Tienari, J., Thomas, R. and Davies, A. (2008). Hegemonic academic practices: Experiences of publishing from the periphery. *Organization*, 15, 584–597.

Mewburn, I. and Thomson, P. (2013). Why do academics blog? An analysis of audiences, purposes and challenges. *Studies in Higher Education*, 38(8), 1105–1119.

Miller, C. R. (1984). Genre as social action. *Quarterly Journal of Speech*, 70(2), 151–167.

Miller, C. R. (1994). Rhetorical community. The cultural basis of genre's understanding how to participate in the actions of a community. In A. Freedman and P. Medway, eds., *Genre and the New Rhetoric*. Abingdon: Taylor & Francis, pp. 67–78.

Miller, C. R. (2011). Exploring genres in cultural contact zones. Featured Presentation. *22nd Penn State Conference on Rhetoric and Composition: Rhetoric and Writing across Language Boundaries*. Penn State University, July 2011.

Miller, C. R. and Kelly, A. R., eds. (2017). *Emerging Genres in New Media Environments*. London: Palgrave Macmillan.

Miller, C. R. and Shepherd, D. (2004). Blogging as social action: A genre analysis of the weblog. In L. Gurak, ed., *Into the Blogosphere: Rhetoric, Community, and the Culture of Weblogs*. Minneapolis: University of Minnesota Libraries. Retrieved from http://hdl.handle.net/11299/172818 [last accessed on 5 July 2020].

Mišák, A., Marušić, M. and Marušić, A. (2005). Manuscript editing as a way of teaching academic writing: Experience from a small scientific journal. *Journal of Second Language Writing*, 14, 122–131.

Mogull, S. A. and Stanfield, C. T. (2015). Current use of visuals in scientific communication. *Proceedings of the IEEE*, 1–7. DOI: 10.1109/IPCC.2015 .7235818

Mort, P. and Drury, H. (2012). Supporting student academic literacy in the disciplines using genre-based online pedagogy. *Journal of Academic Language and Learning*, 6(3), A1-A15. Retrieved from https://journal.aall .org.au/index.php/jall/article/view/173

Motta-Roth, D. (2009). Popularização da ciência como prática social e discursiva. In D. Motta-Roth and M. E. Giering, orgs., *Discursos de popularização da ciência. Hipers@beres*. Santa Maria, RS: PPGL Editores, pp. 131–195.

Motta-Roth, D. and Scherer, A. S. (2016). Science popularization: Interdiscursivity among science, pedagogy, and journalism. *Bakhtiniana*, 11(2), 171–194.

Mufwene, S. (2001). *The Ecology of Language Evolution*. Cambridge: Cambridge University Press.

Mufwene, S. (2013). Globalization, Global English and World English(es), myths and facts. In N. Coupland, ed., *The Handbook of Language and Globalization*. Chichester: Wiley-Blackwell, pp. 31–55.

Mühlhäusler, P. (1996). *Linguistic Ecology*. London: Routledge.

Mühlhäusler, P. (2003). *Language of Environment, Environment of Language: A Course in Ecolinguistics*. London: Battlebridge Publications.

Muresan, L.-M. and Nicolae, M. (2015). Addressing the challenge of publishing internationally in a non-Anglophone academic context: Romania – a case in point. In R. Plo Alastrué and C. Pérez-Llantada, eds., *English as a Scientific and Research Language. Debates and Discourses*. Amsterdam: John Benjamins, pp. 281–310.

Muresan, L.-M. and Pérez-Llantada, C. (2014). English for research publication and dissemination in bi-/multiliterate environments: The case of Romanian academics. *Journal of English for Academic Purposes*, 13, 53–64.

Myers, G. (1990). Stories and styles in two molecular biology review articles. In C. Bazerman and J. Paradis, eds., *Textual Dynamics in the Professions*. Madison: University of Wisconsin Press, pp. 45–75.

Myers, G. (2010). *The Discourse of Blogs and Wikis*. London: Continuum.

Negretti, R. (2012). Metacognition in student academic writing: A longitudinal study of metacognitive awareness and its relation to task perception, self-regulation, and evaluation of performance. *Written Communication*, 29(2), 142–179.

Negretti, R. and McGrath, L. (2018). Scaffolding genre knowledge and metacognition: Insights from an L2 doctoral research writing course. *Journal of Second Language Writing*, 40, 12–31.

Nicholas, D., Huntington, P. and Watkinson, A. (2005). Scholarly journal usage: The results of deep log analysis. *Journal of Documentation*, 61(2), 248–280.

Nieman, A. (2000). *The Popularisation of Physics: Boundaries of Authority and the Visual Culture of Science*. Unpublished thesis. Faculty of Applied Sciences and Faculty of Humanities, University of the West of England, Bristol.

North, B. and Piccardo, E. (2016). Developing illustrative descriptors of aspects of mediation for the Common European Framework of Reference (CEFR), a Council of Europe project. *Language Teaching*, 49(3), 455–459.

O'Donnell, M. B., Römer, U. and Ellis, N. C. (2013). The development of formulaic sequences in first and second language writing. Investigating effects of frequency, association, and native norm. *International Journal of Corpus Linguistics*, 18(1), 83–108.

Okamura, A. (2008). Citation forms in scientific texts: Similarities and differences in L1 and L2 professional writing. *Nordic Journal of English Studies*, 7(3), 61–81.

Olmos-López, P. (2019). Back and forth between languages: An early-career bilingual academic's writing odyssey. *Critical Multilingualism Studies*, 7(1), 32–43.

O'Neil, D. (2018). English as the lingua franca of international publishing. *World Englishes*, 37(2), 146–165.

Organisation for Economic Co-operation and Development (OECD). (2008). *Main Science and Technology Indicators 2008*. Paris: OECD.

Orlikowski, W. J. and Yates, J. (1994). Genre repertoire: The structuring of communicative practices in organizations. *Administrative Science Quarterly*, 39(4), 541–574.

Orpin, D. (2019) #Vaccineswork: Recontextualizing the content of epidemiology reports on Twitter. In M.-J. Luzón and C. Pérez-Llantada, eds., *Science Communication on the Internet. Old Genres Meet New Genres*. Amsterdam and Philadelphia: John Benjamins, pp. 173–194.

Ostergren, M. (2013). *How Scientists Develop Competence in Visual Communication*. Doctoral dissertation. Retrieved from http://faculty.washington.edu/ostergrn/Dissertation/OstergrenDissertationFINAL.pdf [last accessed on 1 March 2020]

Owen, R., Macnaghten, P. and Stilgoe, J. (2012). Responsible research and innovation: From science in society to science for society, with society. *Science and Public Policy*, 39(6), 751–760.

Paltridge, B. (2020). Writing for academic journals in the digital era. *RELC Journal*, 51(1), 147–157. DOI: https://doi.org/10.1177/0033688219890359

Paltridge, B. and Starfield, S. (2007). *Thesis and Dissertation Writing in a Second Language: A Handbook for Supervisors*. London and New York: Routledge.

Paltridge, B., Starfield, S. and Ravelli, L. J. (2012). Change and stability: Examining the macrostructures of doctoral theses in the visual and performing arts. *Journal of English for Academic Purposes*, 11, 332–344.

Pasquali, M. (2007). Video in science. Protocol videos: The implications for research and society. *EMBO reports*, 8(8), 712–716.

Patrão, A. (2018). Linguistic relativism in the age of global 'lingua franca' reconciling cultural and linguistic diversity with globalization. *International Review of General Linguistics*, 210–211, 30–41.

Paulus, T. M. and Roberts, K. R. (2018). Crowdfunding a real-life superhero: The construction of worthy bodies in medical campaign narratives. *Discourse, Context and Media*, 21, 64–72.

Pauwels, L. (2006). *Visual Cultures of Science: Rethinking Representational Practices in Knowledge Building and Science Communication*. Lebanon, NH: Dartmouth College Press.

Pennycook, A. (2007). *Global Englishes and Transcultural Flows*. London and New York: Routledge.

Pennycook, A. (2010a). The future of Englishes: One, many or none? In A. Kirkpatrick, ed., *The Routledge Handbook of World Englishes*. Abingdon: Routledge, pp. 673–688.

Pennycook, A. (2010b). *Language as a Local Practice*. London and New York: Routledge.

Pennycook, A. (2018). Repertoires, registers and linguistic diversity. In A. Creese and A. Backledge, eds., *The Routledge Handbook of Language and Superdiversity*. London: Routledge, pp. 3–15.

Pérez-Llantada, C. (2010). The discourse functions of metadiscourse in published writing. Culture and language issues. *Nordic Journal of English Studies*, 9(2), 41–68.

Pérez-Llantada, C. (2011). Heteroglossic (dis)engagement and the construal of the ideal readership: Dialogic spaces in academic texts. In V. Bhatia, P. Sánchez and P. Pérez-Paredes, eds., *Researching Specialized Languages*. Amsterdam and Philadelphia: John Benjamins, pp. 25–45.

Pérez-Llantada, C. (2012). *Scientific Discourse and the Rhetoric of Globalization. The Impact of Culture and Language*. London and New York: Continuum.

Pérez-Llantada, C. (2013a). 'Glocal' rhetorical practices in academic writing: An intercultural rhetoric approach to L2 English discoursal hybridisation. *European Journal of English Studies*, 17(3), 251–268.

Pérez-Llantada, C. (2013b). The Article of the Future: Strategies for genre stability and change. *English for Specific Purposes*, 32(4), 221–235. DOI: https://www.sciencedirect.com/science/article/abs/pii/S1475158515300059

Pérez-Llantada, C. (2014). Formulaic language in L1 and L2 expert academic writing: Convergent and divergent usage. *Journal of English for Academic Purposes*, 14, 84–94.

Pérez-Llantada, C. (2015). Genres in the forefront, languages in the background: The scope of genre analysis in language-related scenarios. *Journal of English for Academic Purposes*, 19, 10–21. DOI: 10.1016/j.jeap.2015.05.005

Pérez-Llantada, C. (2016). How is the digital medium shaping research genres? Some cross-disciplinary trends. *ESP Today*, 4(1), 22–42.

Pérez-Llantada, C. (2018). Bringing into focus multilingual realities: Faculty perceptions of academic languages on campus. *Lingua*, 212, 30–43. DOI: https://doi.org/10.1016/j.lingua.2018.05.006

Pérez-Llantada, C. (2019). Ecologies of genres and an ecology of languages of science: Current and future debates. In D. R. Gruber and L. Walsh, eds., *Routledge Handbook of Language and Science*. New York: Routledge, pp. 361–374.

Pérez-Llantada, C. (2021a). Grammar features and discourse style in digital genres: The case of science-focused crowdfunding projects. *Revista Signos. Estudios de Lingüística*, 54(105), 73–96.

Pérez-Llantada, C. (2021b). Genres and languages in science communication: The multiple dimensions of the science-policy interface, Language & Communication. 78, 65–76. DOI: https://doi.org/10.1016/j.langcom.2021.02.004

Pérez-Llantada, C. and Swales, J. M. (2017). English for Academic Purposes. In E. Hinkel, ed., *Handbook of Research in Second Language Teaching and Learning III*. New York: Routledge, pp. 42–55.

Phillipson, R. (1992). *Linguistic Imperialism*. Oxford: Oxford University Press.

Phillipson, R. (2003). *English-Only Europe? Challenging Language Policy*. London: Routledge.

Phillipson, R. and Skutnabb-Kangas, T. (1993). Sproglige menneskerettigheder. In A. Holmen, R. Phillipson and T. Skutnabb-Kangas, eds., *Minoriteter og uddannelse. Københavnerstudier i tosprogethed 18*. Copenhagen: Danmarks Lærerhøjskole, Center for multikulturelle studier, pp. 8–19.

Phothongsunan, S. (2016). Thai university academics' challenges of writing for publication in English. *Theory and Practice in Language Studies*, 6(4), 681–685.

Pienemann, M. (2005). *Cross-Linguistic Aspects of Processability Theory*. Amsterdam: John Benjamins.

Pienemann, M., Di Biase, B., Kawaguchi, S. and Håkansson, G. (2005). Processing constraints on L1 transfer. In J. F. Kroll and A. M. B. DeGroot, eds., *Handbook of Bilingualism: Psycholinguistic Approaches*. New York: Oxford University Press, pp. 128–153.

Piller, I. (2015). Language ideologies. In K. Tracy, C. Ilie and T. Sandel, eds., *The International Encyclopedia of Language and Social Interaction*. West Sussex: Wiley-Blackwell, pp. 917–927.

Plastina, A. F. (2017). Professional discourse in video abstracts: Re-articulating the meaning of written research article abstracts. In G. Garzone, P. Catenaccio, K. Grego and R. Doerr, eds., *Specialised and Professional Discourse across Media and Genres*. Milano: Ledizioni, pp. 57–74.

Plo Alastrué, R. and Pérez-Llantada, C. (2015). *English as a Scientific and Research Language. Debates and Discourses*. Amsterdam and Philadelphia: John Benjamins.

Pluchino, A., Burgio, J., Rapisarda, A., Biondo, A. E., Pulvirenti, A. Ferro, A. and Giorgino, T. (2019). Exploring the role of interdisciplinarity in physics: Success, talent and luck. *PLoS ONE*, **14**, 6. DOI: https://doi.org/10.1371/journal.pone.0218793

Politzer-Ahles, S., Holliday, J. J., Girolamo, T., Spychalska, M. and Berkson, K. H. (2016). Is linguistic injustice a myth? A response to Hyland (2016). *Journal of Second Language Writing*, 34, 3–8.

Porter, J. E. (1986). Intertextuality and the discourse community. *Rhetoric Review*, 5(1), 34–47.

Prior, P. A. (1998). *Writing/Disciplinarity. A Sociohistoric Account of Literate Activity in the Academy.* Mahwah, NJ: Lawrence Erlbaum Associates.

Prior, P. A. (2009). From speech genres to mediated multimodal genre systems: Bakhtin, Voloshinov, and the question of writing. In C. Bazerman, A. Bonini and E. Figueiredo, eds., *Genre in a Changing World.* Fort Collins: Parlor Press, pp. 17–34.

Prior, P. A. (2013). Multimodality and ESP research. In B. Paltridge and S. Starfield, eds., *The Handbook of English for Specific Purposes.* 1st ed. Boston: Wiley-Blackwell, pp. 519–534.

Prior, P. and Bilbro, R. (2012). Academic enculturation: Developing literate practices and disciplinary identities. In M. Castelló and C. Donahue, eds., *University Writing: Selves and Texts in Academic Societies.* Bingley: Emerald, pp. 20–31.

Prior, P. and Hengst, J. (2010). Introduction: Exploring semiotic remediation. In P. Prior and J. Hengst, eds., *Exploring Semiotic Remediation as Discourse Practice.* New York: Palgrave, pp. 1–23.

Puschmann, C. (2014). (Micro)blogging science? Notes on potentials and constraints of new forms of scholarly communication. In S. Friesike and S. Bartling, eds., *Opening Science.* New York: Springer, pp. 89–106.

Putnam, L. L. (2009). Symbolic capital and academic fields: An alternative discourse on journal rankings. *Management Communication Quarterly,* 23(1), 127–134.

Rakedzon, T., Segev, E., Chapnik, N. Yosef, R. and Baram-Tsabari, A. (2017). Automatic jargon identifier for scientists engaging with the public and science communication educators. *PLoS ONE.* 12(8), e0181742. DOI: https://doi.org/10.1371/journal.pone.0181742.

Rayson, P. and Garside, R. (2000). Comparing corpora using frequency profiling. In *Proceedings of the Workshop on Comparing Corpora, held in Conjunction with the 38th Annual Meeting of the Association for Computational Linguistics (ACL 2000).* 1–8 October 2000, Hong Kong, pp. 1–6.

Reid, G. (2019). Compressing, expanding, and attending to scientific meaning: Writing the semiotic hybrid of science for professional and citizen scientists. *Written Communication,* 36(1), 68–98.

Reid, G. and Anson, C. M. (2019). Public- and expert-facing communication: A case study of polycontextuality and context collapse in Internet-mediated citizen science. In M.-J. Luzón and C. Pérez-Llantada, eds., *Science Communication on the Internet. Old Genres Meet New Genres.* Amsterdam and Philadelphia: John Benjamins, pp. 219–238.

Riboni, G. (2020). Vlogging science: Scholarly vlogs between scholarship and popularisation. In M. Gotti, S. Maci and M. Sala, eds., *Scholarly Pathways. Knowledge Transfer and Knowledge Exchange in Academia.* Bern: Peter Lang, pp. 255–280.

Ringdal, K. G., Lossius, H. M. and Søreide, K. (2009). Getting your message through: An editorial guide for meeting publication standards. *Scandinavian Journal of Trauma, Resuscitation and Emergency Medicine,* 17, 1–4. Retrieved from www.ncbi.nlm.nih.gov/pmc/articles/PMC2804571/?tool=pubmed [last accessed on 10 April 2020].

Römer, U. (2011). Corpus research applications in second language teaching. *Annual Review of Applied Linguistics*, 31, 205–225.

Roque, G. (2017). Rhetoric, argumentation, and persuasion in a multimodal perspective. In A. Tseronis and C. Forceville, eds., *Multimodal Argumentation and Rhetoric in Media Genres*. Amsterdam and Philadelphia: John Benjamins, pp. 25–50.

Rounsaville, A., Goldberg, R. and Bawarshi, A. (2008). From incomes to outcomes: FYW students' prior genre knowledge, meta-cognition, and the question of transfer. *WPA: Writing Program Administration*, 32(1–2), 97–112.

Royal Society (2011). *Knowledge Networks and Nations: Global Scientific Communication in the 21st Century*. London: The Royal Society.

Rozycki, W. and Johnson, N. H. (2013). Non-canonical grammar in Best Paper award winners in engineering. *English for Specific Purposes*, 32(3), 157–169.

Rubin, D. L. and Kang, O. (2008). Writing to speak: What goes on across the two-way street. In D. Belcher and A. Hirvela, eds., *The Oral-Literate Connection*. Ann Arbor: The University of Michigan Press, pp. 210–225.

Russell, D. (1995). Activity theory and its implications for writing instruction. In J. Petraglia, ed., *Reconceiving Writing, Rethinking Writing Instruction*. Mahwah: Lawrence Erlbaum, pp. 51–78.

Salager-Meyer, F. (2008). Scientific publishing in developing countries: Challenges for the future. *Journal of English for Academic Purposes*, 7(2), 121–132.

Salö, L. (2015). The linguistic sense of placement. Habitus and the entextualization of translingual practices in Swedish academia. *Journal of Sociolinguistics*, 19(4), 511–534.

Salö, L. and Hanell, L. (2014). Performance of unprecedented genres. Interdiscursivity in the writing practices of a Swedish researcher. *Language & Communication*, 37, 12–28. DOI: https://doi.org/10.1016/j.langcom.2014.04.001

Salter, A. J. and Martin, B. R. (2001). The economic benefits of publicly funded basic research. A critical review. *Research Policy*, 30, 509–532.

Samraj, B. and Swales, J. M. (2000). Writing in conservation biology: Searching for an interdisciplinary rhetoric? *Language and Learning across the Disciplines*, 3(3), 36–56.

Sancho-Guinda, C. (2019). Promoemotional science? Emotion and intersemiosis in graphical abstracts. In J. L. Mackenzie and L. Alba Juez, eds., *Emotion in Discourse*. Amsterdam, Philadelphia: John Benjamins, pp. 357–386.

Schmidt, R. (1993). Awareness and second language acquisition. *Annual Review of Applied Linguistics*, 13, 206–226.

Schryer, C. F. (1994). The lab vs. the clinic: Sites of competing genres. In A. Freedman and P. Medway, eds., *Genre and the New Rhetoric*. London: Taylor & Francis, pp. 105–124.

Schryer, C. F. (2011). Investigating texts in their social contexts: The promise and peril of rhetorical genre studies. In D. Starke-Meyerring, A. Paré, N. Artemeva, M. Horne, and L. Yousoubova, eds., *Writing in Knowledge Societies*. Anderson: Parlor Press, pp. 31–52.

Schulson, M. (2018). Science's 'reproducibility crisis' is being used as political ammunition. *Wired, 20 April 2018*. Available online: www.wired.com/story/sciences-reproducibility-crisis-is-being-used-as-political-ammunition/ [last accessed on 10 April 2020].

Science Europe (2017). The rationales of Open Science: Digitalisation and democratisation in research. *Science Europe High-Level Workshop*, September 14, 2017, Berlin.

Scollon, R. (1998). *Mediated Discourse as Social Interaction*. London: Longman.

Scott, M. (2008). *Wordsmith Tools 5*. Liverpool: Lexical Analysis Software.

Selinker, L. (1972). Interlanguage. *International Review of Applied Linguistics in Language Teaching*, 10(1–4), 209–231.

Shaw, P. and Vassileva, I. (2009). Co-evolving academic rhetoric across culture: Britain, Bulgaria, Denmark, Germany in the 20th century. *Journal of Pragmatics*, 41(2), 290–305.

Shema, H., Bar-Ilan, J. and Thelwall, M. (2012). Research blogs and the discussion of scholarly information. *PLoS ONE*, 7(5), e35869. DOI: https://doi.org/10.1371/journal.pone.0035869.

Shih, R. (2011). Can Web 2.0 technology assist college students in learning English writing? Integrating 'Facebook' and peer assessment with blended learning. *Australasian Journal of Educational Technology*, 27, 829–845.

Shohamy, E. (2006). *Language Policy. Hidden Agendas and New Approaches*. London: Routledge.

Shohamy, E. (2017). Linguistic landscape: Interpreting and expanding language diversities. In A. de Fina, D. Ikizoglu and J. Wegner, eds., *Diversity and Superdiversity*. Washington, DC: Georgetown University Press, pp. 37–64.

Silverstein, M. (2015). How language communities intersect: Is 'superdiversity' an incremental or transformative condition? *Language & Communication*, 44, 7–18. DOI: https://doi.org/10.1016/j.langcom.2014.10.015

Simpson-Vlach, R. and Ellis, N. C. (2010). An academic formulas list: New methods in phraseology research. *Applied Linguistics*, 31(4), 487–512. DOI: https://doi.org/10.1093/applin/amp058

Sivertsen, G. (2018). Balanced multilingualism in science. *BiD: textos universitaris de biblioteconomia i documentació*, 40. Retrieved from http://bid.ub.edu/en/40/sivertsen.htm [last accessed on 10 April 2020].

Skutnabb-Kangas, T. (2000). Human rights and language wrongs – A future for diversity? *Language Sciences*, 20(1), 5–27. DOI: https://doi.org/10.1016/S0388-0001(97)00008-9

Skutnabb-Kangas, T. and Phillipson, R. (2001). Language ecology. Dominance, minorisation, linguistic genocide and linguistic rights. In M. Østergaard, ed., *Images of the World. Globalisation and Cultural Diversity*. Copenhagen: Center for kultursamarbejde med udviklingslandene, pp. 32–47, 206–208.

Skutnabb-Kangas, T. and Phillipson, R. (2011). Language ecology. In J. Verschueren, J.-O. Östman, J. Blommaert and C. Bulcaen, eds., *Handbook of Pragmatics*. Amsterdam and Philadelphia: John Benjamins, pp. 1–18.

Smart, G. (2011). Argumentation across web-based organizational discourses: The case of climate change. In S. Sarangi and C. Candlin, eds., *Handbook of Communication in Organisations and Professions*. Berlin, DE: Mouton de Gruyter, pp. 363–386.

Smart, G. and Falconer, M. (2019). The representation of science and technology in genres of Vatican discourse: Pope Francis's encyclical Laudato Si' as a case study. In M.-J. Luzón and C. Pérez-Llantada, eds., *Science Communication on the Internet. Old Genres Meet New Genres.* Amsterdam and Philadelphia: John Benjamins, pp. 195–218.

Spencer-Oatey, H. and Dauber, D. (2015). How internationalised is your university? From structural indicators to an agenda for integration. *GlobalPAD Working Papers.* Available at GlobalPADOpen House www.warwick.ac.uk/globalpadintercultural [last accessed on 10 April 2020].

Spicer, S. (2014). Exploring video abstracts in science journals: An overview and case study. *Journal of Librarianship and Scholarly Communication,* 2(2), eP1110.

Spinuzzi, C. (2003). *Tracing Genres through Organizations: A Sociocultural Approach to Information Design.* Cambridge: MIT Press.

Spinuzzi, C. (2004). *Describing Assemblages: Genre Sets, Systems, Repertoires, and Ecologies.* Austin, TX: Digital Writing and Research Lab.

Spinuzzi, C. and Guile, D. (2019). Fourth-generation Activity Theory: An integrative literature review and implications for professional communication. Paper presented at the *2019 IEEE International Professional Communication Conference (ProComm),* Aachen, Germany, 2019, pp. 37–45.

Spinuzzi, C. and Zachry, M. (2000). Genre ecologies: An open-system approach to understanding and constructing documentation. *ACM Journal of Computer Documentation,* 24(3), 169–181.

Stilgoe, J., Lock, S. J. and Wilsdon, J. (2014). Why should we promote public engagement with science? *Public Understanding of Science,* 23(1), 4–15. DOI: https://doi.org/10.1177/0963662513518154

Stockemer, D. and Wigginton, M. J. (2019). Publishing in English or another language: An inclusive study of scholar's language publication preferences in the natural, social and interdisciplinary sciences. *Scientometrics,* 118(2), 645–652. DOI: https://doi.org/10.1007/s11192-018-2987-0

Stotesbury, H. (2003). Evaluation in research article abstracts in the narrative and hard sciences. *Journal of English for Academic Purposes,* 2, 327–341.

Street, B. (1984). *Academic Writing. Theory and Practice.* Cambridge: Cambridge University Press.

Stubbs, M. (2001). *Words and Phrases: Corpus Studies in Lexical Semantics.* Oxford: Blackwell Publishers.

Sugimoto, C. R., Thelwall, M., Larivière, V., Tsou, A., Mongeon, P. and Macaluso, B. (2013). Scientists popularizing science: Characteristics and impact of TED talk presenters. *PLoS ONE,* 8(4), e62403. DOI: https://doi.org/10.1371/journal.pone.0062403

de Swaan, A. (2001). *Words of the World: The Global Language System.* Cambridge: Polity Press.

Swales, J. M. (1990). *Genre Analysis. English in Academic and Research Settings.* 1st ed. Cambridge: Cambridge University Press.

Swales, J. M. (1996). Occluded genres in the academy. The case of the submission letter. In E. Ventola and A. Mauranen, eds., *Academic Writing: Intercultural and Textual Issues.* Amsterdam and Philadelphia: John Benjamins, pp. 45–58.

Swales, J. M. (1997). English as tyrannosaurus rex. *World Englishes,* 16, 373–382.

Swales, J. M. (1998). *Other Floors, Other Voices: A Textography of a Small University Building.* Mahwah: Lawrence Erlbaum.

Swales, J. M. (2004). *Research Genres: Explorations and Applications.* 1st ed. Cambridge: Cambridge University Press.

Swales, J. M. (2009). Worlds of genre – metaphors of genre. In C. Bazerman, A. Bonini and E. Figueiredo, eds., *Genre in a Changing World.* Fort Collins: Parlor Press, pp. 3–16.

Swales, J. M. (2019). The futures of EAP genre studies: A personal viewpoint. *Journal of English for Academic Purposes,* 38, 75–82. DOI: https://doi.org/10 .1016/j.jeap.2019.01.003

Swales, J. M. and Feak, C. B. (2009a). *Abstracts and the Writing of Abstracts.* Ann Arbor: University of Michigan Press.

Swales, J. M. and Feak, C. B. (2009b). *Telling a Research Story.* Ann Arbor: Michigan University Press.

Swales, J. M. and Feak, C. B. (2012). *Academic Writing for Graduate Students. Essential Tasks and Skills.* 3rd ed. Ann Arbor: Michigan University Press.

Swales, J. M. and Leeder, C. (2012). A reception study of the articles published in English for Specific Purposes from 1990–1999. *English for Specific Purposes,* 31(2), 137–146.

Tannen, D. and Trester, A., eds. (2013). *Discourse 2.0. Language and New Media.* Georgetown: Georgetown University Press, pp. 1–25.

Tardy, C. M. (2004). The role of English in scientific communication: Lingua franca or tyrannosaurus rex? *Journal of English for Academic Purposes,* 3(3), 247–269.

Tardy, C. M. (2016). *Beyond Convention. Genre Innovation in Academic Writing.* Ann Arbor: Michigan University Press.

Thelwall, M., Bailey, C., Tobin, C. and Bradshaw, N. (2019). Gender differences in research areas, methods and topics: Can people and thing orientations explain the results? *Journal of Informetrics,* 13(1), 149–169. DOI: https://doi .org/10.1016/j.joi.2018.12.002

Thomson, J. W. (2002). The death of the scholarly monograph in the humanities? Citation patterns in literary scholarship. *Libri,* 52, 121–136.

Trachtenberg, Z. M., Burns, T. J. de Beurs, K., Ellis, S. E., Gates, K. K., Kelly, J. F. et al. (2016). The Anthropocene biosphere: Supporting 'open inter-disciplinarity' through blogging. *Trends in Ecology and Evolution,* 32(1), 1–3.

Trappes-Lomax, H. and Ferguson, G., eds. (2002). *Language in Language Teacher Education.* Amsterdam and Philadelphia: John Benjamins.

Trench, B. (2008). Internet: Turning science communication inside-out? In M. Bucchi and B. Trench, eds., *Handbook of Public Communication of Science and Technology.* New York: Routledge, pp. 185–198.

Tribble, C. (2001). Small corpora and teaching writing. Towards a corpus-informed pedagogy of writing. In M. Ghadessy A. Henry and R. L. Roseberry, eds., *Small Corpus Studies and ELT: Theory and Practice.* Amsterdam and Philadelphia: John Benjamins, pp. 381–408.

Tusting, K. (2018). The genre regime of research evaluation: Contradictory systems of value around academics' writing. *Language and Education,* 32(6), 477–493.

Tusting, K., McCulloch, S., Bhatt, I., Hamilton, M. and Barton, D. (2019). *Academics Writing: The Dynamics of Knowledge Creation*. London: Routledge.

United Nations Educational, Scientific and Cultural Organisation (UNESCO). (2010). UNESCO Science Report 2010. The Current Status of Science around the World. Paris: UNESCO Publishing. www.sciencequestinternational.com/facts-and-figures-from-the-unesco-science-report-2010/ [last accessed on 5 July 2020].

United Nations Educational, Scientific and Cultural Organisation (UNESCO). (2015). *UNESCO Science Report: Towards 2030*. Retrieved from https://en.unesco.org/unesco_science_report/sdg-9-5-2 [last accessed on 5 July 2020].

Uzuner, S. (2008). Multilingual scholars' participation in core/global academic communities: A literature review. *Journal of English for Academic Purposes, 7*, 250–263.

Van Parijs, P. (2007). Tackling the Anglophones' free ride: Fair linguistic co-operation with a global lingua franca. *AILA Review, 20*, 72–86.

Veltri, G. A. and Atanasova, D. (2015). Climate change on Twitter: Content, media ecology and information sharing behaviour. *Public Understanding of Science, 26*(6), 721–737.

Vitak, J. (2012). The impact of context collapse and privacy on social network site disclosures. *Journal of Broadcasting and Electronic Media, 56*, 451–470.

Wadman, M., Couzin-Frankel, J., Kaiser, J. and Matacic, C. (2020). How does coronavirus kill? Clinicians trace a ferocious rampage through the body, from brain to toes April 17, 2020. Retrieved from www.sciencemag.org/news/2020/04/how-does-coronavirus-kill-clinicians-trace-ferocious-rampage-through-body-brain-toes# [last accessed on 17 April 2020].

Wardhaugh, R. (1998). *An Introduction to Sociolinguistics*. Oxford: Blackwell.

Wei, L. (2018). Translanguaging as a practical theory of language. *Applied Linguistics, 39*(1), 9–30. DOI: https://doi.org/10.1093/applin/amx039

Wendel, J. N. (2005). Notes on the ecology of language. *Bunkyo Gakuin University Academic Journal, 5*, 51–76.

White, P. R. R. (2003). Beyond modality and hedging: A dialogic view of the language of intersubjective stance. *Text & Talk, 23*(2), 259–284.

Wickman, C. and Fitzgerald, E. (2019). Writing and science: An editorial perspective. *Written Communication, 36*(1), 3–8. DOI: https://doi.org/10.1177/0741088318809701

Wilcox, B. J. (2014). Word and image in academic writing: A study of verbal and visual meanings in marketing articles. *ESP Today, 2*(2), 113–133.

Willis, A. J. (1997). The ecosystem: An evolving concept viewed historically. *Functional Ecology, 11*(2), 268–271.

Witte, S., Latham, D. and Gross, M. (2019). *Literacy Engagement through Peritextual Analysis*. Chicago: ALA Editions.

World Bank (2016). *World Bank Annual Report 2016*. Available at Washington, DC: World Bank Group. http://documents.worldbank.org/curated/en/763601475489253430/World-Bank-annual-report-2016 [last accessed on 5 July 2020].

WrELFA (2015). *The Corpus of Written English as a Lingua Franca in Academic Settings*. Director: Anna Mauranen. Compilation manager: Ray Carey. www .helsinki.fi/elfa/ [last accessed on 29 January 2020].

Wu, X., Mauranen, A. and Lei, L. (2020). Syntactic complexity in English as a lingua franca academic writing. *Journal of English for Academic Purposes*, 43, 100798. DOI: https://doi.org/10.1016/j.jeap.2019.100798

Wynne, B. (2006). Public engagement as a means of restoring public trust in science – Hitting the notes, but missing the music? *Community Genetics*, 9(3), 211–220.

Yakhontova, T. (2006). Cultural and disciplinary variation in academic discourse: The issue of influencing factors. *Journal of English for Academic Purposes*, 5(2), 153–167.

Yang, W. (2017). Audioslide presentations as an appendant genre – Key words, personal pronouns, stance and engagement. *ESP Today*, 5(1), 24–45.

Yates, J. and Orlikowski, W. J. (1992). Genres of organizational communication: A structurational approach to studying communication and media. *Academy of Management Review*, 17(2), 485–510.

Yoon, C. (2011). Concordancing in L2 writing class: An overview of research and issues. *Journal of English for Academic Purposes*, 10(3), 130–139.

Yoon, J. W. and Chung, E. K. (2017). An investigation on graphical abstracts use in scholarly articles. *International Journal of Information Management*, 37(1), 1371–1379.

Zinchenko, V. P. (1996). Developing activity theory: The zone of proximal development and beyond. In Bonnie A. Nardi, ed., *Context and Consciousness: Activity Theory and Human-Computer Interaction*. Cambridge: The MIT Press, pp. 283–324.

Index

Academic Englishes, 114.
  See also English as a Lingua Franca
  codification, 122
academic prose, 84, 86, 93, 148
activity theory, 23, 65–66, 213, 243.
  See Spinuzzi, C.
add-on genres, 20, 28, 32, 57, 67–68,
  70, 77, 80, 140, 147, 150, 172, 199,
  201
agendas, 27, 31, 40–42, 66, 85, 90–91, 98,
  103, 133, 173, 198–199, 201, 203,
  205–208, 210, 214
agency, 49, 56, 58, 63, 70, 98
argumentation, 97, 153–154, 166
  contrasting arguments, 153
  joint arguments, 153
  parallel arguments, 153
Atkinson, D., 216
audience(s)
  consumers of science, 98
  diversified audiences, 45, 59, 84,
    111–112, 169. *See also* context
    collapse
  expectations of diverse audiences,
    152
  heterogencous audience, 91. *See also*
  lay audiences, 24, 35, 80, 161
Ayers, G., 216

Bakhtin, M., 55–56, 66, 80, 110, 199, 211,
  216
  heteroglossia, 110
  theory of heteroglossia, 55
  intertextuality, 17, 21, 41, 51, 55, 57,
    82–83, 86, 168, 211
  multivoicedness, 54
  paratext, 55
  peritext, 55, 80–81, 125, 168
  polyglossia, 128
Barton, D., 216
Bateman, J. A., 217. *See* literacy
Bauman, Z., 55, 57, 70, 80
  liquid modernity, 70
Bawarshi, A., 217

Bazerman, Ch. 4, 16, 32, 42, 51, 58, 72, 80,
  83, 115, 129–130, 134, 136, 138,
  144, 188, 190, 206, 217, 233, 237,
  241
Berkenkotter, C., 217
Berkenkotter, C. and Huckin, T.
  See socioliteracies
Bhatia, V. K., 40, 55, 57, 137, 144, 148,
  164, 209, 212, 218, 235
bibliometric indicators, 8, 185
  alternative metrics, 106
  altmetrics, 213
  citation indexes, 71
  metrics, 12
biliteracy, 148, 165, 194, 209, 224
  See Gentil, G.
  bilingualism, 148
  dynamic multilingualism, 7
Blommaert, J., 218
  mobility, 5–8, 14, 22–23, 61, 66, 99, 119,
    155, 185, 201
  sociolinguistics of mobility, 23
Briggs, C. L., 219

Campbell, J., 45, 85, 99, 228
Canagarajah, S., 115, 219
Casper, C. F., 10, 31–32, 50, 58, 175,
  220
citizen science, 11
  climate change, 102, 159
  crowdfunding, 11, 111
  project launchers, 20, 112, 158–159, 162,
    209
cognition, 114, 144
  cognitive processes, 134
  cognitive strategies, 123
  situated cognition, 139
Common European Framework of
  Reference for Languages (CEFR), 37
communities of practice, 210
context collapse, 1, 17, 20, 22, 34, 73, 77,
  158, 169, 173, 194, 207, 210, 212,
  231, 237, 242
  collapsing of social contexts, 158

244

250   *Index*

CPSIA information can be obtained
at www.ICGtesting.com
Printed in the USA
LVHW010042290721
693947LV00003B/372

9 781108 834940